D1549499

# OBJECT LESSONS

# CLEVELAND CREATES AN ART MUSEUM

Frontispiece: In November 1912 a plaster scale model of the Museum's proposed south facade was shown to the public. It met with an enthusiastic response.

Among the landscaping and sculptural features included to enhance the building was a proposed fountain designed by Herman Matzen at the north end of the lake. It embodied the idea that Commerce and Industry make possible Science, Literature, and Art.

# OBJECT LESSONS

# CLEVELAND CREATES AN ART MUSEUM

# LESSONS

EDITED BY

EVAN H. TURNER

Published by The Cleveland Museum of Art

1991

A generous contribution from Bank One, Cleveland
made possible the exhibition which this publication
accompanies.

WITHDRAWN

BQ (CLE)

Cover: South facade of The Cleveland Museum of
Art, designed by Hubbell and Benes, architects, 1916.
Spring 1988. Photo by Emily S. Rosen © 1991.

Copyright 1991 by The Cleveland Museum of Art
All rights reserved

Designer: Thomas H. Barnard III
Editors: Jo Zuppan and Rachel G. Feingold
Production Coordinator: Emily S. Rosen
Printed by Eastern Press, New Haven, Connecticut

Library of Congress Cataloging-in-Publication Data
    Object Lessons: Cleveland creates an art museum /
edited by Evan H. Turner.
        p.   cm.
    ISBN 0-940717-08-5
    1. Cleveland Museum of Art—History. I.
Turner, Evan H.    II. Cleveland Museum of Art.
N552.025     1991
708.171'32—dc20                              91-3397
                                                CIP
                                                 r91

# CONTENTS

# PREFACE

The history of an institution as complicated as The Cleveland Museum of Art is not un-like the story of a large family. There are many different elements—in the case of the Museum: its donors, Board, and staff; art collectors and dealers; and in turn, its many audiences. The last have particular significance in the tale because responding to their just expectations becomes one of the Museum staff's greatest satisfactions. As each member of a family would narrate quite a different story in detailing essentially the same set of facts, so would each element in treating the history of the Museum.

Thus, when the decision was made to write a new history of The Cleveland Museum of Art, on the occasion of its seventy-fifth anniversary, there was much consideration as to the wisest approach. Twenty-five years ago, in 1966, Carl Wittke, the well-known professor of history at Western Reserve University, wrote an account of the Museum—*The First Fifty Years.* However, since it conveyed little of that energetic spirit of commitment that had created such a remarkable Museum in so little time, we decided to take a somewhat different approach. And to a significant degree our route was dictated by the single most unusual factor in this Museum's evolution, one that makes its history distinctly unlike that of most American museums. The greater part of the Cleveland Museum's existence has been dominated by two brilliant Directors, each quite different in character but absolutely comparable in their dedication to the Museum's goals. So we chose to pursue this version of the Museum's history in terms of the accomplishments occurring under each of the Museum's four Directors, concentrating primarily upon the first three, Frederic Allen Whiting (1913-1930), William S. Milliken (1930-1958), and Sherman E. Lee (1958-1983). The essay on each man's directorship was written by a person who seemed particularly appropriate. We were especially pleased that Sherman Lee agreed to discuss his own years at the Museum (like William Milliken, he had first been a Curator). But William Milliken was given the opportunity to speak as well by a selection of quotes from his unpublished history of the Museum now in our Library.

As it turned out, one of the most interesting results of this handling of the Museum's story is the differing approaches of the authors to their subjects; the thoughtful reader can therefore adopt the point of view characterizing one account and consider each of the other periods similarly. Ultimately, the goal has been to present the facts so that readers can define their own picture of the Museum's history.

In doing so we must always recognize the single most important factor of all: the evidence of the collection. Each object in the Museum's galleries bears a number, the first digits of which indicate the years of acquisition (36.20, or *1936.20*; except for the Hinman B. Hurlbut collection which has its own numbering system). Assessing the impact of each person's particular taste upon the development of the collection becomes one of the most fascinating aspects of the Museum's history. Such an exercise is possible here as virtually nowhere else because few of our great city art museums are so totally the creation of the professional staff, at all points remarkably supported by its Board of Trustees.

In turn, certain aspects of the Museum's history have been examined in somewhat greater depth by other writers, whose contributions have proven invaluable. Those authors might be said to represent a microcosm of the many professional colleagues whose visits to the Museum over the years have enriched the lives of all on the staff: T. G. H. James, long the Keeper of the British Museum's Egyptian antiquities, who is now deeply involved in writing a book on Howard Carter, the archaeologist who became a matinee idol when he discovered Tutankhamen's tomb; Neil Harris, the University of Chicago's distinguished historian whose brilliant writings have elucidated so many aspects of the American cultural experience; Hubert Landais, for years the head of the Réunion des Musées Nationaux in France, equally the respected friend and merry companion of three of this Museum's Directors; and Louise S. Richards, our former colleague whose standards of connoisseurship remain an example for us all. Their essays as well as the frequently lengthy captions for illustrations contribute to a fuller understanding of the Museum's story.

The creation of this history has depended upon the help, the suggestions, and the stimuli of many people on the Museum's staff. Obviously no one knows the collection as well as the Curators who have each searched for necessary information with an admirable patience. By policy, few members of the present staff have been mentioned by name in this volume—but let it be said that the Museum is blessed in having a staff today that is as committed as it is perceptive and distinguished of taste.

The planning for this history has been essentially the work of Bruce Robertson, Henry Hawley, and myself. However, two other people have been absolutely focal to its realization. Virginia M. Krumholz joined the staff in 1988 as Archivist to gather together for the first time the Museum's widely scattered papers to create the long-needed Archives. Her knowledge of that material as well as the ingenuity with which she has ferreted out new material and many photographs has repeatedly been startling. The photographs were of particular interest. We particularly sought casual ones because so often the posed cabinet photographs generally favored in the past may have captured the formal public persona yet suggested none of the warmth of personality surely nurtured by a delight in the visual arts. In turn, Jo Zuppan, the Museum's Editor, has coordinated the endless overlaps inevitably occurring with so many authors with exemplary patience; and she has also introduced her own fine sense of style, again and again, not only as an editor but also as the author of many of the captions.

Unceasingly the staff of the Museum's Library and the Registrar's office dealt with a myriad of questions from all of us with a truly monumental patience which was greatly appreciated. The Museum's Photographer, Howard T. Agriesti, and his staff provided both fresh prints from aging negatives and copy prints from vintage photographs that have immeasurably enhanced the text.

The ingenuity of the Graphic Designer in coordinating the many elements of this publication becomes an essential factor in the success of the book. The inspiration with which Tom Barnard constantly resolved what at times have seemed endless numbers of quirks complemented the great quality of the layout as a whole. Production Manager Emily Rosen made it all happen.

Clearly, many have been involved in the preparation of this history and the exhibition that accompanies it—most generously underwritten by Bank One, Cleveland—but it may safely be said that all are united in their commitment to this great Museum and to the many rewards of the works of art it houses. In this fashion the goals of the founders remain a lively example today and, we trust, will continue so for years yet to come.

E.H.T.

# PROLOGUE: TO 1917

EVAN H. TURNER

W ith a few hundred residents, Cleveland was little more than a pioneer village in 1825, but by 1900 the city had grown to such a degree that it was the seventh largest in the United States, with 382,000 residents. Cleveland had prospered mightily, thanks first to the opening of both the Erie and Ohio canals and then, because of a happy geographical location, to the rapid development of a thriving steel industry. Almost as soon as the city's leaders could catch their breath, they applied the same energies that had been so essential in Cleveland's growth to procuring those cultural amenities that in late nineteenth-century America were proof that a city had attained maturity. In the early 1880s, for example, Western Reserve University and the newly founded Case School of Applied Science were established in a developing neighborhood adjoining the park land just given the city by Jeptha H. Wade, a founder of Western Union. In the coming years, the city's most important cultural institutions would also be centered on this parcel of land.

With such a spirit of proud commitment alive in the city and with the example of such nearby cities as Pittsburgh, Cincinnati, Toledo, Chicago, and most recently, Buffalo, it is no wonder that the creation of an art museum should have been in the air. It was, however, a source of some surprise that between 1881 and 1890 three Clevelanders—Hinman Hurlbut, Horace Kelley, and John Huntington—had written wills designating the greater part of their estates for building an art museum. Although traditionally it has been believed that each drew up his will knowing nothing of the others, both Huntington and Kelley must have known of the Hurlbut plan since his entire will was published in the newspaper.[1] Furthermore, all three named one Trustee in common, one of the city's most respected leaders, the lawyer Henry C. Ranney.

Some twenty years, however, passed between the death in 1893 of the last and the wealthiest of the three, John Huntington, and the actual incorporation of The Cleveland Museum of Art that we know to-

Excavations for the privately endowed art museum dedicated to the people of Cleveland began on May 20, 1913. The architects were Benjamin S. Hubbell and W. Dominick Benes of Cleveland, with Edmund M. Wheel-wright of Boston, consulting architect, and Hollis French and Allen Hubbard of Boston, engineers. The Crowell-Lundoff-Little Company, Cleveland, served as general contractors. Work on the steel structure, with foot-ers extending 30 ft. to rest on bed rock, occupied the winter of 1913-14, while the white marble for the exterior of the 300-by-120-ft. building was being quarried in Georgia.

Hinman Barret Hurlbut (1818-1884) was born in Vermont. At the age of 18 he joined a brother in Cleveland to read law in his office. Enjoying success as a lawyer in Massillon, Hurlbut returned to Cleveland and entered banking. His interest in art, shared by his wife, Jane Elizabeth, was aroused during an extended European tour 1865-1868 for his health.

When Hurlbut died in 1884 most of his estate, including a highly acclaimed art collection, was left to found an art museum in Cleveland. A life annuity for his wife, however, delayed action on his bequest until her death in 1910.

Although it turned out that not enough money remained to build a museum, the Hurlbut paintings became the nucleus of a collection for the new Art Museum being built with Kelley and Huntington monies. There was enough capital for the Hurlbut Trustees to set up a small operating and purchase fund from which the Museum still receives annual revenues.

day. Although the details of their efforts are difficult to chart fully today, during those years various city leaders invested much effort and ingenuity, never hesitating in their goal, to meld the three visions into one effective reality. In 1899 the Kelley Trustees actually established a corporate identity, known as The Cleveland Museum of Art, that eventually involved the Hurlbut interests, while the Huntington executors pursued the realization of the Art and Polytechnic Trust that Huntington had outlined in his will.[2] Not too surprisingly, it soon became evident that if the three Trusts could work in concert, it would be to their mutual advantage. Thus, in 1905, at the suggestion of the Huntington Trustees, they joined forces and formed a Building Committee representing their respective interests. Two years later, the committee chose as architects the young firm of Hubbell and Benes over the better known J. Milton Dyer, quite possibly because the committee was impressed by the restrained good taste evident in the firm's recently designed Wade Memorial Chapel.[3]

It was agreed that a museum should be constructed near the University and the Institute on a parcel of land still held by the Wade family from the earlier grant to the city, which J. H. Wade (Jeptha Wade's grandson and namesake) agreed to give for that purpose. Reflecting the need of each corporation to have its own space and recognizing the relative means of

each, one half of that building was set aside for the Huntington Trust and one fourth each for the Kelley and Hurlbut interests. The committee's great sense of responsibility was demonstrated by its visit to Buffalo to talk with John J. Albright about his new museum building. It also retained as its advisor Edmund M. Wheelwright, who had been traveling far and wide gathering information to assist Boston's Trustees in the construction of the newest building for their Museum of Fine Arts. Of even greater importance during these founding years, however, was the wide-ranging advice given by the Assistant Secretary of the Metropolitan Museum of Art in New York, Henry W. Kent. Repeatedly, his judgment assumed *ex cathedra* proportions.

The Building Committee quickly realized that the site's dimensions required orienting the main axis of the proposed building from north to south; this would mean that only an end of the building would be seen from Euclid Avenue—or at best a corner— hardly the most propitious view. Far more serious, however, was Wheelwright's insistence that appropriate natural lighting for the picture galleries could only be achieved with an east-west axis. The committee also expressed the concern that the parcel of land was not large enough to handle future expansion. Lengthy discussions with the appropriate city officials led to an exchange of land parcels. The negotiations

Horace Kelley (1819-1890), a native of Cleveland and a real estate entrepreneur, was responsible for the second large bequest for an art gallery, made in 1890. Shown here with a niece in a photograph taken in Meron süd Tyrol, Kelley often traveled abroad.

In consultation with his wife (Fannie Miles of Elyria), who probably deserves credit for his visiting the European museums that inspired his bequest, Kelley left most of his estate "for the purpose of purchasing land and ... [erecting] a suitable fireproof building to be used forever as a gallery of art ... and said building also to be used in part as a school ... for designing, drawing, painting and other fine arts...."

Kelley believed in the "refining and educating influence of art, ... to which all the people can have access...." He hoped his gallery—possibly named the "National Gallery of Fine Arts and College of Instruction of Cleveland"—would attract other gifts but only if they were of "acknowledged merit." The Horace Kelley Art Foundation continues to appropriate funds for Museum use today.

were even more complicated because the Populist Mayor Tom Johnson apparently preferred a downtown site for the Museum, one nearer the heart of the city.

Even as the city administration changed in 1910 and the Building Committee finally won the day, it made the disconcerting discovery that, with the release of the Hurlbut funds upon the death of his wife, the estate was in fact only a fraction of what had been generally assumed. There were no means for paying the Hurlbuts' proposed quarter of the anticipated $1 million construction costs. At best there was only a modest endowment of about $75,000 besides their collection of modern American and European paintings—of no small consequence since it was all the founders had in the way of an art collection.

Despite this considerable setback, the Building Committee, with characteristic vision, responded by preparing a lengthy, well-reasoned report summarizing all that had been achieved to date.[4] The committee then recommended that the plans proceed and the proposed 61,107-square-foot structure be built, the Huntington Trust to pay seven-tenths of the cost and the Kelley three-tenths. The one hesitation was the use of funds so gravely needed to buy works of art. But already displaying the reasoned courage that

John Huntington (1832-1893) was born in England but had to leave after becoming involved in a textile workers' strike. Settling in Cleveland with his wife (Jane Beck), he started out as a slate roofer and soon prospered.

By 1867 Huntington was involved in oil-refining and wisely accepted 500 shares in Rockefeller's Standard Oil at an opportune time. Branching out into other investments, he became one of the wealthiest men in the city.

His deep sense of civic responsibility led to six terms on the Cleveland City Council, although he was accused of conflicts of interest in sponsoring certain civic improvements.

Travels abroad with his second wife, Mariett L. Goodwin (his first wife had died), awoke Huntington's interest in art. Written in 1889, his will created the John Huntington Art and Polytechnic Trust to set up not only a "gallery and museum" but also a "free evening polytechnic school," among other philanthropies.

Provisions for his heirs, plus some contested debts, delayed the final distribution of his estate—the largest of the three—until 1928. The Huntington Fund still makes annual contributions to the Museum's operating fund besides occasional major donations for specific needs.

would repeatedly characterize the Museum at major turning points in the future, the committee urged forward progress.

However, since the busy committee members were also concerned with many other projects in Cleveland at the same time, all concerned felt that there should be a professional person on hand to oversee the construction and then, an even more daunting task, to furnish it with a collection and a program as a proper art museum. So even as excavations began on May 20, 1913, final negotiations were in progress with Frederic Allen Whiting, who was formally appointed Secretary of the Building Commitee on June 5.

Acceding as well to the reality that it was not legally possible for the three Trusts to unite, the committee agreed that a new body with the name *The Cleveland Museum of Art*, used earlier by the Kelley Trust, should be established. That museum would have a Board responding to each Trust as appropriate. The Museum was thus incorporated on July 2,

1913; and at its first meeting, on December 15, its Board of Trustees appointed Whiting, Director.

Finally, the pivotal question had to be faced: What was the new Museum to be like? In response to a request from the Board, Whiting's first weeks were devoted to preparing a lengthy memorandum addressing that issue.[5] He opined that essentially there were two kinds of museums. The Metropolitan Museum in New York and the Museum of Fine Arts in Boston represented one group: each was "rich in collections and devoted almost exclusively to the exhibition of objects owned by, or lent to, them and rarely having special exhibitions of modern work."[6] Also, each had a chosen area of specialization—for Boston, oriental art, for New York, Egyptian. (The Cleveland Board had already enjoyed the benefits of the latter commitment since Kent's agent in Cairo had enabled the Huntington Trustees to make some acquisitions.) Whiting's second group of museums included Pittsburgh, Buffalo, Chicago, Toledo, St. Louis,

Among works of art purchased by the Trustees of the John Huntington Art and Polytechnic Trust for the Museum is an Egyptian Dynasty XXI *Coffin Case and Cover of Bekenmut* (CMA 14.561) from Thebes. Dating to about 1070-945 BC, it illustrates the early Trustees' interest in obtaining works with historical interest and educational value.

Cincinnati, and Indianapolis. They had "permanent collections of varying importance" but attracted the public "largely through a continuous series of temporary exhibitions of works by modern artists."[7] Although he felt that Cleveland was part of the latter group, he argued that its Museum "should strive for a happy medium between the restlessness which goes with constantly changing exhibitions and the monotony of a comparatively small building filled with permanently installed exhibits"[8]—a position that the Museum has maintained for much of its existence.

While Whiting clearly viewed Cleveland as belonging to the second group of museums, he must have yearned to associate it with the first. He was concerned that the Museum should develop its own "distinct individuality among Museums throughout the world." He argued, "We should at the outset determine upon some branch of art which is not adequately represented in any American Museum, selecting if possible a field in which a sufficient collection

could be secured without too large an expenditure of time and money."[9] Curiously, given future developments, he suggested concentrating upon the art of India, discussing possible opportunities offered by Lockwood de Forest, the brother of the Metropolitan's President, who was then traveling in India, and by Berthold Laufer of Chicago's Field Museum, who knew of "unexpected ruins in Northern India, of which he has learned from old Chinese manuscripts...."[10] A joint expedition was even mentioned in passing.

Whiting's suggestion fell upon responsive ears. Before the next year was out the Museum had raised $30,000—a considerable sum for the time—to fund research in China and proposed travels in Turkestan by the famed Harvard orientalist, Langdon Warner. Warner was retained by the Museum for two years—with remarkable scholarly success although with rather dim results in terms of the collection's growth—but in 1917 he became the new Director of

The Museum's efforts to collect Asian art were evident in the *Inaugural Exhibition* rooms that displayed gifts from the Ralph Kings and Worcester R. Warner, as well as Mr. and Mrs. J. H. Wade, the John Huntington Collection, and Mrs. Langdon Warner. Interspersed with them were loans from private collectors and dealers, including: Paul Mallon, Langdon Warner, Grenville L. Winthrop, A. W. Bahr, T. Kuroda, Loo Ching Tai, S. T. Peters, Frederic Moore, Yamanaka and Company, and Messrs. Duveen.

Loans from dealers were also included in other galleries in the hope that Clevelanders might purchase some of the objects for their new Museum. Open June 7-September 20, 1916, the exhibition drew 191,547 visitors.

Dudley Peter Allen (1852-1915) was born in Kinsman, Ohio. A graduate of Oberlin College and Harvard Medical School, he settled in Cleveland in 1883. The first physician in the city to specialize in surgery, he practiced at both

Charity and Lakeside hospitals, and taught at Western Reserve Medical College. He married Elisabeth Severance in 1894.

Considered a connoisseur, Dr. Allen was one of the founding Trustees of the Art Museum. Writing to Whiting in 1913, he maintained that the Museum

should enlist "the interest and active cooperation of a large number of citizens from many different classes." He mentioned being "very greatly impressed by the bearing ... the Museums of Germany have upon the[ir] commercial activities...."

the Pennsylvania Museum (now the Philadelphia Museum of Art), and was promptly granted a year's leave of absence for further study in China!

In retaining Langdon Warner, Cleveland established a route with which it intermittently experimented for the next few years until it developed its own staff. Briefly, Charles Ricketts represented the Museum's interests in London;[11] and more effectively (until he discovered Tutankhamen's tomb), Howard Carter did so in Egypt. A longer, and not always advantageous, commitment was made with Harold Parsons who represented the Museum's interests in Italy until 1941.

Although archival evidence does not suggest that the issue was formally addressed, there may have been a disparity lurking between the expectations of the two bequests. Kelley's will clearly spoke of a traditional art museum—one for paintings, drawings, and sculpture—whereas, by implication, given a concern for the city's industrial workers, Huntington at least opened the way for broader interests.

The complexities of the various influences on the formation of the Museum are discussed at length elsewhere, but Dudley Peter Allen may at the outset have been the focal figure in the development of the collection. Other than Allen, the new Board was made up of representatives from the Huntington and Kelley Trustees, while he was unanimously chosen

because of his notable interest in the arts. As a medical student years before at Harvard, Allen had first begun collecting Old Master prints, and this early passion had been consolidated by extensive travel abroad. His leadership in the initial formulation of goals, however, sadly ended with his death in 1915, before the Museum building was completed. His enthusiastic advocacy of the need to democratize[12] the Museum led to his calling for "a department which should collect artistic implements and articles of common use as models for the handicraftsmen of Cleveland."[13] He gave funds for such acquisitions even as he urged an aggressive pursuit of the city's various industries for annual appropriations to enable the Museum to buy historic works made of the materials focal to Cleveland's current manufacturing economy. Without question, the frenzied effort to open the new Museum with a major collection of armor was motivated in part by the local importance of steel, although admittedly such material complemented the Museum's educational goals in its own right.[14] And J. H. Wade's early purchase—in 1914—of more than 1,000 pieces of lace from the collection formed by Thomas Wilson, a Curator of Prehistoric Anthropology at the Smithsonian Institute in Washington, for exhibition at the 1893 Columbian Exposition, spoke to Cleveland's major textile industry. Indeed, Wade's enthusiasm for textiles became the

The first gift to the Museum by another founding Trustee, J. H. Wade, was the Wilson collection of over 500 type pieces of lace. Collecting lace was a particular preoccupation of his wife, Ellen Garretson Wade, in whose memory their children gave a wonderful Milanese *Flounce* (CMA 23.997). A detail of it is shown here.

basis for the Museum's unusual early commitment to developing a collection of textiles (as opposed to the costumes favored by so many other American museums).

Thus, in deciding to acquire examples of the so-called decorative arts to encourage higher standards in local industries, the Museum emulated the example of the South Kensington Museum (today the Victoria and Albert) in London, England, and the museum in Philadelphia. Each had been the outgrowth of a great exposition proudly extolling the marvels of modern industry. Indeed, some of the Museum's finest acquisitions, especially in its first fifteen years, fall into the area of the decorative arts.[15]

The commitment to the decorative arts was firmly entrenched, collecting activity in Egypt and the Orient was at least well launched, and the Huntington Trustees were prepared to purchase the plaster casts[16] and architectural fragments that seemed to be an inevitable first step for virtually every new American museum. But the Museum's position on paintings was more ambivalent, perhaps because of its modest means.

The 122 paintings of the Hurlbut collection—largely American and modern—were an essential start. While paintings graced the various famed Euclid Avenue mansions, the city was not distinguished for its holdings, and how could anyone know which

ones might be given to the Museum?[17] Without question the most ambitious local collection was the group of Italian "primitives" that Liberty Holden's wife, Delia, had persuaded him to purchase from James Jackson Jarves in 1884. Holden's great personal interest in the proposed Museum was repeatedly evident in his skillful chairmanship of the Building Committee; it was surely no surprise, therefore, when in the year following his death, his widow gave to the Museum the greater part of her beloved collection of "early sacred art."[18]

In July, as the new galleries were being completed, an initial acquisition policy was announced in the Museum *Bulletin*.[19] The meager funds were to be spent on forming a "collection representing the important American painters" and the first purchase was John Singleton Copley's *Portrait of Mrs. John Greene* (CMA 15.527). The policy was justified for two reasons: "it seems the normal beginning point for an American museum and it offers the field in which paintings can be bought to good advantage and at low prices as compared with the European schools." That a collection of earlier American paintings would complement Hurlbut's gathering of later nineteenth-century American painting must surely have been a factor in the decision.

The first Trustees may have been hesitant in the development of collection policies, but once defined,

Consultant Edward Hamilton Bell noted in the Museum's February 1916 *Bulletin:* "It must be admitted that the building, like all newly erected edifices, stands ... a little stark and box-like on its recently graded hilltop, but time and judicious planting will soften that and break up the white mass which now is a little startling in our strong American sunlight. However, it has the rare distinction of expressing a purpose and an idea in a really beautiful manner."

Writing for *International Studio,* Raymond Wyer found the Museum building: "imposing and graceful when viewed from any point."

their commitment to education was unwavering. The Building Committee, in its pivotal 1910 report, had urged the appointment of a Director because such a person was needed not only to watch over the construction but also:

*to create an art interest* [in the community]. *A building filled with art objects is not necessarily a successful museum of art. A community must be interested and its active cooperation secured. A campaign of education should* [therefore] *be carried on simultaneously with the growth of the institution.*[20]

The 1913 Articles of Incorporation confirmed this commitment: the Museum would expect "to provide instruction and maintain courses of lectures upon art" and to "maintain an industrial training school for the best interests of mechanics, manufacturers and artisans, for the more general diffusion of knowledge in such classes...."

Clearly, the very prosperity that had made the Museum a reality depended upon the city's many different industries, but even so, the Museum's constant

The entrance on the north side of the building served visitors arriving by automobile and offered access to the gallery level via a passenger elevator as well as stairs. It also provided a direct route to classrooms, library, lecture hall, and lunch room, so that non-gallery visitors could avoid disturbing people in the galleries.

Neither this nor the original service entrance remain because of subsequent additions.

awareness of them in planning an education program is remarkable. Huntington's vision had, of course, seen an art museum as part of a much larger concept, specifically incorporating a free polytechnic school for, as he expressed it in his will, "the promotion of scientific education for the benefit of deserving persons ... who are unable to acquire a collegiate education."[21] Whiting was sympathetic to such intentions. In his 1914 report he observed "how eagerly certain elements in the community are reaching out for any form of sympathetic cooperation in their efforts to develop higher capacities in the rising generation." Espousing a position that may seem rather more self-serving today than was surely intended then, Whiting thus presented a potential policy:

*The Museum should ally itself positively with the industries of Cleveland. By enlarging the outlook of artisans and giving them a needed opportunity to spend their leisure hours pleasantly and well, we can positively increase their efficiency ... by special exhibitions and talks for particular trades. The imagination of craftsmen can be beneficially stimulated and they can be made to realize the possible development of their capacity in a remarkable way.*[22]

The Museum acted quickly. By the end of 1915 Emily Gibson, the newly appointed head of education, was meeting with local schools, libraries, and social clubs; and an exhibition of Babylonian and Assyrian tablets was already being shown in the branch libraries where Mrs. Gibson spoke. Also, plans were well underway for the creation of an interactive children's museum within the new Museum. Its quite different orientation encompassed "art, ethnological and natural history material, as well as the many objects on the borderland between the scientific and art classifications."[23]

So the busy three years between incorporation and the actual opening of the new building—on June 6, 1916—presented many problems and policy options to be discussed; but impressively the Museum did open with its new gallery space jammed with pictures. The extensive *Inaugural Exhibition* could leave no doubt as to the Board's ambitious goals. Important works came from museums and collectors throughout the country—but numerous objects loaned by dealers were deliberately chosen with the hope that Clevelanders would be tempted to purchase them for the new Museum. Imposing gifts were proudly displayed: the Severance armor, the great suite of seventeenth-century tapestries illustrating the story of Dido and Aeneas (CMA 15.79-.86) that Mrs. Allen purchased as a memorial to her husband, Mrs. Holden's paintings (insistence upon correct attributions in gallery labels and the exhibition catalogue, insofar as the scholarship of the day permitted, was ample proof of the Museum's professional integrity), Asian objects from the Ralph Kings and Worcester Warner, and examples of the decorative arts from the Wades. The names that would dominate the Museum's records in the coming years were already appearing in leadership roles.

As Secretary of the Board, Hermon A. Kelley (Horace Kelley's cousin) gave the annual report at the close of the first year after the building opened. Besides proudly noting the 376,459 visitors and 2,744 members, he pointed out that the Trustees "are determined that this institution shall be a live educational force in the community and not a mere cold storage warehouse for works of art."[24] The efforts of so many over more than thirty years had made an improbable dream a successful reality!

For the *Inaugural Exhibition* the Armor and Tapestries Court was suitably furnished with armor purchased by Mr. and Mrs. John L. Severance for the Museum and the magnificent tapestries presented by Mrs. Dudley P. Allen as a memorial to her husband.

According to a 1930 report by a staff member: "Not the least of his [Whiting's] brilliant achievements was the installation of the Armor Collection which was obtained at so late a date that no one without the energy of a dynamo would have thought its exhibition for the opening possible. After its purchase, for some reason, it did not arrive. During a trip East Mr. Whiting investigated. He was told the car was 'on its way.' Looking out the window of his berth the next morning, he saw a van on a flat car on a siding near a small Ohio town which he mysteriously divined as the one he needed. It was. As soon as he arrived in Cleveland, Mr. Whiting did some rapid telephoning. The armor arrived speedily. But it would never have been put in place had not the late Dr. Bashford Dean, Curator of Armor at the Metropolitan, literally taken off his coat and attacked the Chinese puzzle of some hundreds of unconnected pieces of iron strewn over the floor of the Armor Court."

1. *Cleveland Leader*, April 22, 1884, clipping in Archives of The Cleveland Museum of Art (hereafter cited as CMA Archives).

2. Those Articles of Incorporation also allowed for "a museum of natural or other curiosities of art" and "the establishment and maintenance of a Polytechnic School and an academic School of Art." Articles of Incorporation of The Cleveland Museum of Art [now the Horace Kelley Art Foundation], February 27, 1899, CMA Archives. Huntington was insistent that his name should not be associated with the new Museum.

3. The first Jeptha H. Wade had died in 1890, and his family had a chapel built in his honor at the fashionable Lake View Cemetery, which he had founded in 1869. In fact, his much loved grandson, Jeptha Homer Wade II, had moved the appointment of Hubbell and Benes as the architects of the new Museum at the Building Committee meeting on September 4, 1906. The great success of Louis Comfort Tiffany's mosaics at the chapel may also explain the suggestion that Tiffany should create mosaics for the rotunda of the new Museum, an idea that was never realized. Records of the Building Committee of the Cleveland Museum of Art, CMA Archives.

4. Records of the Building Committee of the Cleveland Museum of Art, July 13, 1910, CMA Archives.

5. Attached to the Board Minutes, January 2, 1914, pp. 11-21.

6. Board Minutes, January 2, 1914, p. 11.

7. Board Minutes, January 2, 1914, p. 11. In discussing how Cleveland might respond to the challenge of presenting modern art he suggested (1) a biennial or triennial international exhibition such as the show already done by the Carnegie in Pittsburgh, (2) an exhibition of Ohio-born or trained artists judged by a jury chosen by the artists, and (3) an annual exhibition of American artists. The second alternative, the local show, did become a reality in 1919 and still exists today as the *May Show*; and for fifteen years, until 1935, the third alternative was shown as well.

8. Board Minutes, January 2, 1914, p. 11.

9. Board Minutes, January 2, 1914, p. 12.

10. Board Minutes, January 2, 1914, p. 12. Interestingly, in arguing for Indian art the Director noted, as the Board was establishing its collecting goals, that "their native traditional art has more of suggestion for our designers than that of any other of the old civilizations." How curious that, with few exceptions, the pursuit of Indian material with any method waited for almost fifty years!

11. Ricketts and his friend, the artist Charles Shannon, were elegant figures in the London art world in the years following World War I. There is no evidence that anything resulted from the Museum's appropriating $2,500 for Ricketts to spend at the famous sale of the Hope Collection of Greek vases (Sotheby's, July 23, 1917). Board Minutes, July 3, 1917, p. 142. The significant development of this section of the Museum collection did not really occur until after 1958.

12. To quote the word used by Hermon A. Kelley in his "Address," given at the Memorial Service for Allen on January 24, 1915, which outlines the importance of Allen's leadership to the new Trustees. *CMA Bulletin* 1, 4 (February 1915): 7.

13. Ibid.

14. Initially the collection of a Mr. Keasebey of Philadelphia was considered for purchase; then, when that fell through, a major loan from the private collection of Bashford Dean, Curator of Armor at the Metropolitan Museum, was negotiated. Finally, however, John Severance was able to purchase the Macomber collection, which he and his wife gave to the Museum.

15. A later paper, "The Relation of the Museum to Local Industry" (*CMA Bulletin* 5, 10 [December 1918]: 122-127), consolidates these attitudes at length. It refers to Allen's position, namely, "to be really useful, the modern museum should bind itself in the most intimate way to the life and industry of the community," and that any museum not doing so was failing in its trust. The goal of this particular *CMA Bulletin* was essentially a fund-raising pitch for acquisition funds from the city's various industries.

16. The outbreak of World War I prevented the Museum from purchasing casts in Europe, so this good idea was not pursued. By the time the opportunity was again available, the Museum's goals had become more ambitious. Nonetheless, acquisitions were made. The Director reported to the Board of Trustees at its June 24, 1938, meeting that the Cleveland Board of Education was delighted to have been given the Museum's casts of the Hermes and infant Dionysus (by Praxiteles), the Two Fates (from the Acropolis), an Athena, a Theseus, and the Winged Victory.

17. Numbers of pictures were given over the years, but faint evidence of that remains today because of considered programs of de-acquisition in the 1950s and the 1960s. Sadly, the city's most important collection, that formed by Alfred A. Pope, had quietly left town in 1900. Much of it can be seen today at the Hill-Stead Museum in Farmington, Connecticut.

18. Much is known about Liberty E. Holden's business affairs, among other things that he was the owner and President of *The Plain Dealer*, but there is surprisingly little information on his art collecting. We know that while traveling in Egypt early in this century he purchased a mummy of Dynasty XXI, which over the years has delighted countless children at the Western Reserve Historical Society. There is a reference in the Museum's memorial on his death in 1913 that he had negotiated the possible purchase of an important classical collection—nothing came of it because the Museum was not sufficiently advanced—but there is little else. The circumstances of his buying those Jarves paintings that Yale had not acquired as settlement of a debt are not even clear; the Holdens bought as well in 1889 the "Kellogg Gallery,"

which had been collected by the painter Minor Kellogg in Europe and was also part of the 1916 gift.

19. "The Collection of Paintings," *CMA Bulletin* 2, 2 (July 1915): 4-5; "The Holden Collection," ibid., 4, 2 (February 1917): 17-21.

20. Report of the Building Committee, July 13, 1910, p. 8, CMA Archives.

21. Will of John Huntington, Harold T. Clark papers, CMA Archives.

22. "Recommendations as to Fundamental Policies ... prepared at the request of the Special Committee," dated June 25, 1914, CMA Archives.

23. Minutes of the Executive Committee, February 4, 1916.

24. *CMA Bulletin* 4, 5 (June-July 1917): 77.

*Orchid Blossoms* by
Martin Johnson
Heade, American
(1819-1904). Hurlbut
Collection. CMA 461.15

*Mother and Children,*
1879, by William
Adolphe Bouguereau,
French (1825-1905).
Hinman B. Hurlbut
Collection. CMA 432.15

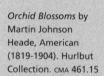 inman Barret Hurlbut, like so many men in his circumstances, decided to go to Europe to recover his health when he collapsed from overwork in 1865. There he and his wife, Jane Elizabeth, discovered the arts and began to collect paintings. By 1873 the Hurlbut collection was considered the finest in Cleveland. Five years later, in Cleveland's first significant art exhibition, Hurlbut's loans were the major attraction.

Typical of the American collections formed after the Civil War, before the taste for Old Master paintings became the rage, Hurlbut chose a selection of works by popular modern European painters balanced by a group of the leading Americans. Painters from almost every European school, but especially the Munich and Barbizon, were represented: Karl von Piloty, Michael Munkacsy, and P. A. Kaulbach; Constantin Troyon, N. V. Diaz de la Pena, Jules Breton, and Adolphe Bouguereau. Among American artists, Hurlbut collected Martin Johnson Heade, Thomas Moran, Sanford Gifford, Eastman Johnson, and Frederic Edwin Church. From 1917 on the Museum Board adopted the policy of selling Hurlbut collection paintings, mostly the European works, that did not stand the test of time. Particularly carried out in the 1940s, the funds from such sales were used to acquire works by American artists for the Hinman B. Hurlbut Collection.

*The Monastery of Our Lady of the Snows* by Frederic Edwin Church, American (1826-1900). Hinman B. Hurlbut Collection. CMA 363.15

*Winding Yarn* by Eastman Johnson, American (1824-1906). Hinman B. Hurlbut Collection. CMA 355.15

A prominent Cleveland businessman, Liberty Emery Holden (1833-1913) used his fortune, made mostly in western mining, to buy *The Cleveland Plain Dealer* and local real estate, and to promote cultural activities. Holden's personal interest in Cleveland's proposed Art Museum was manifest in his adept chairing of the Building Committee formed by the Kelley and Huntington Trustees.

Liberty Holden's wife, Delia, had persuaded him in 1884 to purchase a group of Italian "primitives" from an exhibition of foreign art in Boston. These paintings had been purchased in Europe by James Jackson Jarves, the first important American collector of early Italian paintings. The Boston exhibition handbook explicitly stated that the works "were not presented as masterpieces, but as types of the greater men and their schools...." Stella Rubinstein in the Museum's *Inaugural Exhibition* catalogue noted: "the collection as a whole admirably shows the progress of painting from the early Italian schools to the end of the Renaissance." When the Holdens bought the paintings, Bostonians were shocked that the collection was going to an upstart Midwestern city.

The Filippino Lippi tondo was acquired when William Milliken was Director. In *Time Remembered*, he recalled that "In the late twenties, following the death of Edward P. Warren, the great tondo of Filippino Lippi became a possible purchase.... A small painted replica was shown to Mrs. Bole, and she, her brother and her sisters ... wished to give it to the Museum in memory of their mother...." Afterward, "Mrs. Bole made a trip to California to tell her mother, who was still alive but completely blind. When the name Filippino Lippi was mentioned, Mrs. Holden's face brightened as she remembered the Filippinos in Florence, in Santa Maria Novella, in the Badia, and in the Uffizi."

Delia E. Bulkley (Mrs. Liberty E.) Holden (1838-1932); is shown here on July 25, 1921, with seven of her great-grandchildren. They have tentatively been identified as (left to right): Holden Higbee, Robert Morse (?), Robert White (?), and Jeanette Norweb (in front); Philip Morse, Mrs. Holden, R. Henry Norweb, and Windsor White (in back).

*The Holy Family with the Infant St. John and St. Margaret* by Filippino Lippi, Italian (about 1457-1504). Purchase from the Delia E. Holden Fund and from a fund donated as a memorial to Mrs. Holden by her children: Guerdon S. Holden, Delia Holden White, Roberta Holden Bole, Emery Holden Greenough, Gertrude Holden McGinley. CMA 32.227.
Paintings of the Virgin Mary as an ideal of motherhood delighted Mrs. Holden, so this memorial to her is quite apt.

The Holden Gallery at the time of the *Inaugural Exhibition*. The architect Arthur Loomis Harmon of New York attempted to emulate "an apartment in an Italian Palazzo.... The vaulted ceiling, enriched with ornament and colour, the doorways and surbase of travertine and the cool brown velvet on the walls produce an impression of dignity and subdued splendour which should greatly enhance the effect of the early paintings which are to hang there...." (February 1916 *Bulletin*)

Once attributed to Leonardo da Vinci, the painting *Madonna and Child* (CMA 16.779) is now believed to be the work of Francesco Napolitano (Italian, active about 1500), an imitator of Leonardo.

Probably the work of an Italo-Flemish painter, *Portrait of a Married Couple* (CMA 16.793) is an example of the "masterly portraiture" found in The Holden Collection.

# OVERVIEW: 1917-30

EVAN H. TURNER

World War I clouded the Museum's first years. Such specific concerns as the coal-less Mondays or closing the Museum for five weeks because of the terrible influenza epidemic added drama to the early days; but the grim state of the world only made Cleveland the prouder of its Museum of Art.[1]

As 1919 drew to a close, Judge William B. Sanders indicated that in a year's time he wished to step down as President of the Board of Trustees. Ever since the very first meeting of the Building Committee in 1905, he had been a leading figure—probably the single most important person—in the realization of the Museum. His ingenuity had solved countless problems, while his legal wisdom had repeatedly clarified the conflicting issues presented by the interested bequests. A unanimous endorsement of Whiting's Directorship in 1920 neatly pinpoints the essential problems that Judge Sanders's Board had faced:

*Mr. Whiting came to Cleveland at a time when there was much public dissatisfaction with the progress which had been made in the building of the Museum. That this dissatisfaction was unwarranted does not affect the fact that it existed. A further handicap was encountered in the public impression that the Museum was more or less a monument to its two or three founders. Mr. Whiting and the Board had before them the difficult task of making the people of Cleveland see and realize that the Museum was theirs.... It took vision and constructive ability and hard work to bring it about.*

With just pride the report then continued: "The results accomplished are evidenced by the largest attendance per capita of population of any museum in the United States."[2]

With those basic concerns now well resolved, it was essential to concentrate all energies upon the creation of the best possible art museum. This meant developing as distinguished a collection as possible as well as planning stimulating programs. There was one man with the knowledge and enthusiasm, discreet charm of manner, and personal generosity needed to further the realization of those goals: Jeptha Wade's grand-

William Brownell Sanders (1854-1929), after resigning as judge of the Court of Common Pleas, went into partnership with Andrew Squire (right) and James H. Dempsey (center) in 1890. The firm quickly became one of the largest and best known in Ohio. Besides his law practice Sanders had extensive business interests.

As a Trustee of both the Huntington Trust and the Kelley Foundation, Sanders had been a leader in consolidating the three art museum projects into one adequately financed enterprise. An active member of the Building Committee, he also prepared the Museum's Articles of Incorporation in 1913 and served as its first President.

son, J. H. Wade II. As proof yet again of Judge Sanders's wisdom, by stepping down he made way for a man with a superior understanding of the arts to guide the Museum through this second phase of development.[3] Wade was elected the Museum's President in November 1920, while Ralph T. King, John L. Severance, and William G. Mather were elected its Vice Presidents, thus establishing the Museum's leadership until 1949. At the end of the year Leonard C. Hanna, Jr., also became a member of the Board.

No one could question the choice of Wade. He had given the land upon which the Museum was built and, within months of its incorporation, even before col-

lecting policies had been established, had begun making gifts. As the *Inaugural Exhibition* was being dismantled, he and his wife gave thirty-four of the finest paintings in their personal collection to help fill the empty galleries, and in the summer of 1920 he established a trust fund, the income of which was preferably to be used for acquiring "European and American paintings, rugs, embroideries, brocades, laces, jewelry, and artistic objects in gold, silver and enamel."[4] Subsequently he added major sums to that fund (at his death in 1926 its value was close to $1,300,000) and also gave $200,000 as a challenge to encourage others to establish an operating endowment since he recog-

Jeptha Homer Wade II (1857-1926), a financier and philanthropist—the grandson of a founder of Western Union Telegraph Company, Jeptha H. Wade—had given the land on which to build an art museum as a Christmas gift to the city in 1892. By the time of his death Wade had given the Museum 2,855 works of art, besides setting up a $1.3 million art purchase trust fund.

Wade's knowledge and enthusiasm about art, his personal charm, and his generosity more than qualified him for assuming the Museum's leadership when Judge Sanders stepped down in November 1920.

Acquired in May 1927 for $120,000, this marble figure of Athena was believed, on the advice of competent experts, to belong to a group produced in an ancient Greek colony. Suspicions, however, led to further research, and in May 1928 it was returned to the dealer for a full refund.

The statue, the work of the now-famous art forger Alceo Dossena, had never been exhibited at the Museum; Director Whiting reported the full story in the April 1929 *Bulletin*.

nized that all too soon the income from the Huntington Trust and Kelley Foundation would no longer suffice. These and countless other gifts—2,855 objects before his death—are well known; the impact of his thinking upon every aspect of the emerging Museum is not as widely recognized.

Since the Museum was now well established and its professional staff was growing, any former dependence upon the Metropolitan Museum of Art disappeared. In turn, as Cleveland came to realize that it could be—and indeed was—a competitor on the international art market, its goals became more ambitious. The earlier enthusiasm for numbers of Egyptian artifacts ended, although—reflecting the new sense of standards characterizing the Museum in the 1920s—one or two much more important works were acquired, most notably a Dynasty VI tomb relief in 1930 (CMA 30.736). Instead, attention was directed toward Greek and Roman art. Late in 1923 Wade urged "taking advantage of opportunities to increase our small classical collection, when suitable opportunities arose."[5] Simultaneously Harold Parsons wrote Whiting at length.[6]  He pointed out that, while it was no longer possible to do what Boston had done between 1892 and 1904,[7] there were important opportunities still available on the European market even as there was less competitive activity from European collectors hard-hit by the war. Wade led the way by purchasing three Roman marbles, and to the delight of all, the Huntington Trustees made a handsome grant even as Leonard Hanna's mother, Coralie Walker Hanna, became actively interested—so there was money for classical sculpture. The enthusiasm was slightly diminished when it turned out that an archaic Greek Athena, acquired for the largest amount yet spent by the young Museum on a single object, was discovered to be wrong; by 1929 it emerged that this piece was among the numerous Dossena fakes which had duped so many of the major public and private collectors in America.[8]

Perhaps the classical material was not at the level later expected of this Museum, but several works acquired during these years remain major elements in the collection today.[9] In contrast, however, and providentially Wade took great delight (as suggested by the terms of his trust fund) in fine metal and precious objects. The initial acquisitions made with the income of his new trust fund were three pieces of American silver, including a Paul Revere, Jr., cream jug (CMA 21.38);[10] but Wade soon turned his attention to an earlier period where the greater part of his fund's income was spent in the last few years of his life. The Museum had the perfect match: a committed, perceptive donor, J. H. Wade, delightedly working with a brilliant, knowledgeable Curator, William M. Milliken. The standards that were to characterize the Museum's acquisitions for the next sixty-five years were established almost overnight. The first hint of the new direction was evident in 1922 with the acquisition of three compelling Rhenish walrus, or morse, ivories of the second half of the eleventh century (CMA 22.307-.309). The goals were evident a year later with the acquisition of a Limoges enamel known as the Spitzer Cross (CMA 23.1051), dating to about 1190. This was followed in 1924 by the Bethune casket (CMA 24.747)—a Byzantine ivory of the eleventh-twelfth century (given by Wade along with Severance, Prentiss, and Mather)—as well as the French table fountain (CMA 24.859) of the first half of the fourteenth century found by Milliken as he scoured the market in Paris, and finally in 1925 the Strogonoff ivory plaque of the eleventh century (CMA 25.1293)—each object a world-famous work of art that would be the envy of any museum. Paul J. Sachs, the distinguished collector who was also the Director of Harvard's Fogg Art Museum, wrote apropos of the Strogonoff ivory: "it is a triumph for all concerned. Every serious student and every lover of truly *great* things must now visit The Cleveland Museum of Art if only to see this one object"—truly music for the young Board's ears.[11]

The policy on acquiring paintings evolved more hesitantly. The earlier assumption that buying American paintings was sensible because such material was

William Milliken remembered that when "word came that the ivory [an 11th-century Byzantine *Plaque: Madonna and Child Enthroned with Angels* (CMA 25.1293) from Count Strogonoff's collection] was on the market ... [it] seemed almost incredible."

J. H. Wade was willing to help, "but how to transmit ... [the offer]? It had become evident that time was of the essence, a letter might be too late in those days before Air Mail. A clear cut offer of a large amount by cable might raise questions and encourage counter offers."

Relief efforts fortuitously provided a suitable cover: "The cable read: 'Cleveland will be glad to contribute (X number of) dollars for Near Eastern Relief.'" And it won a positive reply.

He added: "Many years later, Arthur Sachs recounted how that was the first time that the Cleveland Museum had come in his way. In fact it was the first time that Cleveland had appeared as a purchaser of prime objects in the international market." Later still, the Museum was to buy some of Sachs' famous paintings.

less costly than the European Old Masters was quickly disproved. After much hemming and hawing, the Board decided in 1924 to approve the purchase of Winslow Homer's late, grand marine painting *Early Morning after a Storm at Sea* (CMA 24.195)—in all likelihood spurred by Wade's offer to provide the funds —but the Board was troubled that a contemporary painting should cost the staggering sum, for the day, of $50,000. This figure is put in perspective when one considers the prices of the Museum's first two major European paintings—both acquired as the result of efforts by a new group, called The Friends of The Cleveland Museum of Art, established at the end of 1925 to raise funds for the acquisition of paintings. An early Poussin *Landscape* (CMA 26.26) was purchased for $6,000 (although chosen as the Friends' first gift, it was instead given by Wade, to convey to the Friends his delight in their new efforts) and the El Greco *Holy Family* (CMA 26.247), which became the Friends' memorial to Wade, for $35,300.[12] Given the Museum's modest resources, however, it was obvious

that other means would have to be found to suggest the evolution of European painting. Wade pointed the way by funding the acquisition of ten important manuscript illustrations in 1925, thereby launching the Museum in its unusual pursuit of distinguished material in this area.

The Museum moved in other, more unorthodox directions as well. In 1920 the Board supported Whiting's suggestion that space should be allocated for "exhibits representing the art of primitive Americans, such as Peruvian, Mexican and North American Indian ... which should be the first attempt of an American art museum to show in a constructive way [i.e., not as anthropological material] the art of those who lived here before the white man came."[13] Given this unusual, broad perspective, it is not surprising that the Board was quite receptive in 1928 to the suggestion of the Gilpin Players of Karamu House that monies raised from certain performances would be sent to the Cleveland painter, Paul Travis, in Africa, to purchase African material for the collection.

*Early Morning after a Storm at Sea*, 1902, by Winslow Homer (1836-1910), American. Gift from J. H. Wade. CMA 24.195

Shortly afterward Charles F. Ramus was appointed Assistant in charge of Primitive Art.

The diverse background of the city's population had a greater impact upon the Museum's thinking than has been generally realized. On the one hand, Cleveland was very much aware of its New England origins. In April 1919 the Curator of Colonial Art Lawrence Park urged the creation of American period rooms illustrative of "Colonial Life" (1650, 1750 or 1775, and 1800 to 1820), pointing out that such rooms would be "instructive ... in a part of the country populated largely by people of New England birth or ancestry."[14] At about this time, too, the Bostonian Hollis French started to deposit his important collection of American silver on indefinite loan. His attitudes were mentioned in the Board's memorial at the time of his death in 1940, which noted that he saw "in Cleveland and the Western Reserve an outpost of the New England spirit in the lands beyond the Alleghenies. He realized profoundly the importance of the old bonds of tradition which drew together the new and the old."[15]

On the other hand, responding to the city's many different ethnic communities, in 1919 the Museum presented its *Homelands Exhibit* made up of "objects brought from home countries by the foreign-born residents of Cleveland."[16] During these early years specific programs—especially in the area of music— were energetically pursued to attract these various communities to the Museum.

In just ten years[17] the new Museum had gone through a succession of steps leading to a policy on acquisitions that would serve the new institution remarkably well; henceforth the goals were clear, the variations in carrying them out would result from the means available. Wade served the collection well in yet another most important way. As the Director noted in his memorial in 1926: "Mr. Wade definitely stated that it would be contrary to his wishes to have a room set aside for his collection, or to bear his name, as he believed this would be contrary to the best policy for the Museum." Whiting rightly observed "this declaration by Mr. Wade was one of the most important gifts which he made to the Museum. It established a precedent of the utmost value in the upbuilding of its collections."[18]

While the policy on the collection became increasingly ambitious, the education program developed with a steady energy, much as planned from the outset. The Board recognized, with pride, "The work of our Director, in popularizing Art and bringing the advantages of [the Museum] ... to the people" and observed that his work "has been recognized all over the country as a departure from traditional methods, which bids fair to revolutionize museum management."[19] The single important departure from the original plan was the decision in 1920, after two years of experimentation, to establish the first Department of Musical Arts in an American art museum.[20]

The program of the Children's Museum was proof of the Museum's early commitment to the curious concept that "the natural approach of the child to an understanding of the art of man is through the beauties of nature."[21] It is hardly surprising, therefore, that on February 6, 1920, the Museum enthusiastically hosted the meeting that led to the creation of the nearby Cleveland Museum of Natural History. And in 1924 the evident success of the Children's Museum and Wade's satisfaction with its varied programs inspired him to give another piece of land upon which a separate wing could be built, when the funds were raised, to develop that program even further. This effort was, of course, put off by the Depression—but the need for more space for an ever-expanding, if redirected education program (as opposed to the needs for the collection) became a leitmotif appearing in the Board minutes and staff discussions until it was realized many years later, in 1971, with the completion of the Breuer wing.

Wade's death in 1926 was a terrible blow—but he left the Museum well launched. Indeed, even before the year was out, the Huntington Trustees were making acquisitions quite as ambitious as those Wade had championed: the Perseus tapestry (CMA 27.487), a pair

The Roman *Orestes Sarcophagus* dates to the early 2nd century AD. Gift of the John Huntington Art and Polytechnic Trust. CMA 28.856

of Northern Italian thirteenth-century marble griffins (CMA 28.861-.862), a Roman bronze portrait bust dating to the first century BC (CMA 28.860), a second-century Roman marble *Orestes Sarcophagus* (CMA 28.856), and a sculpture from about 1300 of *Christ and St. John* (CMA 28.753). And so the Museum's acquisitions would continue for the next few years leading to the spectacular acquisition of the Guelph Treasure in 1930 and 1931.

By common agreement the city's other most important collector, John L. Severance (who had been greatly influenced by his brother-in-law, Dudley P. Allen), was considered the appropriate successor to J. H. Wade.

1. See Judge Sanders's remarks at the opening ceremonies of the Museum, William B. Sanders Correspondence, 1914-24, Harold T. Clark Papers, CMA Archives.

2. Quoted in Hermon A. Kelley to Worcester R. Warner, dated December 17, 1920, and appended to the December 16, 1920, Board Minutes, pp. 279-281.

3. The Board's memorial to Sanders notes: "In 1920 he withdrew from the presidency to secure the election of Jeptha H. Wade, who was so successful in carrying the Museum through its second stage of development." "The Death of Judge Sanders," *CMA Bulletin* 16, 3 (March 1929): 39-40.

4. Bequest, wills, estates: Wade, CMA Archives.

5. Board Minutes, November 16, 1923, p. 466.

6. Board Minutes, December 6, 1923, p. 466. Parsons had been suggesting European acquisitions since 1914. After much discussion, and recognizing that the Museum was spending more, the Board officially appointed Parsons as the Museum's "European Representative" in 1925; clearly a retainer was more to the Museum's advantage than a commission on each object. By the early 1930s Parsons was also representing the interests of the new Nelson Gallery in Kansas City. He retired in 1941, although he maintained friendships with the staff thereafter.

7. The expatriate Bostonian, Edward Warren, working with his companion, John Marshall, bought brilliantly, first for the Museum of Fine Arts, Boston, and then, when all funds there were concentrated instead upon a new museum building, for the Metropolitan. Cleveland did try unsuccessfully to work with Warren, late in his life; and it did work with Marshall through Parsons. But following Warren's death in 1929, Mrs. Holden's children acquired for the Museum the greatest treasure of his not inconsiderable private collection, the Filippino Lippi tondo, as a memorial for their mother.

8. The Museum had in fact bought two Dossena fakes; the other was a *Madonna and Child* in the manner of the fourteenth-century Pisano family. Thanks to William Valentiner, the Museum first discovered its mistakes before the attribu-

This *Griffin* is one of a pair created in North Italy, about 1220. Gift of the John Huntington Art and Polytechnic Trust. CMA 28.861

tion to Alceo Dossena was recognized or the extent of his fraudulent activity known. The money for each was fully returned and subsequently well spent, primarily on medieval objects. Following lengthy discussions of the matter at its October 18, 1928, meeting, the fascinated Board displayed its new sophistication in urging full publication of all the Dossena forgeries in America and agreed that the Museum must immediately publish the facts about its acquisitions. See "The Dossena Forgeries," *CMA Bulletin* 16, 4 (April 1929): 66-67.

9. Among them are the 8th-century vessel known as the Dipylon *Amphora* (CMA 27.6), the so-called Cleveland *Krater* of about 470 (CMA 30.104), the Roman bronze portrait (CMA 28.860), and the *Orestes Sarcophagus* (CMA 28.856).

10. A Bostonian collector of eighteenth-century American silver, Hollis French, who had been one of the engineers working on the new Museum, lent his own personal collection of American silver to Cleveland; Wade's acquisitions may well have been a contributing factor in French's giving his own collection to the Museum in 1940, just before his death.

11. As is seen by its inclusion in the Board Minutes for the November 27, 1925, meeting (p. 635). Sachs had hoped to buy this ivory for his brother Arthur, from whom the Museum bought several major paintings in the early 1950s.

12. Only six paintings were given by the Friends during their short-lived existence between 1926 and 1937, but each was a major work: besides the El Greco, the Friends gave the anonymous Spanish painting, *A Bishop Saint with Donor* of about 1420 (CMA 27.197), the Bernardo Strozzi *Minerva* (CMA 29.133), a work by the German Master of the Fröndenberg Altarpiece, *Coronation of the Virgin* (CMA 29.920), *Bouquet of Flowers* by the Cleveland artist Henry Keller (CMA 38.374), and the Austrian Master of Heiligenkreuz's *Death of the Virgin* (CMA 36.496), the last given as a memorial to the Museum's third President, John L. Severance.

13. Board Minutes, July 1, 1920, p. 230.

14. *CMA Bulletin* 6, 3 (April 1919): 53-54.

15. Board Minutes, November 1940, p. 1850.

16. *CMA Bulletin* 6, 3 (April 1919): 56.

17. During these years there had been over 3,000,000 visitors and the operating budget had gone from $57,353 to $242,920. *CMA Bulletin* 13, 7 (July 1926): 167.

18. "A Joint Memorial Meeting of the Trustees and Councilors," *CMA Bulletin* 13, 4 (April 1926): 72.

19. Hermon A. Kelley to Worcester R. Warner, December 17, 1920, Board Minutes.

20. Whiting's firm commitment to this effort may have been influenced by his wife, Olive Cook Whiting, who cared greatly for music and must have had some professional competence since she was initially the conductor of the Museum's Children's Orchestra.

21. "The Cleveland Museum of Natural History," *CMA Bulletin* 7, 2 (February 1920): 24.

This Roman bronze *Portrait Bust of a Man* dates to 40-30 BC. Gift of the John Huntington Art and Polytechnic Trust. CMA 28.860

Ambrose Swasey (1846-1937) and Worcester Reed Warner (1846-1929) were photographed at the age of 80, on January 13, 1927, in their office.

aving met in Exeter, New Hampshire, Warner and Swasey formed their pioneering machine tool partnership in 1880. First located in Chicago, Warner & Swasey Company moved a year later to Cleveland, due to its better location and supply of skilled mechanics. Both men were active in scientific and professional societies, and the Cleveland Chamber of Commerce. Both were invited to serve on the Art Museum's Advisory Council when it was formed on July 13, 1914, by the Trustees. The by-laws called for appointing an Advisory Council that "shall ... consider and report upon to the Board all such questions as shall be submitted to it by the Board."

Worcester Warner and Ambrose Swasey continued their connection with and interest in the Museum until their deaths. Ralph King is credited with arousing Warner's interest in Asian art with notable results even before the Museum's doors opened. The marble *Buddha* illustrated here featured prominently in the *Inaugural Exhibition*. On that occasion it was noted: "ere long our Museum will have, in the Warner Collection, a splendid exhibit of the art of the far East. Nothing could have been done for the Museum more timely or adding more substantially to its attractions and usefulness than that which Mr. Warner has done."

Carved in the North-
ern Qi period (550-
577), this marble
*Seated Amitayus
Buddha* is displayed
on a pedestal dated

647 (Tang dynasty).
Worcester R. Warner
Collection. CMA
15.334,a

This gilt-bronze
*Guanyin* dates to
about 1450 (Ming
dynasty). Worcester R.
Warner Collection.
CMA 16.19

Box with Cover is part
of a set of five 12th-
century Korean inlaid
celadon ware boxes
within a larger box.
Worcester R. Warner
Collection. CMA
16.1186

The Japanese Imari ware porcelain *Vase with Dutchmen and Foreign Vessel* (CMA 19.837) is an unusual and important work in the shape of a double gourd, and is an example of the Asian ceramics and sculpture that King gave to the Museum.

*The Age of Bronze* (CMA 18.328) is one of the most famous pieces by the contemporary French artist Auguste Rodin. Like the over-lifesize cast of *The Thinker* at the Museum's south entrance, it was ordered from the artist himself by the Kings.

As a student of prints and a wise collector, Ralph Thrall King was the Print Department's first, volunteer Curator, 1920-1922, and helped train his successor Theodore Sizer. In its early days the Print Club considered King its leader as well as a founder, though he declined its presidency. With his wife King gave at least 870 objects to the Museum, over 700 of which were in the graphic arts. Among the most notable, according to Curator Sizer, were "the magnificent collection of etchings, lithographs, and drawings by James McNeill Whistler ... Fantin-Latour lithographs ... seventy-five etchings by Legros ... the Lepéres and Lautrecs."

King's contribution to the Museum, however, is broader than such tangible evidence might indicate. As the Board's memorial put it: "His enthusiasm for the work the Museum was doing, and for its service to the community, was a source of constant encouragement and inspiration to all who were associated with him." Perhaps more to the point however, is the sentiment of Rossiter Howard: "Though we shall miss his help in meeting our large problems, what we will miss most will be ... his personality and a feeling of his warm friendliness."

*Sultry Afternoon*
(CMA 19.843) by the
American artist Arthur
William Heintzelman
(b. 1891) was given
by Ralph King for
The Frederick Keppel
Memorial. The me-
morial was initiated

with a gift of 47 etch-
ings from members of
the Keppel firm for
the purpose of "en-
couraging among art
institutions a better
understanding of
prints and engrav-
ings."

*Elles: The Seated
Clown* (CMA 25.1205)
by Henri de Toulouse-
Lautrec shows King's
evolving taste.
   He presented the
Museum with the

entire *Elles* set—ten
lithographs, frontis-
piece, and original
folder.

Ralph Thrall King
(1855-1926) with
Webb Hayes (right),
the son of Rutherford
B. Hayes, the 19th
President of the
United States.
   A graduate of
Brown University,
King gained his first

business experience in
his father's lumber
firm, but came into
his own as President
of Realty Investment
Company, one of the
largest holders of
property in down-
town Cleveland.

*Venus Reclining in a Landscape (after Giorgione)* by Giulio Campagnola, Italian (about 1482-after 1515). Gift of The Print Club of Cleveland. CMA 31.205

Formed after World War I in late 1919, The Print Club of Cleveland was the vision of one man, Ralph Thrall King, generously supported by 15 other charter members. It was the first group of Museum friends interested in a special subject to unite in order to increase their knowledge and to sponsor suitable additions to the Museum collection. Though the membership has inevitably changed during the past seventy-two years, the Club's enthusiastic commitment to the Museum has not wavered. It maintains a vital, close relationship with the Museum and remains dedicated to the founders' twin purposes of enhancing the Museum's collection by gifts and stimulating a general interest in collecting.

Over the years the Club's gifts—sometimes drawings rather than prints—have more than satisfied the Museum's standards of quality. Many members—too many to name here—have followed Ralph King's example in giving works to the Museum's print collection themselves as well as contributing toward Club purchases. Few Club members, however, have been as dedicated as Leona E. Prasse, long-time Secretary of the Club and former Associate Curator of Prints and Drawings. As Sherman Lee pointed out on the Club's fiftieth anniversary in 1969, "Through good times and depression she nurtured the interests of the Club and found ways to continue its programs. She has given guidance to the budding collector and a sense of direction to the experienced who come to the Print Study Room. The Mr. and Mrs. Charles G. Prasse Collection established with her personal gift is an important segment within the Museum's collection."

The Print Club also supports the Museum in other ways. It sponsors exhibitions and programs open to the public concerning the graphic arts. The Club has provided funds to the Museum Library for the purchase of materials related to prints and drawings, and to the Education Department for special projects.

*The Apocalypse: The Four Horsemen* by Albrecht Dürer, German (1471-1528). Gift of The Print Club of Cleveland. CMA 32.313

*The Virgin with a Spindle* by Jacques Bellange, French (about 1594-about 1638). Gift of The Print Club of Cleveland in honor of Louise S. Richards. CMA 86.244

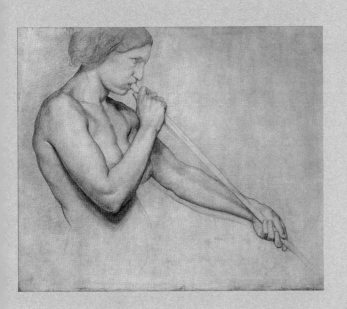

*Study for an Angel Blowing a Trumpet* by Edgar Degas, French (1834-1917). Gift of The Print Club of Cleveland. CMA 76.130

# FREDERIC A. WHITING: FOUNDING THE MUSEUM WITH ART AND CRAFT

BRUCE ROBERTSON

Bruce Robertson is the Museum's Associate Curator of Paintings.

At first glance, Frederic Allen Whiting seems to have been an unlikely choice as the founding Director of The Cleveland Museum of Art. Secretary of the Society of Arts and Crafts in Boston for twelve years, he had only just taken up his first museum job, as Director of The John Herron Art Institute of Indianapolis, Indiana, when he was offered the position at Cleveland. Whiting was nationally known as a promoter of the industrial arts and an educator, not as a museum professional or connoisseur of the fine arts. But the selection of Whiting as Director reveals much about the Trustees' initial conception of the Museum and its role in the community. The Museum's subsequent development under Whiting, until his resignation in 1930, confirmed and strengthened the wisdom of their choice.

The Whiting family had originally come from Massachusetts, but Frederic was born on January 26, 1873, in Oakdale, Tennessee, where his father was president of an iron company. After a few years in Tennessee and New Jersey the family returned to Massachusetts, to the manufacturing town of Lowell. They remained there from 1890 to 1895 before moving closer to Boston. As a teenager, Whiting went into business, as had his father and brothers. He had no formal education after grammar school and was tutored at home. While in Lowell, his essential interests became clear. As he recalled later: "I think the most important factor was the social work in the mill town of Lowell, where I ... spent a good deal of time in club work with mill boys." Whiting served as treasurer of the Unity Guild, the charitable arm of the Unity Congregational Church (Unitarian) of Lowell, from 1895 to 1897, before rejoining his family who had moved on to Framingham. He remembered that he began preparing for the ministry "but bad eyes made a halt necessary, and I decided I could serve effectively as a layman."[1] This idea of service among working-class, often immigrant communities inspired the rest of his life, however shadowed by the threat of exhaustion and illness.

Frederic Allen Whiting (1873-1959), the new Director of The Cleveland Museum of Art, had been recommended to the Cleveland Trustees by the Metropolitan Museum's Secretary Henry W. Kent. Whiting was nationally known as a proponent of the Arts and Crafts movement and an educator.

In 1900 Whiting took his first step into the world of professional art and artists when he was appointed the first full-time, paid secretary of the Society of Arts and Crafts, Boston. Two years before, he had met C. Howard Walker, a prime mover in the Society, on board a ship going to England. Whiting had been heading for Liverpool to study the utopian worker's community of Port Sunlight, founded by Lord Leverhume. When the opportunity—thanks to Arthur Carey's gift—came to hire a secretary for the Society, Walker remembered Whiting and recommended him.[2]

The Arts and Crafts movement was a loose coalition growing out of the aesthetic reform of British artists and critics like William Morris and John Ruskin. Bringing together social visionaries who despised what the factory system did to people, and lovers of beauty who preferred handmade objects to mass-produced goods, the movement represented a natural step for anyone interested in bettering the working classes, since it aspired to improve society by raising the quality of workmanship.

The Boston Society, after a tremendous start in 1897, had stalled for a few years, but Whiting's arrival augured a new enthusiasm and dedication on the part of its directors. It soon emerged as the leading Arts and Crafts group in the country, inspiring scores of similar societies and guiding them by the example of its salesroom and its periodical *Handicraft*. As H. Langford Warren, the Society's President, declared at Whiting's farewell dinner, Whiting had been largely responsible for this growth.[3]

As Secretary, Whiting had two major concerns. The first was education. He lectured to all the smaller societies—from Minnesota to Maryland and throughout New England—organized meetings, and formed coalitions between interested groups. He founded and edited *Handicraft* as another means of inspiring and uniting the movement. Whiting declared: "There is a crying need for the education of the general public in matters of culture and appreciation; an education leading to better standards of individual taste which will in turn bring about a simpler manner of life."[4] Education was, for Whiting, the way to achieve that "flowering of art in common things which shall be expressive of a new realization of the importance of beauty as a necessary element of daily life."[5]

Achieving the first goal led naturally to the second, that of putting "before the discriminating purchasing public the product of the craftsmen."[6] As Whiting wrote, "this involves, in the end, a reorganization of society through a changed point of view as to the value of artistic work. It means an appreciation by the purchaser of his responsibility for the welfare and happiness of the producer of what he purchases."[7] Thus, Whiting's other primary concern was the Society's shop, always a source of irritation that consumed endless amounts of time. Whiting wanted it to be commercially successful and to provide a solid income for the Society's other activities. He oversaw a growth in sales from $4,000 in 1900, the year it opened, to $37,000 in 1905, when the Society became self-supporting.

His attempts to guide the Society professionally, however, were not always welcome, and he attempted to resign twice, in 1903 and 1908. For the more radical, Socialist members, Whiting's businesslike pragmatism ran counter to the spirit of communal support. In 1903 Arthur Carey and Mary Dennett both resigned from the Board over the issue. Dennett ap-

preciated "the lovable, intimate, family, friendly side of Fred's character," she declared to Whiting's wife Olive, although she deplored his "general attitude of compromise."[8] In the effort to rouse the Society against him, she and Carey involved the staff of the shop, taking depositions about his behavior as a "boss." Whiting prevailed then and again in 1908 when craftsmen dissatisfied with how their work was being displayed tried to get him fired on charges of favoritism. Whiting, concerned that the shop produce revenue for the Society, had insisted on the highest standards for the merchandise. The Board again supported him completely.

Recognition of his stature as a national spokesman for the Arts and Crafts came quickly. In 1904 he was asked to organize the Division of Applied Arts at the Louisiana Purchase Exposition in St. Louis. There, in testimony to his success (and perhaps bias), the Boston Society accounted for over half of the 863 exhibits and both he and Mrs. Whiting received gold medals for their participation.

By 1911 his increasing national reputation had begun to make him consider leaving the Society, which in any case had long questioned—or rather some of its members had—the need for him to devote so much of his time to a national platform at the expense of local matters. Also, Whiting could barely support his family on his salary. On June 4, 1903, he had married Olive Cook, and their only child, Frederic Allen Whiting, Jr., was born in 1906. For the rest of his life, Olive was also his colleague and co-worker.

At first Whiting thought he might go back into business, and he explored the possibility of working with Tiffany's, which had contributed a major display to the St. Louis exhibition.[9] But The John Herron Art Institute of Indianapolis offered him the post of Director, enabling him to continue his educational work, as well as paying him four times more than the Society had.

Arriving in Indianapolis in May 1912, Whiting stayed less than a year. By September the Cleveland Museum had approached him, and by the end of

January 1913 he had accepted their offer. But in that year he accomplished a surprising amount, a revealing prelude to his efforts in Cleveland. In a sense, he saw the Herron Art Institute as a permanent version of the Arts and Crafts hall at the St. Louis Exposition, augmented with far-reaching educational programs. His first efforts went, not toward the collection, but for education. Among other innovations, he arranged for a teacher's training college to provide docents, and inaugurated a special edition of the museum bulletin for children, establishing a pattern that he would follow in Cleveland: using the resources of other educational institutions and aiming his efforts at young people.[10]

When Cleveland approached him, only months after his arrival in Indianapolis, Lockwood de Forest—the brother of Robert de Forest, President of the Metropolitan Museum, and someone on whom Whiting relied for advice—wrote him: "[Cleveland] is a bigger place, and you would have all the advantages of starting out at the beginning and of having your views of what a museum should be carried out."[11] De Forest described those views in the same letter: "Your idea of developing the museum on industrial art lines has created new interest in Indianapolis. The picture and sculpture business has been overdone, and really has very little if any educational value." Earlier he had written: "You will have done a valuable piece of real missionary work if you are able to convince your directors that modern paintings have probably less value than any other form of art work in educating our people."[12]

De Forest's comments cast an interesting light on Whiting's views about building collections, one of the things for which the Cleveland Museum would become most famous. Such a prejudice against painting was common among progressive art educators of the time. It arose from a commonly held perception of the nature of the American audience and how to educate it. In the last decades of the nineteenth century progressive institutions of all kinds, museums included, understood that the primary audience in need

of education was working-class children, which really meant immigrant children. In a sense, upper- and middle-class children were already served, but there seemed to be a real danger that an underclass would develop which would have nothing in common with and would not share traditional, Anglo-Saxon cultural expectations. Such a class might well want to overthrow them: anarchist threats and industrial actions scared those in power into periodic fits of abuse and cajolery. Immigrants, mainly from Eastern Europe and the Mediterranean, needed to be educated into American ways if they were going to become Americans; and it was much easier to start with the children than with their parents. Progressive educators realized that as far as art was concerned, what was needed for these children was not high-falutin' and incomprehensible pictures but immediate and concrete objects, things closer to their experience and their needs as future workers and craftsmen in American industries. Decorative arts were considered most suited to attract the interest (and intellects) of children.[13]

Both schools and museums were seen as agents of social order: "The development of the artistic sense is often a preventive of mischief making and modifies the chronic restlessness so common in young people."[14] "Mischief making" had a larger political meaning than just childish behavior. Most politicians feared the anarchism and socialism believed to run rampant among communities of foreign workers. But art could quiet even them: "So long as [art] schools for the building up of society are heartily sustained by all classes of ... citizens, the delusive sophistries of 'Socialist' agitation, the destructive activities of foreign 'Nihilists' can find no footholds."[15]

Successful industrialization required not only docile but skilled workers, and the Arts and Crafts movement in this country insisted that the most successful products were those made by workmen with taste. Dedicated to fitting children to their lives as workers, industrial high schools were set up throughout the United States beginning in the 1880s, a decade or more before the Arts and Crafts movement began. In Massachusetts training in design formed a major part of the school curriculum and provided the most important model for the rest of the country. As Secretary of the Boston Society, Whiting had been intimately involved in organizing a statewide conference on Industrial Education, bringing together "representatives of educational, industrial and labor interests."[16]

The "art" taught to these students was naturally largely devoted to designing objects for domestic use, an activity which was not merely useful but upright. It is hard now to comprehend the fervor with which the moral import of interior decoration was preached. At the turn of the century, the Arts and Crafts movement was imbued with the certainty and ethical strictness shared by ecological organizations today. People stenciled walls as earnestly as they now recycle paper. This passion to perfect the home—something we seem to have given up on—was manifested not only in behavior but in objects. Correctly designed objects indicated the moral orderliness of the owner and could inculcate rectitude in the user. The decorative arts reeked of purity in a way that painting, even purged of the naked ladies who seemed to frolic in it, could never achieve.

Hand in hand with this "practical" emphasis on design went a major change in the nature and goals of art education, even in the art academies. Since the Italian Renaissance, drawing and study of the human body—whether from plaster casts of ancient sculpture or live models—had been the foundation of study and the prime concern of the artist. The American realist painter Thomas Eakins, for example, as a professor at the Pennsylvania Academy, spent most of his time teaching life drawing, with little attention to any of the other aspects of an artist's craft. By 1900, however, a more democratic and universal method was desired and developed. Formal issues of pattern and color theory moved to the forefront. One of the leaders of this movement was the influential teacher and theorist Arthur Wesley Dow, whose book *Theory and Practise of Teaching Art* went through countless

editions. In it, he dispensed with the human figure almost entirely, relying instead on patterns as a way of teaching students to draw and to develop compositions and techniques of design.

The belief of Dow and other reformers in the fundamental need to begin with pattern in art education underpinned the desire to collect patterned artifacts which dominated American museums at the turn of the century. Ceramic tiles, ironwork, baskets, bowls, all were grist for their collections, but the most important were textiles, a craft that seemed to embody old-world traditions, as well as being particularly suited for the education of young women (as ironwork was for young men). Textiles evoked an earlier time, so that a nineteenth-century American quilt could elicit extravagant response: "The hand-woven coverlet tells you that the humblest artisan who kneels at the altars of Beauty received from the hand of the god his share of that priceless draught."[17] Lace was usually the focus of this activity—not only the lace produced in the great centers of Italy and France but even examples that were essentially folk art. The avidity with which early nineteenth-century lace from obscure, isolated Eastern European or Greek Island communities was sought after is hard to comprehend today. Such laces served as a way of both recognizing and rewarding the ethnic communities from which so many immigrants had come. Normally prominently displayed, textiles were often the only artifacts from the homelands of many new Americans represented in American museums. Handmade textiles also represented a stand against the premier symbol of the Industrial Revolution, the textile mill, which had been the focus of conservative wrath from the eighteenth century. Ironically this late nineteenth-century fixation on textiles came just at the point when steel, not textiles, became the industrial leader: the fixation on lace was therefore doubly old-fashioned. Not surprisingly, the Wade family's collection of lace was one of the first major collections given to the Cleveland Museum; it was made available to the public to examine in the Textile Study Room (which preceded the Print and Drawings Study Room). Like the Metropolitan's lace collection, it focused not on folk examples but on the "high art" of sixteenth- and seventeenth-century Italian lace making.

Finally, most American museums shied away from paintings because they felt that they had no chance in building up collections comparable to the great picture galleries of Europe. They chose as their model something more recent and more useful, the South Kensington Museum (now called the Victoria and Albert Museum) in London. It took a world war and the Great Depression, which dispersed so many private collections, before Andrew Mellon's vision of a National Gallery of Art modeled on the National Gallery in London could materialize, and before other great collections of Old Master paintings could be assembled and opened to the public.

Whiting's vision of a new kind of art museum which would put paintings in their place was shared by many progressive reformers, including the man Cleveland's Trustees had first approached to direct the Museum, Henry Watson Kent. A Bostonian by birth as Whiting was by blood and inclination, Kent was Secretary of the Metropolitan Museum of Art and a major force in the American museum world. Trained as a librarian, he aimed his major efforts at organizing information and institutions: he was the first Curator and Librarian of both the Slater Memorial Museum and the Grolier Club. But he was not the kind of librarian who liked to keep books on the shelves. His ideal, like Whiting's, was public service, an ideal he interpreted imaginatively. Kent believed in new technologies and systems: he devised the registration methods of the Metropolitan and Cleveland museums, initiating the use of catalogue cards. It is typical of the man that he should have organized the first slide library at the Metropolitan in 1907 and have installed it at the information desk in the lobby, available for visitors to borrow. He was also instrumental in developing the Metropolitan's educational programs and its cooperation with local school systems, beginning in 1905.[18] In all his efforts, with the

full support of the President of the Museum, Robert De Forest (who was greatly interested in children's education), Kent expanded the notion of the public service of museums, quite as much as his famous contemporary and good friend, John Cotton Dana, Director of the Newark Museum. Kent declared: "Art for the people's sake is the motto of the American museum today."[19] Furthermore, Kent had practical experience in building museums: as Secretary, he had supervised the construction of a new wing at the Metropolitan in 1910 and had advised on installing cast collections in Springfield, Providence, New York, Pittsburgh, and Buffalo.

Offered the job of Director at Cleveland on November 28, 1911, Kent turned the Trustees down. But he did agree to help out and advised them for several years about the design of the new building, concentrating as much on such practical matters as storage and office space (as well as new technological matters like skylights and a climate control system), as on the design of the galleries. With his help, the Cleveland Museum became the first in the country to be built with the three primary functions of a museum firmly in mind—"acquisition, exhibition and exposition."[20] Later, until the curatorial departments were established, he served as an *ex officio* New York agent for the Museum, advising on acquisitions.

Kent also suggested names to the Trustees as candidates for the directorship. One of them was Whiting, whom Kent would have known through several sources, as they shared interests in fine printing and children's education, besides a good many friends and acquaintances. Both, for example, were well-known to Tiffany's; in fact, George Kunz of Tiffany's had recommended Kent to J. H. Wade. In a sense Whiting and Kent came from the same mold, and their careers remained intertwined in later years. Offered the job in September 1912 by Judge Sanders, the President of the Board of Trustees, Whiting accepted on January 27, 1913.

The Trustees' choice was consonant with the tenor of similar appointments made then at most new institutions in Cleveland. The Trustees wanted the best and most professional help they could find, and they wanted someone nationally prominent. Later, when the Trustees of the Cleveland School of Art, a group essentially the same as the Trustees of the Art Museum, began looking for an academic director of the art school, they chose Henry Turner Bailey, the most prominent figure in industrial art education in Massachusetts and one of the leading educators in the country. Kent and Whiting were equally well known in their own fields. Moreover, whether or not the institution was narrowly defined as educational, the trustees of most Cleveland philanthropies saw their mission as educational. Another reason for choosing Kent and Whiting concerned their pronounced views on education, backed by a great deal of experience. Finally, most philanthropies in Cleveland preferred to cooperate, to pool resources and increase efficiency (another leitmotif of progressive movements at the time). As we shall see, they could not have chosen a more dedicated coalition builder than Whiting.

As far as the Museum collection was concerned, the Trustees may not have been as united, given that few were real collectors themselves. Not all were ready to write off Old Master pictures as a worthwhile goal. After all, they felt they had some pretty fine paintings in town (although time has removed many of the Holden and a few of the Wade paintings from the gallery walls). Nonetheless, all were well aware that Cleveland was an industrial town and that the Museum, in its educational mission and community presence, should at least reflect that fact if not somehow promote it. The most vocal in this regard was Dudley Peter Allen. The Trustees memorialized him for his dedication to creating a museum that would be a "living agency for the education of the people," with a collection that would serve "as a model for the handicraftsmen of Cleveland."[21]

Along with their recognition of the industrial basis of Cleveland—which was, after all, the source of most of the city's wealth—came the knowledge that factory workers were mostly foreign-born. By 1910

first-generation Americans and immigrants accounted for three-quarters of Cleveland's population, and the development of the eastern suburbs had already begun. Whether for self-serving reasons or as a defensive reaction to the progressive city forming downtown—Sanders, for example, was on the losing side of the greatest legal fight the city had ever known, when he represented the private trolley-car companies against the Progressive Mayor Tom Johnson—the fact remains that nearly all the Trustees also served on the boards of charitable institutions of one kind or another. The focus of all this effort was single-minded and overwhelming: Cleveland's philanthropists saw children as the hope for a better future.

The choice of Whiting embodied this belief. Now the task was to put plans into action. Although consumed with building the Museum during his first three years, Whiting still found time to consider the future. Staff had to be selected (a task at which he achieved a remarkable level of success); the galleries had to be filled. These were matters that had to be attended to immediately and yet solved in a lasting way. Some proposals were merely pipe-dreams; others established lasting patterns within which the Museum still works.

In his initial presentation to the Trustees, Whiting characterized two types of American museums: New York's Metropolitan and Boston's Museum of Fine Arts with their rich permanent collections and few "special exhibitions of modern work" on the one hand, and all the other museums in the country with a few objects but a "continuous series of temporary exhibitions of works by modern artists" on the other. Whiting recommended the latter course, while urging "a happy medium." He stressed the need for the Museum to find some individuality in its collection and suggested that it acquire art from India since no other museum at the time specialized in it. Some of his other suggestions for the collection were pure flights of fancy. Writing to a Trustee in 1914, for example, Whiting set out his plans to woo Henry Clay Frick:

The Museum's Education Department soon achieved national distinction, under the leadership of Emily G. Gibson. Following Louise Dunn's innovation in 1919 of letting children draw while seated on the floor in the galleries, Katherine Gibson (Mrs. Gibson's daughter) is shown here with a class in the American room.

Peale's *George Washington at the Battle of Princeton* (CMA 17.946) can be seen next to Copley's *Portrait of Mrs. John Greene* (CMA 15.527) on the wall. Displayed in the case was a collection of American silver on loan, and later given, to the Museum by Hollis French.

Later Mrs. Frank Scott Corey Wicks, Gibson remained active on the staff until 1946, when she left to work for the Artists and Writers Guild.

*To the west of the entrance lobby is the large painting gallery which I have set aside for Mr. Frick's collection of Old Masters, fifty of which he lent to the Boston Museum some years ago. This is an exceedingly important collection and with the Cleveland Associations with Mr. Frick, I believe it will be possible to secure this if early measures are taken toward this end. I consider that this is the most important thing by far that we can concentrate on and that certain members of the Advisory Committee should be of particular help to us in this connection ... [I]t will draw an enormous attendance and will establish the standard of our exhibition on the highest plane so that I feel it is a matter that cannot be too strongly urged.*[22] Although correct in his estimation of Frick's pictures, Whiting underestimated Frick's independence.

The new Director concluded his first presentation to the Board: "The Museum of today is primarily an Educational institution.... Closely allied to the Educational function of the Museum is what may be called its social responsibility." The latter, Whiting suggested, could be fulfilled by having a club room.[23] In this first statement of his plans, Whiting could hardly have foreseen the distinction the Museum would gain in all areas of its permanent collection—the work of other people and the happy fortune of great bequests and gifts. But the educational aspects, something over which Whiting did have power, he managed to impress indelibly on the psyche of the Museum.

Activities outside the Museum were as important as those inside it; The Cleveland Museum of Art had to become part of the community. While expectation was high, few had any idea of what an art museum might actually accomplish in Cleveland. Whiting's sense of a museum's mission may be summed up in remarks he made in 1922, emphasizing aesthetic appreciation.[24] On the one hand, he declared, "I am not at all ashamed to go into a gallery and be unable to clip off the dates of the artist's birth and death but it would deeply grieve me not to be sensitive to the real quality of the thing itself." On the other hand, speaking of Sunday visitors, he said: "Many of them are curiosity seekers only, they bring nothing and therefore they take nothing away." In Whiting's view, it was a museum's task to provide "something" to those who wanted it. He had firm ideas about how to go about it, and devised a number of ways to reach beyond the Museum's walls. He himself constantly gave lectures with lantern slides to every kind of group. He hired a professional membership developer (a failure), but his primary method was through education. Despite the objections of some Board members who had wanted to wait until there was a collection and a building to hold classes in, almost the first person Whiting hired was Emily G. Gibson, who had run a school in Indianapolis. The Museum had begun accepting objects in 1914, so that when Mrs. Gibson

On June 7, 1916, the day the Museum first opened to the public, Whiting showed a group of students from the University School, including his son, through the Armor and Tapestry Court.

arrived in November 1915, she could organize exhibitions in high schools and libraries at once. Before the Museum opened its doors to the public on June 7, 1916, the Education and Extensions departments were already in operation. After the first member of the public walked through the doors—Alice Cole, who lived a few blocks away—Frederic Whiting led a group of fourth-grade boys from University School, including his son, through the galleries. The Museum was ready to take up its tasks.

Aside from the structure itself—which was a model of modern museum building—the first department to achieve national distinction was that of Education. While Mrs. Gibson tried little that had not been tried elsewhere—the only "first" the department claimed was Louise Dunn's decision in 1919 to let children draw freely in the galleries seated on the floor—she and her staff were happy to experiment and change to fit the situation. Several decisions made that first year had long-lasting consequences. Professional docents, for example, were employed from the start; the only volunteers were teachers from the Cleveland School of Art who helped out on Sunday afternoons. Such standards marked the rest of their efforts. After the first two months Mrs. Gibson reported: "It is clearly recognized that it is the quality of service rendered and not the numbers reached, which counts." This point had to be emphasized again and again to a Board interested in attendance figures.[25]

Children were the focus of her work. She noticed that they seemed first interested in the armor (nothing has changed in that regard!); then came the tapestries, because of "the rudimentary knowledge of handweaving taught in the schools." But after that, as she noted, "'Little Italy' came with the greatest frequency for the first week and a half. The novelty wearing off they became somewhat inclined to use the rotunda as a race track."[26] With the beginning of a new school year, the Director negotiated an agreement with the Superintendent of Cleveland's Public Schools to permit children to come during class time, so that the summer efforts were not wasted.

Not only the children but their mothers came, and Mrs. Gibson was equally observant of their behavior and their backgrounds. She commented on the diversity of those coming in 1917: "from groups of women who had left their washing and other household duties for a glimpse of objects suggestive of widely separated 'home lands' to those who approached the collection with very different experiences of foreign travel and study."[27]

The Education Department was game to try new technologies as well. Almost Whiting's last action as Director was to request the installation of fifty-four Radioears for the deaf in the auditorium.[28] One of his earliest had been to show movies to children. From the first year until 1923, movies were used in Saturday afternoon children's classes. The Cleveland Museum was probably the first in the country to have had facilities designed for showing films: a movie projector was planned for the auditorium from the beginning. Whiting was interested in films and their uses.[29] The movies were deemed to "have proved to be a most interesting phase of a much discussed problem."[30] The highlight of these films—most of which were severely instructional—must have been *Snow White*, produced by Eleanor Flynn, a dance teacher, and her pupils in 1922. The next year, for some reason, movies were discontinued. Puppet shows and small-scale theatricals, however, remained a vital part of the Museum's children's activities for years; one of the department's great triumphs was the creation of a small stage in the Museum suitable for these productions. The members of the department also published widely on the subject, one of national interest.[31]

Music was fundamental both to Whiting's notion of the arts to be represented in the Museum and in his educational efforts. The first Curator of Music, Thomas Surette, was appointed in 1918, and in 1922 the organ was dedicated. The musical offerings ranged from serious, all-Bach programs to sing-alongs for children, comparable to the range of lectures with which they were balanced. Of special interest were the nationality nights during World War I, when dif-ferent ethnic communities were invited to present songs in both their own languages and English.

In 1923, the same year in which movies were discontinued, the Education Department got down to some serious business. Cleveland's schools had become infected with the mania for testing pupils in 1912, with the appointment of one of the national leaders in the school efficiency movement, Frank Spaulding, as Superintendent. Before long, all Cleveland Public School pupils had been tested and sorted into three categories: X, Y, and Z—or high, normal, and below normal intelligence—according to the results of intelligence tests. When the Art Museum joined the game, it became the first in the country to apply "scientific" testing to study the efficiency and efficacy of museum educational methods. Begun by Katherine Gibson (Mrs. Gibson's daughter) and completed by Marguerite Bloomberg, several approaches were tried, varying both the methods of imparting the information and the location and timing of it. Success was measured by the retention rate of information among 2,024 children from twenty-six schools, measured against intelligence, home environment, race, and other factors. The outstanding result was the surprise that Z children did much better than expected, which was interpreted to mean that concrete objects were especially suitable for slow children (it did not occur to anyone then that the categories themselves might be worthless). The tests, funded and published by the Carnegie Corporation, New York, seemed to confirm nationally the importance of the Museum's Education Department.

Whiting hoped to crown these efforts with the creation of a permanent Children's Museum—one of his greatest dreams. Rooms had been set aside on the second floor for the use of children from the start, but Whiting had grander ambitions. In many annual reports, he expressed the hope that a small building would be constructed on the slope of the hill rising to the Museum, connected to the main building by a tunnel, providing an independent, safe space for children only. Never built, it was probably the failure among Whiting's many plans that rankled the most. The children's museum was also a beloved scheme of his best friend and closest collaborator among the Trustees and donors, Sanders's son-in-law, Harold T. Clark. Clark was the mainstay of the Natural History Museum (founded in 1920) and later became President of the Art Museum's Board of Trustees. His real interest in both institutions was the education of children. Whiting later recalled, with regret, that had Clark been President of the Board in 1930 things might have been different. As it was, Clark maintained several of Whiting's goals for the Museum long after his departure.

Given his burning desire to reach out to the community, Whiting eventually expanded the reach of the Museum to include all the other educational institutions in the city. From his first day he thought big. He worked quickly to establish a close relationship with the Cleveland School of Art. In 1917, Henry Turner Bailey, a friend and long-time colleague of Whiting's from Boston, was brought in as Dean of Instruction at the School. Within months of his appointment, Whiting also added Bailey to the staff of the Museum, to serve as an interim advisor after the premature death of Emily Gibson. The next year the Huntington Trustees finally established the Polytechnic School required in Huntington's will, with Bailey at that helm as well: Whiting's hand should be seen in these events.

Whiting conceived of the Museum and art schools as partners, serving different audiences but the same goal. The art classes at the Museum were designed, in part, to identify talent and encourage it. The most talented students in the Museum classes were offered scholarships to go to the Art School. As productive artists they in turn would exhibit at the Museum. In the meantime, the Art School faculty and the Museum staff volunteered and gave lectures in each other's institutions. During the 1920s, for example, doing research in the Museum collection was a formal part of the Art School's curriculum in ceramics and interior decoration.

Western Reserve University was a slightly harder nut to crack, although staff at the Museum shared appointments with the University, and the classes Bailey taught at the Museum counted for college credit. Whiting lent prints to the Music School Settlement and offered the services of Thomas Surette, the Museum's Curator of Music. Even the Case School of Applied Science required the Museum's courses for senior engineering students.

At the city-wide level, Whiting found a receptive colleague in Linda Eastman—who became Director of the Cleveland Public Library in 1918—and from 1915 organized exhibitions in Cleveland's branch libraries. The public schools were also amenable to the Museum's aid. Not only were students permitted to spend school-time in the Museum, but teachers were assigned by several school boards to work at the Museum from 1918 to help teach students and other teachers about the Museum collection. All these efforts resulted quite directly in the Cleveland Conference on Educational Cooperation or, as it is known today, University Circle. But that story belongs to the second half of Whiting's career in Cleveland.

Recognizing that an art museum necessarily gains its greatness from the art it houses, Whiting did not ignore that aspect of his job, although he was never passionate about collecting. Nonetheless, his interest in craft, reflected in the curatorial departments he created and the appointments he made, as well as many of the early collections and gifts he accepted, is still reflected in Cleveland's galleries: it is a museum of objects.

Whiting's "plan" for Indianapolis and its progressive implications have already been discussed. But Whiting's plans for Cleveland were old-fashioned in a fundamental aspect. Many experts (as disparate as Kenyon Cox, the artist, critic, and arch-enemy of modern painting, and John Cotton Dana, the iconoclastic Director of the Newark Museum) in thinking about the educational mission of museums implicitly modeled their plans on schools or more often on libraries: collections were to be useful above all else.

They imagined museums as places that stored and catalogued works of art like books, producing them on demand to a public that wished to study them and then return them to the shelves. Whiting, no doubt partly in response to the Board's inclinations and Kent's experiences, however, never truncated the aesthetic experience so abruptly. He understood well the difference between museums and their comrade institutions. He agreed with Sanders that the Museum should be a "holiday house," not a laboratory or a "school of instruction in the industrial arts."[32] He understood, as well, the need for the quiet contemplation of beauty in hospitable circumstances. He was proud of the Holden gallery, with its elaborate decor built to match its Italian Renaissance paintings. His concern for properly lighting works of art, evidenced in the construction of the galleries with the help of Kent and Edward P. Hyde (the Chief Engineer at the National Electric Lamp Works), extended into experimentation with temporary displays.

Both the Trustees and Whiting were interested in a broad range of art and aspired, like most American museums, to imitate the encyclopedic breadth of the Metropolitan Museum. Whiting's specific interest in Indian art, mentioned earlier, was also competitive: Boston had a great Chinese and Japanese collection, while the Metropolitan had its Egyptian collection. Although the Cleveland Museum did not seriously pursue Indian art at this time, its first Curator, J. Arthur MacLean, appointed in 1914, specialized in Asian art.

One of the first dilemmas facing the Museum was the issue of reproductions and originals: given the need to fill galleries and to educate the public, which was the right road? Typical (and fortunate) was the dilemma over plaster casts. The debate was sharp on this issue, with respected voices on both sides holding differing opinions. Although Sanders agreed with Charles Freer of Detroit that casts were not desirable, Cleveland did originally intend to have casts (something Kent strongly favored).[33] But fate intervened. In a letter to Dudley Allen, Whiting described his plans

Interested in all art, Whiting felt that the art of primitive cultures was the product of direct, authentic experience and as such could inspire modern artists.

Such art also had its place in the progressive educational theories of the day that proposed that children could respond more directly to it. This photograph of the Children's Museum conveys something of the activities focused there.

Particularly interested in native American art, Whiting planned to build a series of galleries devoted to it, especially the basketry collected so avidly by the Victorians.

Left to right: J. Arthur MacLean, the Museum's first Curator, an orientalist; E. Hamilton Bell, who wrote the *Inaugural Exhibition Catalogue*; and Frank Pool, the Museum's first Registrar.

for the galleries in the Museum. Planning the *Inaugural Exhibition*, he hoped to:

*secure the Keasebey collection of armor and additional important pieces sufficient to use the court of casts as a court of armor since the present war has interfered with securing the casts from abroad. The walls will be covered with important tapestries and the whole effect can be made very splendid and this exhibit should, it seems to me, be of particular interest to the men interested in the steel industry in Cleveland.*[34]

Here another and equally meritorious educational point replaced the first.

It is typical of Whiting that having thought of the space in aesthetic terms, he then wanted to make it practical and useful to the community. He got a chance shortly after the Museum was opened, when he decided that it should join the war effort by holding dances for soldiers. After the first successful one, held on the ground floor, he decided he would hold the next in the armor court. Enamored with the vision of modern soldiers waltzing (or fox-trotting) beneath the tapestries and against the backdrop of the ancient armor, he nonetheless wisely decided to get the approval of the Board. The younger members either liked the idea or were indifferent to it; but a few of the older members were emphatically horrified. Ever pragmatic, Whiting dropped the idea.

While the issue of plaster casts had been happily resolved in absentia, as it were, reproductions were collected in other areas. During the mid-1920s the Museum acquired Old Master drawing reproductions for educational purposes. Decrying the high prices and the lack of good drawings to buy, Curator Sizer declared: "The present-day public collection in order to be workable and worthwhile must of necessity be based upon reproductions."[35] Only the Great Depression and the next world war would prove him wrong.

Perhaps the greatest force in the institution on the side of original art was J. H. Wade, whose attitudes were a crucial corrective to Whiting's. Not only had Wade insisted that the galleries be organized by country or chronology, but he would not permit his

collections to be placed together, a valuable precedent for a young museum in desperate need of objects. Whiting's fight with Worcester Warner over displaying the latter's collection of Asian art was his first major policy struggle in the matter of accessions. The Director wrote to Wade: "Mr. Warner has made it very evident in many ways that he wants to have his exhibit continued permanently in a room by itself, despite the fact that it interferes with the regular sequence of the Galleries. We have no room which can be easily spared for such an exhibit."[36] Wade agreed: "I feel as I always have that the only proper way to exhibit works of art is by periods or countries."[37] Wade also trusted the professional expertise of the staff. As Whiting had earlier written: "I cannot tell you how much I appreciate the extended precedent which you and Mrs. Wade are establishing in putting the matter of selections into the hands of the Museum staff in this way. It is one of the most splendid offers which I know of having been made to any Museum and should facilitate greatly the work of accessions on objects offered in the future."[38] But Wade also insisted on quality, something that Whiting needed to be reminded of occasionally. Despite his own protestations, the Director was sometimes seduced by a work's documentary or educational function. Wade reprimanded him for the plethora of little objects brought to the Accessions Committee. As another Trustee, Hermon Kelley, declared to Whiting: "I believe that so far as possible expenditures for minor objects should be avoided, and that these funds should be conserved until they amount to enough to warrant the purchases of really important museum material."[39]

Whiting's most significant act in regard to collecting was his choice of staff for the curatorial departments he established in 1919. Having chosen them, he then left them largely alone to develop collections. A Curator of Oriental Art had been in place since 1914, albeit with responsibility for the entire Museum collection (MacLean went to Chicago in 1922, but was replaced by Theodore Sizer, who was also Curator of Prints). Next Whiting added a Curator of Co- lonial Art (renamed Early American Art in 1923), Lawrence Park, and a Curator of Decorative Arts, William Milliken. The following year (1920) a sepa- rate Print Department was established, with Ralph King as volunteer Curator. No Paintings Curator, however, was appointed; the Decorative Arts Curator assumed the responsibilities for paintings by Decem- ber 1923, a clear indication of Whiting's sense of what was important.[40]

Partly through accident and partly by design, the most important Curator soon became William Mil- liken, the one who collected in the areas closest to Whiting's heart: the decorative arts of Europe, espe- cially those of the medieval period. Not surprisingly for an Arts and Crafts enthusiast who revered John Ruskin and William Morris, the first major area de- veloped under Whiting was the medieval collection. An Anglophiliac, he seems to have visited the Conti- nent only once before 1924, and he had spent most of his time in England.[41] It is unlikely that he spoke any foreign languages. His interest in Continental art was not essentially different from his interest in any other non-English art. All were equally foreign from a Bos- ton perspective, and equally distant. Milliken's cos- mopolitan viewpoint was quite different.

Whiting's greatest interest, judging from the effort expended on it, was American art. Two points stood in its favor: besides representing the nation, it was the art of the present-day. Whiting felt very strongly about the need for showing the origins of American art in the collection and for supporting contemporary American artists. Initially, a few of the Trustees agreed. During the first year of the Accessions Com- mittee, Judge Sanders had urged that the majority of the remaining acquisition funds "should be mainly used for paintings, preferably paintings of the Early American School."[42] His remarks had been prompted by an exhibition by Vose Galleries of Boston at the Statler Hotel downtown (we may perhaps detect Whiting's hand in this appearance of a Boston art dealer in Cleveland). Among several possible acquisi-

tions, the choice was, in the end, between a portrait of a member of the British royal family by Benjamin West painted in England and John Singleton Co- pley's portrait of Mrs. John Greene, the daughter and sister of governors of Rhode Island. The latter, con- sidered more American, was acquired on June 10, 1915, the Museum's first purchased painting (CMA 15.527). Only six months later, the Museum bought Copley's portrait of Nathaniel Hurd (CMA 15.534). Its appeal is obvious, showing as it does an honest crafts- man. Whiting urged its purchase, despite the fact that faint-hearted ladies on the board of the art museum in Worcester, Massachusetts, had turned it down re- portedly because Hurd looked "too sensual and gross in appearance."[43]

This note of warning was one that Whiting might well have heeded. With Park's appointment as the non-resident Curator of Colonial Art, the Museum got the services of a noted authority, but one more interested in the historical associations than in the beauty of the pieces. Up to a point, the Trustees shared his enthusiasm, but that point was quickly passed. Already in 1921, Whiting warned Park that "some of our Trustees feel that, while our Colonial room is interesting, it represents a lot of very plain people and that the paintings themselves are almost entirely of historic interest."[44] Park defended himself by suggesting that there were no pretty women painted in the colonies; besides, what was really wanted were portraits of "a fine type of a New Eng- land woman."[45]

But the fact that Park was non-resident and that his health soon began to fail meant that his influence was never strong.[46] By the time of his death in 1924, the Museum had not bought an early American portrait in several years. Even the collection of nineteenth- century paintings—which had begun so strongly with the purchase of Thomas Cole's *Schroon Mountain, Adirondack* (CMA 1335.17) in 1917 and continued through 1922 with Albert Bierstadt's *Half-Dome, Yosemite Valley* (CMA 221.22)—stopped short, not to be resumed with any vigor until the 1960s.

*Portrait of Mrs. John Greene* by John Singleton Copley, American (1737-1815). Gift of The John Huntington Art and Polytechnic Trust. CMA 15.527

*Portrait of George III of England* by Benjamin West, American (1738-1820). Gift of Mr. and Mrs. Lawrence S. Robbins. CMA 52.17

*Portrait of Nathaniel Hurd* by John Singleton Copley, American (1737-1815). Gift of The John Huntington Art and Polytechnic Trust. CMA 15.534

The Trustees decided that Museum's meager acquisition funds should be concentrated on forming a "collection representing the important American painters." They reasoned that: "it seems the normal point of beginning for an American museum and it offers the field in which paintings can be bought to good advantage and at low prices as compared with the European schools." A desire to complement the Hurlbuts' later nineteenth-century American paintings may have influenced this policy as well.

When members of the Museum's Accessions Committee met for the first time in 1915, they visited an exhibition by Vose Galleries of Boston at Cleveland's Statler Hotel (Vose remains in business in Boston to-day). The committee had the pleasure of choosing between a John Singleton Copley portrait of Mrs. Greene and a portrait purportedly of the Duke of York by Benjamin West. The two most important American artists of the eighteenth century, West and Copley were the first Americans to earn international reputations. In the end, the Copley was selected because it had both an American subject and been painted in America. (The West canvas fortuitously entered the Museum collection in 1952, as a gift, and has since been identified as a portrait of George III.) Later that year Director Whiting persuaded the Board to buy a portrait of Nathaniel Hurd also by Copley. Thus, Cleveland had begun to assemble a distinctive painting collection.

The Trustees, however, were enthusiastic about portraits of George Washington. From the beginning the idea of ancestor portraits had been very much on their minds. With the acquisition of Copley's two portraits within six months of initiating the painting collection, the Museum had acquired perfect representatives of the men and women it would like to claim as its own, both in the past and the present. Mrs. Greene represented American womanly virtue (nothing about her face suggested anything else) and decorative beauty (as she is appropriately draped in swathes of imported finery), while Nathaniel Hurd was a worthy laborer, a craftsman successful enough to dress up in a gentleman's robe—the Trustees might almost have seen their own histories in these two paintings. But George Washington transcended family and spoke to national ideals. The Cleveland Museum, like nearly every other museum in the country, was anxious to crown its collection of ancestors with portraits of Washington.[47] The Trustees eagerly pursued versions of Gilbert Stuart's Atheneum portrait of Washington (the one on the dollar bill) and rued the number that other museums possessed. By an act of purposeful collecting the first work of art bought with the funds from membership dues was *Washington at the Battle of Princeton* by Charles Willson Peale (CMA 17.946); shortly thereafter the Museum was happy to add a portrait of Washington by Joseph Wright (CMA 2553.21). In 1924 the Director announced that, because of two loans, the patriotic visitor could view no less than four portraits of the great man.

Whiting, however, was not content to stop there. He wanted to build American period rooms modeled on Connecticut houses. He sent his Curator scouring Connecticut for the right ironmongery and woodwork. The project, announced to the public in 1921, did not materialize. The Trustees were never that enthusiastic, and when Park died, Whiting decided the effort and expense were not feasible (the crunch of 1922 was another obstacle). The choice of rooms and the tenacity with which Whiting pursued the

*Schroon Mountain, Adirondack,* 1838, by Thomas Cole (1801-1848), American. Hinman B. Hurlbut Collection. CMA 1335.17

*Half-Dome, Yosemite Valley,* 1866, by Albert Bierstadt (1830-1902), American. Hinman B. Hurlbut Collection. CMA 221.22

George Washington
at the Battle of Prin-
ceton (CMA 17.946)
painted about 1780
by Charles Willson
Peale, was the first
work of art purchased
with money from
membership dues.

project, however, reveal that it had more than the usual significance for him. Whiting saw period rooms as one way to connect the present-day, immigrant population of Cleveland with the city's roots in Connecticut. The choice of a kitchen and parlor had purpose: the first was useful, the second civilized, with the definite progress of American civilization laid out for the audience. The kitchen, too, as John Cotton Dana declared: "was the center of education in the Colonies ... it was around the fireplace in the kitchen that, in summer and in winter, the door to learning in the Arts of Life was opened by daily occupations."[48] As the New Haven architect George Seymour wrote to Whiting: "I think you can not possibly overdo 'playing up' the idea of Connecticut and the Western Reserve."[49] The Trustees disagreed, their eyes fixed on broader horizons.

Whiting had much more success with his desire to support contemporary artists, which is embodied in the *May Show* and the other related exhibitions. This annual show of the arts and crafts produced in the area has been a staple of the Museum's annual exhibition schedule since 1919, a record for any American museum. Given Whiting's experience in Boston with the Society of Arts and Crafts shop, a source of constant harassment from envious craftsmen and an endless drain on his time and energy, one would have thought he would have avoided repeating the experi-

ment at all costs. But his interest and his sense of duty in promoting the arts and crafts outweighed his distaste for petty squabbles. After a disastrous experience in 1918, when he let the artists hang their own exhibition, he gamely organized the *May Show* (not coincidentally held at the same time as the Royal Academy *Summer Show* in London). This time, however, the jurors came from outside the Museum and the show was held only once a year; craftsmen and artists had only the one opportunity a year to sell their work at the Museum.

From 1919 to 1929 the *May Show* generated $98,000 in sales, on which the Museum took no commission. But the point was not simply the revenues generated for artists out of sales in the show. In 1918, writing about a modern iron chandelier by Herman Lother of the Boston Arts and Crafts Society, Whiting had noted: "Fine examples of modern craftsmanship should be, when shown in comparison with older work, a tremendous stimulus to the craftsman." He added that he would like someone to support the gift of modern examples which would "in time ... affect the artistic quality and financial output of [the city's] commercial output."[50] The whole point of the Museum for Whiting, perhaps most directly expressed in the *May Show*, was to vitalize the local art community. Nor did Whiting stop at the visual arts. From 1925 to 1929, there was an annual May concert of

The first *Annual
Exhibition of Work by
Cleveland Artists and
Craftsmen* (now
known as the *May
Show*) was held in
1919. *The Cleveland
Plain Dealer* called it
"one of the most
significant events in
which the Cleveland
public has ever been
invited to share."

music written by Cleveland composers as well.

Whiting also decided that Cleveland artists should compete on a national level, trying, as always, for the widest exposure and the most professional stature and behavior. As Whiting recalled in 1947, the Museum had had lots of requests for exhibitions and had offered local artists the gallery space. But the offer had simply occasioned jealousy "as to who should have the central positions, etc." This experience had given birth to the *May Show*. He wrote further: "In 1921, we decided to take another step. To follow the May Show with an American Painting Show and to ask Cleveland painters to submit to the May Show Jury work produced within five years, the Jury to select what they considered the thirty most important Cleveland canvasses, to be hung with sixty canvasses by painters outside of Cleveland to be selected by the Museum curators." Frederick Carl Gottwald, one of the older painters, thought Whiting was "trying to show up the Cleveland painters (to crucify them he said); at the opening they came slipping in, but walked out proud." Whiting added that the *American Painting Show* had improved local sales by showing how strong Cleveland painters were when displayed with nationally known artists.[51] Whiting thought this combination of Cleveland and national painters was one of his most important efforts, and was disappointed when the show was discontinued in the

1930s. The Museum also benefitted since many of its best American paintings from the first half-century were bought out of these national exhibitions.

In line with his Arts and Crafts ideals, Whiting tried to stimulate art among Clevelanders by including the work of people who did not consider themselves artists. Naturally, given the population of Cleveland, this meant the immigrant workers in ethnic neighborhoods. To precede the *May Show* in 1919, the Museum also organized a *Homelands Exhibit* of artifacts produced by members of the many different nationality groups in the city.

In the middle of the hysteria of World War I, when Americanization became an obsession with most established institutions, several homelands shows were held in cities with large Slavic and Italian populations. Cleveland's was the only one organized by an art museum, a direct outgrowth of Whiting's concern for his audience and the wholeness of the arts. His statement of purpose was similar to many others: "That of encouraging the foreign-born residents of Cleveland in the belief that they made their own vital and valuable contribution to the civilization of the country."[52] He worked through settlement houses and branch libraries. During the exhibition he had spinners working in the galleries—textiles were, again, an important focus. During the weekend activities for various ethnic groups, Whiting spoke repeatedly about how the

Held April 6-May 1, 1919, the *Homelands Exhibit* was mounted to demonstrate, "through objects lent by foreign-born citizens of Cleveland, the artistic heritage which those people bring as their contribution to the aesthetic development of our country," to quote Whiting.

"color and gaiety which was the native inheritance of these people was sadly needed in our more drab American life." His speech would then be followed by an address from the city's Americanization Committee. The Museum's success led to an even bigger festival of the dramatic and performing arts throughout the city a few years later.[53]

Whiting's attitude toward the art of other cultures was progressive, in many senses of the term. From the outset, as a proponent of the Arts and Crafts movement, he was interested in the art of every culture. In a lecture on jewelry in 1907, given at the Boston Public Library, he ranged impressively from prehistoric and Eskimo carvings to modern examples, taking in the art of New Guinea, Scythia, India, and almost every other imaginable group. He said: "I hope to show conclusively that through all times the jewelry which has survived ... definitely expressed the life of the peoples by whom and for whom it was created; but this cannot be said of the work of today."[54] The value of the art of primitive cultures, he felt, stemmed from its not being art historically self-conscious. As the product of direct and authentic experience, it could thus inspire modern artists.

To a degree his attitude was patronizing, although it reflected widely held beliefs. As the historian Eileen Boris has written: "The association of childhood with handicraft, early years with primitive people, became part of Progressive Education, where curriculum matched individuals with cultural stages of growth."[55] In progressive education theory the curriculum was adapted to stages of child development and the development of human society, as the child imitated "the past important activities of the race."[56] Thus, all art had its place in the curriculum.

For Whiting, some cultures were definitely more worthy than others, and in others he had an idiosyncratic interest. American Indian art he valued highly, no doubt due to its being in some sense antecedent to colonial art and perhaps, too, because he still had notions of the American Indian as the noble savage. Along with colonial period rooms, Whiting planned

Paul B. Travis (1891-1975) was a graduate of the Cleveland School of Art (now the Cleveland Institute of Art). He taught there from 1920 to 1957, while also offering classes at the John Huntington Polytechnic Institute. His paintings and prints appeared regularly in the Art Museum's *May Shows*.

In 1927-28 Travis took a sabbatical to travel, not to France as advised, but to Africa. "I wanted to see Ujiji and hear how it was pronounced," he later wrote, remembering his fascination with the story of Sir Henry Morton Stanley meeting David Livingstone. Travis was also aware of the fascination of avant-garde European artists for tribal art.

Africa overwhelmed Travis, forcing him to adapt his artistic vision to the grandeur of its landscape and peoples. He also collected artifacts and art objects there, supported by a grant of $1,500 from the Gilpin Players of Karamu House and the African Art Sponsors, who wanted him to purchase objects for their organization and for the Natural History and the Art Museums.

While the Art Museum had always collected African art, it had done so mostly for educational use. The activities of Travis and the Gilpin Players, combined with the Education Department's programs, resulted in the appointment in 1929 of a Curator of Primitive Art, Charles Ramus. The Museum also held its first exhibition of African art, *Primitive African Art*, that year.

for years to build rooms for American Indian art. He wrote to one collector that "many of the older art museums have had a very narrow conception which has in many cases ruled out such work as Indian basketry.... I am hoping that in time we may have additional room and can prepare for such an exhibit a series of galleries devoted to the work of the Indians."[57]

His interest in American Indian art differed from his interest in African art; the latter he seems to have classed with ethnographic material. While American Indian and pre-Columbian art deserved galleries, African art seems to have held the same place as the displays of flora and fauna which the Museum owned in its first years. It was described, in the Extensions Division collection, as "products of a primitive African Tribe" which were interesting more from the perspective of "geography or ethnology than from ... the fine arts."[58] But his attitudes could and did change. Most notably, his appreciation of African art improved perhaps as much for social and community reasons as anything else. Louise Dunn, a member of

the Education Department staff who supported Karamu House and possibly originated the idea of the Cultural Gardens in Wade Park, also encouraged him. Through her, the Museum helped sponsor the Cleveland artist Paul Travis's expedition to Africa in 1928, and held its first exhibition of African art in 1929. Whiting, however, was just as excited about the contribution by the Gilpin Players of scholarships for "colored children" as their gift of African art. It is worth noting that, judging from early photographs, Museum classes were integrated very early on.

Dunn's interests were typical of members of the Education Department, several of whom also served as Curators: Rossiter Howard was Curator of Classical Art and Gertrude Underhill became Curator of Textiles. Whiting's primary interest in objects seems to have been their usefulness for educational purposes. He saw the collection as acting in concert with the educational programs he set in place: aspects of the collection were conceived with different audiences and programs in mind. The Extensions Divi-

*Queen's Stool* created before 1929 in Zaire by a member of the Mangbetu Tribe. Gift of The Gilpin Players of Karamu House. CMA 29.320

*Wild Coast, Newport* by Homer D. Martin, American (1836-1897). Leonard C. Hanna, Jr., Collection. CMA 23.1118

sion was the most obvious expression of this fact, accumulating objects specifically for use in schools and libraries. However, its range of material (in terms of cultures, broader than the rest of the Museum) related to its primary purpose of educating children who would respond directly to "primitive" cultures. Whiting recognized that the needs of a child differed greatly from those of an adult, and that aesthetic experiences could range from an uninformed love for the bright colors and intricate workmanship of a Japanese doll to the meditative contemplation of an Italian Renaissance masterpiece. Each object had its role to play in the grand scheme; each was important in its own way. Even if this developmental view essentially demoted the work of certain cultures, it at least embraced them.

Whiting's vision of the collection at work, along with the exhibition program, was to have a remarkable effect on the art community. If Cleveland ever had a nationally recognized school of artists, it was during and just after Whiting's tenure as Director. In a sense, the *May Show* and the American paintings show were the peaks of the exhibition season, the real *raison d'être* for the Museum. From the perspective of his Arts and Crafts ideals, Whiting succeeded in his mission of creating a community responsive to the needs of artists and able to support and nurture them. Lurking at the back of his mind, as it did for most leaders of the art world at the turn of the century, was a vision of Athens in the time of Pericles or Florence under the Medici: small communities having a distinctive artistic voice and creating masterpieces. If Cleveland did not begin to match that vision, it did at least for a short time in the late 1920s and early 1930s support a cohesive and worthwhile school of artists and craftsmen, which nurtured such important figures as William Sommer, Clarence Carter, Carl Gaertner, Victor Schreckengost, and others. While Whiting would never have taken the credit for this, much of it may be given to him.[59]

Within a decade of its founding, the Museum's successes were recognized widely. Its education and community work were admired. Critics declared that: "The Cleveland Museum has the sanest, the most courageous and the most sympathetic attitude towards helping local artists of any museum in America."[60] Even its collection became a source of pride, as Wade's ideas continued to be felt. *Art News* noted that the Museum justified the principle that one great work conveys its period better than many lesser ones, and astutely compared the *gift* of the Italian Renaissance paintings to the decorative arts which had been *bought* by the professionals on the staff, noting the importance of the latter.[61] The medieval objects in particular garnered praise, while the building itself became a model. Arthur Pope, when building the Legion of Honor in San Francisco, found Cleveland his most important guide.[62] And Paul Sachs, the famous founder of the museum program at Harvard, wrote to tell Whiting how much he admired the Museum's management, team spirit, and fine acquisitions.[63] Perhaps the ultimate compliment was the way that Whiting's staff kept getting raided by other institutions: the Art Institute of Chicago in the space of a few years hired away four heads of departments.

By 1924 the Museum was firmly established. It had survived one national financial crisis in 1922 and was beginning to make significant purchases in several fields. But it was clear that Whiting had a larger sense of the Museum's presence in the community than did the Trustees, and for the rest of his tenure one senses him drawing away from them, proud as he was of the Museum.

The acquisition of Winslow Homer's *Early Morning after a Storm at Sea* (CMA 24.195) reveals a crucial development. The painting was presented with two others, a Homer Martin and a George Inness. The most expensive object the Museum had yet contemplated purchasing, the Homer prompted an important policy debate. J. H. Wade, whose fund supplied the purchase money, wrote to Whiting:

*Regarding the policy of purchasing only one or two masterpieces a year from the Wade Fund nothing would gratify me more, personally, for I would un-*

*doubtedly derive more pleasure and the Museum more notoriety and advertising than if part of the fund were used to gradually build up the various departments necessary to make a balanced Museum. The question is, should we think most of the pleasure it gives to a comparatively few people, or the educational value to the community and its students.... If we had other funds that could be used to build up the various departments to the point where they would fulfill the proper mission of a Museum, I would be a strong advocate of using the Wade fund only for the purchase of masterpieces.*

Then he added: "Perhaps I am unduly solicitous regarding the obligation of a modern Museum."[64] Whiting, disregarding Wade's equivocation, replied: "I am sure that you know that my feeling agrees with yours as to the necessity of building up the Museum collections for the widest use instead of for a few people."[65] Whiting nonetheless recognized the importance of the Homer painting and desired it strongly. But of the other two paintings, he wanted the Inness, while Milliken greatly preferred the Martin. Whiting reluctantly let Milliken's preference stand, a decision confirmed when (perhaps because of Milliken's influence?) Leonard Hanna, Jr., the youngest member of the Accessions Committee presented a check for the Martin (CMA 23.1118). Whiting's backing down demonstrated his relative lack of interest in the collection, except as an educational tool. His inability to bring the colonial rooms to completion despite a public announcement or to hire another Curator of Early American Art suggests that the Trustees felt they had had enough, that that area was complete, and they wanted to put their energies into more exciting things. No better example of the convergence of the Board's and William Milliken's taste could be wanted. The primary task of a museum— building a collection—was obviously not the founding Director's major concern.

Whiting turned instead to the wider community outside the institution. In a sense, now that the home base was in order, that was the logical next step. Almost from his first public statement, the theme which

Whiting sounded was "cooperation."[66] And he sought cooperation on a city-wide level, in a forum called the Cleveland Conference for Educational Cooperation, an organization with two goals. The first was the same one that Whiting had worked for in founding the National Handicraft League and the American Federation of the Arts: efficiency, doing away with duplication of effort, sharing information, and so on. This was quiet work that could go on indefinitely, sometimes resulting in lasting institutional changes among its members but more often simply smoothing paths and egos. The second goal was more monumental and involved reshaping the face of Cleveland: Whiting wanted to create a gathering of institutions around Wade Park that would provide a cultural epicenter for the city to balance the model urban center that had been built downtown.[67]

In a letter to J. H. Wade, Whiting recorded the sequence of events that led to the Carnegie Corporation's support and the momentous decision to develop the area surrounding the Museum as a cultural center.[68] Whiting had modestly proposed to the new President of Western Reserve University that Curator Sizer give a course at the University to bring the Museum and University closer together. University President Robert Vinson had just returned from a meeting with the Carnegie Corporation's president, Frederick Keppel, who had been thinking of selecting Cleveland as a place to try cooperative planning between museums, universities, and libraries. When Vinson asked Whiting to submit his plan, Whiting responded ambitiously. He told Wade:

*As you will perhaps remember, I tried to get President Thwing interested in this plan in 1916, and it seems too good to be true to feel that it is now probably on the verge of working out.... I therefore told [Vinson] of my plan of grouping the museums together on East Boulevard and he expressed great interest in the idea and told me that in his own mind the present campus would always be used probably for a graduate school, if the undergraduate buildings were removed to some place where more room would be available.*

Building on this new enthusiasm, Whiting quickly marshaled all his forces, and the Cleveland Conference for Educational Cooperation was born.

By its own accounts (aimed at the Carnegie Foundation and the press), the Conference was a great success and attracted national attention. The national Adult Education Association, for example, held its first meeting in Cleveland in May 1927 because of the luster of the Conference's reputation. But the results were often hard to see; and although admirable, improvements in scheduling and coordination of curricula are ephemeral, if they do not result in a lasting institution. Whiting also experienced a significant failure: branch museums, which were to be a combination of performing arts center, library, and museum, were never established, although for several years the Carnegie West Library functioned as one. But there was one great success: the Cleveland Educational Group Plan. This ancestor of today's University Circle fulfilled at last Wade's vision of thirty years before. In a series of complicated real estate maneuvers, at the behest of the Natural History Museum and the Conference (in other words, Harold T. Clark and Whiting), Western Reserve University convinced both the Christian Scientists and the Roman Catholics to sell their property on Euclid Avenue and East Boulevard and build their churches elsewhere. Then, along with the Natural History Museum, the Cleveland Orchestra, and the Cleveland School of Art, the University began the planning that many years later resulted in the present locations of those institutions.

The relative failure of the Conference must have strongly influenced Whiting's decision to leave Cleveland. He later lamented to Clark that he could have used more support from the Board.[69] Whether there was a lack of sympathy developing between Whiting and his Board, or whether the chance of a new opportunity was too enticing, Whiting resigned in 1930 to become the President of the American Federation of the Arts (AFA) in Washington, D. C. Given the onset of the Depression it was a courageous move, and one that his sense of service would not let him reject. The AFA was the national lobbying organization for the arts and also a primary sponsor of touring exhibitions. Whiting had been associated with it since its founding in 1909.[70] Thus, Whiting found himself at the helm of a national institution he had helped guide for twenty years.

Upon his resignation, the Trustees credited Whiting for "the deep hold which the Museum has taken upon the people of Cleveland." Rossiter Howard, speaking for the Museum staff in a more personal note and recognizing Olive Whiting's long service as Whiting's assistant, said: "The character of the Museum has been largely determined by the ideals of Mr. and Mrs. Whiting, who together led a pioneer struggle for ideas which are now current among museums. This was accomplished by genuine leadership."[71] Whiting's departure was not universally mourned, to be sure. His relative lack of interest in pure aesthetics as well as his absolute pragmatism, noted by Mary Dennett in her protest in 1903 at the Boston Society of Arts and Crafts, were equally valid aspects of his character and leadership. Frank Pool, the first Registrar of the Museum, for example, writing to Milliken to congratulate him on his appointment as Director, could not resist adding:

*I rejoiced in the certainty of a change in museum policy.... Being a "museum man" and not an ex-store-keeper, your first effort was to establish a sympathetic understanding between yourself and your Staff.... I see new [names] on your advisory council and as lenders who heretofore refused even this passive connection with the museum.*[72]

But you can't please everyone and Frederic Whiting had succeeded where it counted in the long run: the community.

Replacing Whiting was a momentous decision. That the Trustees chose Milliken instead of Rossiter Howard, the Assistant Director, had significant consequences. Henceforth, although little of what Whiting had put in place was dismantled (after all, Milliken had also been trained by him), the wider implications of the Museum as a leader in the adventure of civic cooperation and coalition building would fade, an outcome hastened by the Depression.

Cleveland remained in Whiting's mind even after he left, although he seems seldom to have returned. Whiting was able to use the forum of touring loan exhibitions as a means for promoting the Cleveland art scene he had put so much effort into establishing. But on the whole, the presidency of the AFA turned out to be an unhappy experience. He discovered himself out of sympathy both with contemporary art and with most of his directors. Financial problems for the organization mounted, as the Carnegie Corporation and others cut their annual grants and he failed to find private sponsors. He retired in 1936 at the age of sixty-three. Later he wrote to Clark: "The fact is, Harold, that something very essential to my success in any undertaking died out of me during the disappointing struggle against an uncooperative board in Washington. My enthusiasm and confidence in the value of the work I was doing was an essential part of my success and this was slowly drained out of me."[73] A few years later, his sense of commitment and energy rekindled, he tried to get back in to the world of museums but found no takers.[74]

With few other options, Whiting returned to his first calling. He considered "opening a handicraft shop for local, or Maine handicrafts," intending both to support himself and Olive and to sponsor local craftsmen. Ever the pragmatist, he wrote to a colleague: "We believe that an attractive shop with good local work would appeal to many who would rather buy such things than goods made in Japan or Germany, no matter how attractive and cheap the latter may be."[75] But finally he decided that the venture was too risky.

Shortly after resigning from the AFA, the Whitings had inherited a house in Mt. Dora, Florida, not far from where the Cleveland Museum's Secretary, I. T. Frary, had retired. For the next few years, the Whitings lived there or in Ogonquit, Maine. Despite continuous money problems (without pensions and, in typically Yankee fashion, land rich and cash poor),

Frederic A. and Olive Whiting returned to Cleveland to attend the Museum's 20th anniversary and the 1936-38 Great Lakes Exposition. Ostensibly celebrating the centennial of Cleveland's incorporation, the Exposition brought together representatives of commerce, industry, science, and culture of the entire Great Lakes region including Canada in an attempt to revitalize the area's economy, particularly its iron and steel industry and to revive the city's civic pride. Occupying a large area of downtown Cleveland, the Exposition attracted worldwide attention.

they still thought of public service. They tried to give much of their land in Maine to the village for a park in order to save the trees, but finally had to permit lumbering. Art still played a major part in their lives, and Whiting found the energy to help found two more museums—in Orlando and Ogonquit—putting into practice ideas he had worked for all his life. About the Orlando effort he wrote: "It is an expansion of the plan I worked out with Miss Eastman for the use of distant branch libraries as local cultural centers."[76]

Years later, James Holly Hanford, an English professor at Western Reserve University, wrote to Whiting thanking him for his work on the Cleveland Conference. Declaring that the fruits of Whiting's labors were only then ripening, Hanford recalled the spirit in which Whiting "deliberately and skillfully and lovingly democratiz[ed]" the art museum world.[77] One hopes that Whiting gained some satisfaction

from this reminder that his work in Cleveland had not been in vain. The degree to which the Museum has always been vitally connected to the community, in a myriad of ways—from its joint program with Case Western Reserve University to its commitment to a free admission policy—bears the durable impression of Whiting's influence. His unflagging commitment to community and cooperation, as well as his eye for excellence in people, has never deserted the Museum.

1. Frederic Allen Whiting to Harold Terry Clark, November 14, 1949, Harold T. Clark Papers, 1949-50, Archives of The Cleveland Museum of Art (hereafter cited as CMA Archives).

2. Remarks by Walker on Whiting's resignation, April 23, 1912, Society of Arts and Crafts, Boston, Records 1897-1960, Archives of American Art, Smithsonian Institution (hereafter cited as SACB), microfilm roll 300, 708.

3. See the testimonials of H. Langford Warren and C. Howard Walker, and others, SACB, microfilm roll 300, 706-725. See also Beverly Brandt, "Mutually Helpful Relations: Architects, Craftsmen, and The Society of Arts and Crafts" (Ph.D. diss., Boston University, 1985).

4. Address to the Worcester Art school, 1907/8, SACB, microfilm roll 300, 241.

5. [Whiting?], *Handicraft* 3, 1 (April 1910): 28.

6. Whiting, typescript of a lecture, 1902, SACB, microfilm roll 300, 37.

7. "The Arts and Crafts Movement in the United States," p. 2, 1903-1904, SACB, microfilm roll 300, 151.

8. Mary Dennett to Olive Whiting, October 11, 1903, SACB, microfilm roll 300, 398-399.

9. Whiting to Lockwood de Forest, November 27, 1911, SACB, microfilm roll 300, 679.

10. See Whiting's comments, American Association of Museums, *Proceedings* 7 (1913): 64.

11. De Forest to Whiting, November 13, 1912, Whiting papers, Archives of American Art, microfilm roll 142, 0007. De Forest was also president of the National Handicraft League, founded in 1907 with Whiting as Secretary-Treasurer.

12. De Forest to Whiting, October 25, 1912, Whiting papers, Archives of American Art, microfilm roll 142, 0005. See Sherman Lee's essay for the full extent of Whiting's success.

13. Wendy Kaplan, "Spreading the Crafts: The Role of the Schools," *The Art that Is Life*, exh. cat. (Boston: Museum of Fine Arts, 1987), 302. See also Arthur D. Efland, *A History of Art Education* (New York: Teachers College Press, Columbia University, 1990).

14. A Director of the Chicago Public School Art Society, after 1893, quoted in Eileen Boris, "Art and Labor: John Ruskin, William Morris and the Craftsman Ideal in America" (Ph.D. diss., Brown University, 1981), 196.

15. M. A. Newell, "Art in the Public Schools," 1887, quoted in Boris, 1981, p. 170.

16. See SACB, microfilm roll 300, 177-182. The speakers at the Conference on Industrial Education, February 1908, included Henry Turner Bailey, who later became the head of the Cleveland School of Art.

17. Boris, 1981, p. 260.

18. See Henry Watson Kent, *What I am Pleased to Call My Education* (New York: The Grolier Club, 1949). He and Whiting served on a committee for educational cooperation between museums. American Association of Museums, *Proceedings* 11 (1917): 136.

19. Henry W. Kent, "The Museum and Industrial Art," in Charles R. Richards, *Art and Industry* (New York: Macmillan, 1929), 436.

20. Kent's phrase, quoted by Winifred E. Howe, in *A History of the Metropolitan Museum of Art*, vol. 2 (New York: Metropolitan Museum of Art and Columbia University Press, 1947), 26.

21. Whiting, *CMA Bulletin* 1, 4 (February 1915): 2, 6-7. See also "The Relation of the Museum to Local Industry," *CMA Bulletin* 5, 10 (December 1918): 122-127.

22. Whiting to Dudley P. Allen, November 10, 1914, file 114, Director Whiting (I), CMA Archives.

23. Report to the Trustees, January 6, 1914, Director Whiting (II), CMA Archives.

24. "Mental Photos," *Cleveland News*, Clippings Scrapbook no. 2, June 2, 1922, CMA Archives.

25. Education Department Report, June-July 1916. See also Whiting to Clark, December 7, 1928, Harold T. Clark Papers, 1925-30, CMA Archives.

26. Education Department Report, September 4, 1916, CMA Archives.

27. Education Department Annual Report, June 5, 1917, CMA Archives.

28. Board of Trustees Minutes, February 27, 1929, CMA Archives.

29. Louise Tragard and Patricia E. Hart, *A Century of Color, 1886-1896: Ogonquit, Maine's Art Colony* (Ogonquit: Barn Gallery Associates, 1987), p. 38.

30. Education Department Annual Report, June 5, 1917, CMA Archives. Mrs. Gibson added: "In these programs the department has boldly attacked the problem of moving pictures in their relation to educational work. This has been done at times at the expense of a real connection with material in the galleries. The experiment was tried with the idea of finding out what possibilities the field offers and how to use the little material now available, and has proved to be a valuable addition to the year's work." In the 1925 annual report the Department noted a "falling off" in attendance at the Saturday children's programs "apparently due to the persistent refusal to provide motion pictures."

31. Books by members of the Education Department include: Marguerite Bloomberg's *An Experiment in Museum Instruction* (American Association of Museums, 1929), Louise M. Dunn and Winifred H. Mills's *Masks, Marionettes and Shadows* (Doubleday, Page, 1927), Katharine Gibson's *The Golden Bird* (Macmillan, 1927) and *The Goldsmith of Florence* (Macmillan, 1929), Helen Gilchrist's *The Severance Catalogue of Arms and Armor* (Artcraft Printing, 1924), Ann V. Horton's *My Picture Study Book* (for grades 3-6) (Harter School Supply, 1928), and Alice W. Howard's *Sokar and the Crocodile* (Macmillan, 1928).

32. Sanders to Whiting, June 23, 1914, quoting in part an article by Ernest Gross, H. T. Clark papers, 1914-24, CMA Archives.

33. Sanders to Freer, July 2, 1915, Harold T. Clark Papers, 1914-24, CMA Archives.

34. Whiting to Allen, November 10, 1914, file 114, Director Whiting (I), CMA Archives.

35. *CMA Bulletin* 14, 10 (December 1927): 161.

36. Whiting to Wade, March 27, 1917, file 134, Director Whiting (I), CMA Archives. By the date of publication, Sizer—formerly Curator of Prints as well as Oriental Art—had left and Henry Sayles Francis had replaced him as Curator of Prints.

37. Telegram, Wade to Whiting, March 30, 1917, file 134, Director Whiting (I), CMA Archives.

38. Whiting to Wade, April 1, 1916, file 134, Director Whiting (I), CMA Archives.

39. Hermon Kelley to Whiting, February 17, 1920, file 121, Director Whiting (I), CMA Archives.

40. Milliken added the title Curator of Paintings to his job in 1925, having been listed in the *CMA Bulletin* as Acting Curator of Paintings as early as December 1923; Rossiter Howard was named Curator of Classical Art in 1924 (with the Egyptian antiquities); and a Department of Primitive Art was created in 1929, with Charles Ramus as Curator.

41. In a letter to Wade, Whiting noted that he had been to Paris once briefly and never to Italy. Whiting to Wade, January 18, 1924, file 134, Director Whiting (I), CMA Archives.

42. Accessions Committee Minutes, June 3, 1915, CMA Director's Office. This was also stated in the CMA *Bulletin* 2, 2 (July 1915): 5-6: "The policy of the Trustees as regards paintings is to use such funds as are at present available for this department for the consistent development of a collection representing the important American painters. This policy has been decided on mainly for two reasons; first, it seems the normal point of beginning for an American museum, and second, it offers the field in which paintings can be bought to good advantage and at low prices as compared with the European schools."

43. Lawrence Park to Whiting, January 5, 1921, file 265, Director Whiting (I), CMA Archives.

44. Whiting to Park, December 29, 1921, file 265, Director Whiting (I), CMA Archives.

45. Park to Whiting, January 27, 1922, file 265, Director Whiting (I), CMA Archives.

46. For instance, in 1925 William Mather had never heard of John Smibert, Ralph Feke, and Joseph Blackburn, despite the fact that the Museum had owned works by these artists since 1919. Mather to Milliken, July 10, 1925, file 116, Director Whiting (I), CMA Archives.

47. Even immigrant children admired Washington as their greatest hero. See Boris, 1981, p. 196.

48. *The Museum*, ed. John Cotton Dana, 1, 1 (May 1917): 23.

49. Seymour to Whiting, January 15, 1921, Director Whiting (II), CMA Archives.

50. *CMA Bulletin* 5, 10 (December 1918): 115.

51. Whiting to James Holly Hanford, March 11, 1947, Whiting papers, Archives of American Art, microfilm roll 142, 112.

52. *CMA Bulletin* 6, 2 (March 1919): 31.

53. Allen H. Eaton, *Immigrant Gifts to American Life* (New York: Russell Sage Foundation, 1932), 62 ff.

54. "Jewelry," lecture delivered at the Boston Public Library, April 18, 1907, p. 4, SACB, microfilm roll 300, 183-230.

55. Boris, 1981, p. 174.

56. Ibid, p. 185.

57. Whiting to Miss Ella Hubby, July 30, 1919, H. T. Clark Papers, 1914-24, CMA Archives.

58. Education Department Report, August 1, 1916, CMA Archives.

59. Henry Turner Bailey, President of the Cleveland School of Art, credited the thriving art scene to a cycle of support beginning in the public schools and culminating in the *May Show*. In the seven steps he outlines, the Museum was responsible for three. "The Cleveland Method," *Methods of Teaching the Fine Arts*, ed. William Sener Rusk (Chapel Hill: The University of North Carolina Press, 1935), 71-80.

60. Forbes Watson, *The Arts* 13, 2 (February 1928): 73-74.

61. *Art News* 24, 26 (April 3, 1926): 1.

62. Pope to Whiting, January 7, 1924, Whiting-Clark Correspondence, Director Whiting (II), CMA Archives.

63. Sachs to Whiting, January 12, 1926, Director Whiting (II), CMA Archives.

64. Wade to Whiting, December 28, 1923, file 513a, Director Whiting (I), CMA Archives.

65. Whiting to Wade, December 31, 1923, file 513a, Homer-Martin-Inness Folder, Director Whiting (I), CMA Archives.

66. Whiting wrote in 1902, in the opening statement of *Handicraft:* "Feeling that the Arts and Crafts movement in America has reached that stage where it is necessary to bring about a hearty cooperation between the craftsmen and those who are interested in the way of procuring the product of the craftsmen's skill." SACB, microfilm roll 300, 37. See also Whiting's address at the dedication of the Museum, CMA *Bulletin* 3, 2 (July 1916): 23.

67. Whiting to Wade, February 11, 1924, file 134, Director Whiting (I), CMA Archives.

68. Holly M. Rarick, *Progressive Vision: The Planning of Downtown Cleveland 1903-1930,* exh. cat. (Cleveland, 1986).

69. Whiting to Clark, November 13, 1949, Whiting-Clark Correspondence, Director Whiting (II), CMA Archives: "I cannot tell you how happy this news [of your election] makes me, and I can imagine how different things might have been if you had been elected as President before the spring of 1930, and I could have had the satisfaction and the pleasure of working with you to carry out my plans."

70. See also C. Howard Walker, "The Arts and Crafts Movement in the United States," in Charles R. Richards, ed., *Art and Industry,* p. 440.

71. *CMA Bulletin* 17, 6 (June 1930): 116.

72. Frank Pool to Milliken, February 1935, letter 26, Milliken papers, Archives of American Art.

73. Whiting to Harold T. Clark, December 30, 1949, Clark-Whiting Correspondence, Director Whiting (II), CMA Archives.

74. Whiting applied for the position of Director at the new museums in Sioux City and Colorado Springs, and almost became the Director of the new Delaware Art Museum, Wilmington. See correspondence in the Whiting papers, Archives of American Art, microfilm roll 142.

75. Whiting to Mrs. Heyl, January 23, 1938, Whiting Papers, Archives of American Art, microfilm roll 142, 056.

76. Whiting to Marie Clark, February 20, 1950, Whiting Papers, Archives of American Art, microfilm roll 142, 173.

77. James Holly Hanford to Whiting, March 1947, Whiting Papers, Archives of American Art, microfilm roll 142, 110-111.

**B**esides being a member of the Museum's building committee and one its incorporators, J. H. Wade served as a Trustee of the Huntington Trust, the Kelley Foundation, and the Hurlbut estate. He was the only Museum founder to make his gifts during his own lifetime. By 1920, when he was elected the Museum's President, Wade and his wife had presented over 2,000 objects to the Museum, in addition to the land on which it was built. In the same year he set up a trust fund to generate income for acquiring: "European and American paintings, rugs, embroideries, brocades, laces, jewelry, and artistic objects in gold, silver and enamel." Recognizing the inadequacy of the Huntington and Kelley incomes for covering future Museum operating expenses, Wade made a $200,000 challenge gift to encourage others to contribute to a general endowment fund.

As a collector, Wade set an example both by his own rare discrimination and by specifying that any objects he gave to the Museum should be shown in the appropriate galleries with other examples of the same period or school—not segregated in a special room or collection bearing his name.

His innate modesty and wise counsel, however, received the warmest praise among the many memorial tributes offered: "So unobtrusive was his presence among us, so retiring even in his greatest gifts, so anxious to avoid notice or public acclaim, that we ... feel constrained to an unnatural moderation in our acknowledgment of what his life, his counsel, his friendly advice and criticism, his coöperation, his example have meant to us."

A photographer captured the Wade family on film at their residence in Thomasville, Georgia. Back row: Fred Perkins, Ellen Garretson (Mrs. J. H.) Wade, Ellen Howe Garretson, J. H. Wade, Anna McGaw Wade; bottom row: Sue Harmon Pelenyi, Irene Lowe Wade, George Garretson Wade, Helen Wade Greene, Linda Bole Perkins (later Mrs. James Brooks), Tillie Bole, and J. H. Wade, Jr.; front row: Edward B. Greene and a Mr. Hitchcock.

This pastel drawing of ballet dancers by his contemporary Edgar Degas (CMA 16.1043) demonstrates J. H. Wade's admiration for French painters. It was among the early gifts made jointly by Mr. and Mrs. Wade.

This *Hair Ornament* (CMA 81.49) by René Lalique was given to the Museum in 1981 by Mrs. A. Dean Perry, a granddaughter of J. H. Wade. She thought that it had probably once figured in the Wades' collection of jewelry, fans, snuff boxes, and vinaigrettes, most of which had been donated to the Museum.

The canvas *Landscape with Nymphs and Satyrs* (CMA 26.26) by the seventeenth-century master Nicolas Poussin was given to express Wade's appreciation to the newly organized The Friends of The Cleveland Museum of Art, who would make possible future acquisitions. His check for the purchase price of the painting and a subscription to the Friends was enclosed in a letter dated February 3, just a few weeks before his death on March 6, 1926.

During the course of his extensive travels, J. H. Wade took his extended family to India. There he collected widely, concentrating on colorful textiles from nearly every corner of the Far and Nearer East, as well as jewelry from Tibet and India, and delicate miniatures from Persia and India.

The organization, The Friends of The Cleveland Museum of Art, was formed in the spring of 1926. John L. Severance was the Chairman and Leonard C. Hanna, Jr., the Vice Chairman. Its purpose was "to aid in the development of the collection by augmenting the purchasing funds of the Museum." Annual subscriptions ranging from $1,000 to $100 were first solicited for a period of five years. The membership list published in the January 1927 *Bulletin* includes the names of nearly fifty individuals. Within its ten-year existence the group raised the money to purchase four first-rate paintings for the Museum. The first, a painting by El Greco, was given in 1926 in memory of J. H. Wade, who had subscribed $1,000 and had set such a fine example for the Friends. Their last, the work of the Master of Heiligenkreuz, honored John L. Severance.

*The Holy Family with Mary Magdalene* by El Greco (Domenico Theotocópuli), Spanish (1541-1614). Gift of The Friends of The Cleveland Museum of Art, in memory of J. H. Wade. CMA 26.247

*A Bishop Saint with Donor* was painted by a Spanish master about 1420. Gift of The Friends of The Cleveland Museum of Art. CMA 27.197

*The Death of the Virgin* by the Master of Heiligenkreuz, in Austria, about 1400. Gift of The Friends of The Cleveland Museum of Art in memory of John L. Severance. CMA 36.496

The Fine Arts Garden of Cleveland was formally dedicated on July 23, 1928. Taking part in the ceremony were Mrs. John Sherwin (center), President of the Garden Club of Cleveland; William G. Mather, representing the Trustees of The Cleveland Museum of Art; William R. Hopkins (seated), Cleveland's City Manager; and the Rt. Rev. William R. Leonard, Bishop of the Episcopal Diocese of Ohio.

On the Euclid Avenue side of the Fine Arts Garden a marble balustrade overlooks the Wade Park lake. Flights of steps lead down to the Holden terrace on which stands *Night Passing* *Earth to Day* by the Cleveland sculptor Frank L. Jirouch. The terrace was presented by Mrs. Windsor T. White, while the bronze was the gift of Mrs. B. P. Bole.

The program opened when a group of debutantes—representing families connected to the donors—carried a daisy chain down the Museum stairs into the garden while three cornetists played "The Grand March" from *Aida*. Taking up positions around the garden, the young women unveiled the various gift sculptures.

The Fine Arts Garden, situated between Euclid Avenue and The Cleveland Museum Art, is a tribute to the cooperative efforts of The Garden Club of Greater Cleveland, the Art Museum, private citizens, and the city of Cleveland.  Designed by the Olmsted Brothers, Landscape Architects of Boston, the $400,000 project was originated and sponsored by the Garden Club. Finished in July 1928, it replaced a neglected five-acre park just south of the Museum. Today, the John and Frances Sherwin Fine Arts Garden Endowment Fund helps provide for the garden's maintenance by the Museum's grounds staff. In all seasons the garden provides an enchanted setting for the Museum.

Among major contributors to the garden were Mrs. Leonard C. Hanna, Leonard C. Hanna, Jr., Mr. and Mrs. John Sherwin, J. H. Wade, Mrs. Windsor T. White, Mrs. B. P. Bole, Mr. and Mrs. E. B. Greene, Mrs. S. Prentiss Baldwin, Dr. and Mrs. Charles E. Briggs, Mrs. Williard M. Clapp, Mrs. William McLauchlan, Katherine Mather, Mrs. John E. Newell, Mrs. W. D. Rees, Mrs. Andrew Squire, Mrs. J. E. Ferris, Mrs. George W. Ford, Mrs. J. D. Cox, Mrs. W. S. Tyler, Mrs. Albert W. Russel, Mrs. L. Dean Holden, Mrs. E. R. Grasselli, Mr. and Mrs. F. E. Drury, John L. Severance, William G. Mather, the Estate of Ralph King, Samuel Mather, D. Z. Norton, F. F. Prentiss, John H. Hord, Mrs. Amos N. Barron, Mrs. Arthur St. John Newberry, Mrs. William G. Pollock, Mrs. T. S. Grasselli, Clara Sherwin, and The Cleveland Art Association, as well as the City of Cleveland.

At the dedication dancers performed in the oval garden named the Court of Nature, around *The Fountain of the Waters* by the sculptor Chester A. Beach. Given by Mrs. Leonard C. Hanna, the fountain's two main figure groups represent the flowing waters: the lake and the waters returning to the parent lake. The children on either side stand for the flowers of the river banks.

# HOWARD CARTER AND THE CLEVELAND MUSEUM OF ART

T. G. H. JAMES

A former Keeper of the British Museum's Egyptian Antiquities, T. G. H. James is writing a book on Howard Carter.

hat happens if a museum decides to embark on a new field of collecting for which it has little to build on and no professional expertise? There will be problems, most of which will derive from ignorance; but ignorance coupled with determination may produce a situation from which exploitation and fearful mistakes can result. It is, therefore, with great interest that the development of the Egyptian collection in The Cleveland Museum of Art may be observed, and it says much for the far-sightedness of its Trustees and Director that they even contemplated entering a field which was already beginning to be well represented in the museums of the United States.

The great museums of Europe—the British Museum, the Louvre, Leiden, Berlin, Turin—all had acquired their first Egyptian antiquities early in the nineteenth century. Their core collections were varied and secure, and it was not too difficult to maintain and build on what was in existence by judicious purchasing and by excavation. Yet it was not too late in the early twentieth century for action to be taken on the other side of the Atlantic; the initiative could be seized quite decisively if determination, skill, and finance were deployed with good planning and knowledgeable advice. Since the 1880s the fruits of excavation had been tasted by numerous American institutions through their support for the London-based Egypt Exploration Fund, and useful, well-provenanced objects had been acquired by the Metropolitan Museum of Art, New York, the Museum of Fine Arts, Boston, and the University Museum, Philadelphia. These three were quick to appreciate what could be done by direct action, and of them the first two were spectacularly successful, the Metropolitan in its excavations at Lisht and Thebes, and Boston at Giza, El-Bersha, Naga el-Deir, in Nubia, and elsewhere. In consequence, by 1914 both New York and Boston possessed Egyptian collections which in some respects rivaled, even surpassed, those to be found in Europe. The Metropolitan, supported liberally by wealthy donors, had further strengthened its Egyptian holdings by extensive purchases.

So, any progressive museum that wished to go beyond the traditional fields of the purely fine arts, the decorative arts, and European medieval art, might now look to Egypt for remote antiquity, exoticism, and the mystical seductiveness of hieroglyphs. Cleveland was no exception in wishing to participate in this movement, and the wish was not at all unjustified. There was already a more than useful nucleus of 500 Egyptian objects in the Museum, many acquired by Lucy Olcott Perkins, who had been in Egypt as part of J. Pierpont Morgan's entourage in 1913.[1] It represented a good, though modest, beginning, which needed to be vigorously built on if it were to achieve any kind of respectability. In 1916 ideas began to crystallize; Cleveland's Director, Frederic Allen Whiting, took steps to consult colleagues in the Metropolitan Museum—in particular Henry W. Kent, Secretary of the New York museum, and Albert M. Lythgoe, Curator of Egyptian Art. Their advice was encouraging. In the first place, the time for entering the market was propitious; secondly, Cleveland should try to obtain the services of Howard Carter.

Of these two recommendations, the second was undoubtedly superior to the first. The time was almost certainly not propitious. It was the height of World War I, few excavations were taking place in Egypt, there were no tourists in the prewar sense, and there was no serious market for antiquities. It might have been thought a good time to go buying, but experience has shown that the supply of antiquities in Egypt tends to march with the level of visitors. In times of difficulty the hatches on illicit digging seem to be battened down, and random finds, of which there are always some, are put down by antiquities dealers to mature for better times ahead. By chance, the position is neatly set out in a letter to a friend by Howard Carter himself, to whom Whiting was shortly to turn for help:

*Here things are tedious especially these long summers—though this one on the whole has been abnormally cool*

*which is a blessing. The excavations, what little there has been, have been dull and where [sic] it not for a few interesting things turning up in the shops from time to time this last two years has proved of little interest that way.*

*The best was a large hoard of silvergilt stuff at Dendera [sic] which the [Cairo] Museum got—very late and horribly ugly. Possibly part of the temple treasure.*

*Antiquities like everything else have gone up in price—the natives have become so rich, farm produce being threble [sic] what it was in value. Too much large sums are brought in through the Army contracts etc.—most of which absorbed by the natives and hoarded for future times. So much so that they are now issuing five piastre notes, the whole of the silver being hidden underground.*[2]

Carter, who was to find international fame in 1922 with his discovery of the tomb of Tutankhamen, was in 1917 already very much an old Egypt hand. Forty-three years old, he had spent the whole of his career, from the age of seventeen, in the archaeological life of that country. From 1909 he had been in charge of the excavations financed, and personally supervised, by the fifth Earl of Carnarvon. In 1914 Lord Carnarvon had obtained the concession to work in the Valley of the Kings at Thebes, but throughout the war up to late 1917 Carter had been able to do little there apart from occasional probing and testing when his official duties allowed. Working for Carnarvon, even outside the restrictive circumstances of war, was not a full-time occupation, and Carter had plenty of time while in Egypt to execute business on behalf of friends and a few selected clients. There is good evidence to suggest that in this secondary activity of gentleman dealer he was encouraged by Lord Carnarvon. Above all others Carnarvon had first claim on Carter's acquisitions, but in a good year there would be many pieces not required for the Carnarvon collection at Highclere Castle and therefore available for offer elsewhere. Moreover, Carnarvon was not above advancing funds to Carter for the purchase of expensive items on behalf of other clients. In this arrangement there was, it seems, an eagerness on Carnarvon's part to encourage Carter to exploit his knowledge of antiquities and his familiar relationships with Egyptian dealers so that he could make some provision for a future which would be very uncertain if Carnarvon were to die. This possibility was not remote. Carnarvon had never enjoyed robust health after a serious accident in 1901, and his tragic death in 1923, only a few months after the discovery of the tomb of Tutankhamen, was the consequence more of his poor constitution than of any putative curse.

After consulting with his Trustees, Whiting addressed Carter: "I am writing to you at the suggestion of Mr. Kent and Mr. Lithgoe [sic] of the Metropolitan Museum, New York, who believe that you may be in a position to act for us in the matter of purchases in Egypt, the time for which in their opinion is propitious."[3] After a short statement about the existing Egyptian collection and drawing attention to a list of "priorities" prepared by Mrs. Grant Williams,[4] he continued: "I might say that I feel particularly anxious to secure one or two fine portrait statues if they ever become available at prices within our means." And after a request for Carter's terms he added:

*it is not our plan to develop an extensive Egyptian collection, as it seems to me undesirable to do so in view of the collections already in New York, Boston, and Philadelphia. We desire rather to supplement our present collection with additional material which will round it out so that it will give a fairly adequate idea of Egyptian art, and I shall hope to secure funds from time to time to add important individual examples as they become available.*

Carter's answer is dated September 16, one month later, which says a lot for wartime postal services.[5] From Luxor he sent an encouraging signal: "I shall be happy to undertake such a commission which would receive the outmost [sic] of my ability." He then set out his terms, which were pretty comprehensive, suggesting that he was no greenhorn in business matters. His commission would be fifteen percent; he would obtain best prices (as we shall see) and guarantee the authenticity of purchases. The Museum would defray all costs of packing and transport; he would help in the clearance of objects through the Cairo Museum.

He suggested that the Museum employ the same agencies for insurance and for transport, and the same agents for payment as those employed by the Metropolitan Museum. He added: "from time to time I acquire Egyptian antiquities myself for the purpose of sale. Should at any time your Museum wish to make a purchase from me, I would ask that it be done through a third person accepted or appointed by you." In delicate negotiations strict secrecy should apply. It had been suggested that photographs of projected purchases should always be submitted; in general Carter agreed, but pointed out that it might not always be possible, especially when negotiating with "native" dealers, when quick decisions would often be imperative:

*may I mention that among the numerous and considerable purchases I have made for both public and private collections I have been given a free hand in the matter.... In all cases of objects purchased photographs would be sent, before exportation.*

Carter's terms were acceptable, and his willingness to act delighted Whiting and the Cleveland Trustees. The friends of the Museum elsewhere were most encouraging. Kent from the Metropolitan wrote enthusiastically to Judge William B. Sanders, President of the Cleveland Board: "he [Carter] will produce results for you which will give the Cleveland Museum an enviable place among museums in the Egyptian Art." A cable to Carter on December 1 confirmed the acceptance, and within two days he was able to write to Whiting, sending photographs of objects in the hands of Nicolas Tano, one of the leading Cairo dealers. Initiating a practice that became standard, Whiting passed the photographs to Mrs. Williams for examination and recommendation.

On December 7 Mrs. Williams responded, commenting on the Carter photographs, adding useful information, and stating categorically: "In view of Mr. Carter's discriminating taste I would suggest that you give him practically a free hand, within the limit of what you can spend." So the process was launched. However, it took a little time for positive results to be achieved. By June 15, 1918, Carter could confidently write to Whiting:

*I have at last been able to break the ice in the way of making a few good acquisitions for your museum. They are, I think you will find, good exemplary specimens worthy of any collection, and if I may pat my own back most reasonable in regard to price.*

These first objects included a useful series of Predynastic pottery vessels, picked up for what even then might have been thought a "song" from the Luxor dealer Mohammed Mohassib (CMA 20.1980, 20.1983-88); a royal shawabty figure of King Nectanebo II of Dynasty XXX (CMA 20.1989); a bronze sistrum (CMA 20.1990); a royal relief head—an intriguing figure—of disputed date (CMA 20.1979); and a vulture headdress in gold and glass cloisonné work (CMA 20.1991). All were good, although not very exciting pieces, apart from the vulture headdress, which is a remarkable example of intricate craftsmanship and was later classed as a minor masterpiece by Curator John D. Cooney.[6] He suggested, on the evidence of the Cairo dealer R. H. Blanchard from whom it had been purchased, that it may have formed part of the Dendara treasure about which Carter had written scornfully.

A second group of antiquities that Carter acquired from the leading Cairo dealers Kytikas, Abemayor, and Tano soon afterward contained more substantial pieces. There were three inscribed lintels from tombs of the Old Kingdom at Giza (CMA 20.1992-94), two of them with particularly fine hieroglyphic signs; a painted head in relief of Queen Hatshepsut, probably from her funerary temple at Deir el-Bahri (CMA 20.1995); a grotesquely decorated Roman bowl (CMA 20.1996); and a fine painted pottery vessel possibly from the palace of King Amenhotep III at Thebes (CMA 20.1997). Again, the purchase prices were economical and Whiting had every reason to write to Carter on August 17 with satisfaction at what had so far been obtained. It was, however, a tantalizing time, for there was little chance that the new acquisitions would be seen in Cleveland for quite some months. With the war continuing in Europe, it would have

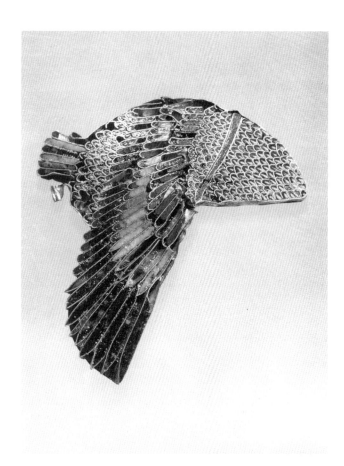

Acquired in 1920 with Carter's assistance, this *Vulture-Form Headdress* (CMA 20.1991) is a remarkable example of the craftsmanship found in Egypt during Dynasty XIX.

been chancy to send antiquities back to America even if space on a boat could have been found. Earlier in the war the Metropolitan Museum had lost a shipment of fine excavated material by enemy action. So they waited for better times.

After the Armistice in November 1918, the prospects for shipping not only improved, but there was also an encouraging relaxation of atmosphere in Cairo which augured well for a lift in the antiquities market. Now able to spend more time on archaeological work for the Earl of Carnarvon, Carter carried out a brief season at Meir in Middle Egypt at the end of 1918, and then in February 1919 resumed his excavations in the Valley of the Kings. In between times he could attend to other things and wrote a most interesting letter to Whiting on January 25:

*I feel, certainly without wish to be pretentious, that the times are without doubt advantageous for making further purchases; and for that reason I am strongly inclined to advise a further and, if I may add, substantial budget. Good specimens of art are rare—they appear as by hazard—one is tugged from all directions by institutions for material—and I should like, as you have asked me to look after your interests, that your museum be well represented. In regard to a sum required: until discoveries come in and are disclosed it is very difficult to estimate requirements; but that a museum, especially of art, should have good specimens as may be obtainable is essential—its collection being judged by its representative pieces—and the powers of obtaining such, while never forgetting prudent selection and value, is the credit for procuration. Hence, I most strongly confirm your views in the matter and would ask for as large a sum as your supporters would feel it possible to subscribe. Think what educative value, importance, not to speak of the public pleasure, a fine piece renders to both the collection and instruction. A fine specimen statue of one of the good periods would I fear not be procurable under four to ten thousand dollars. Nevertheless, I long to have the luck to find and have the permission to procure for your museum such a specimen.*

From a present-day perspective it might be thought that Carter was exercising a little too much

persuasion in urging Cleveland to act so vigorously, but he was not exaggerating the need for readiness and promptitude. Egypt was opening up again to archaeologists and tourists after almost five years of war-closure; it could be expected that the demand for antiquities would accelerate and that material put away for a rainy day would now emerge to meet the metaphorical deluge. Cleveland responded, as Carter hoped, and a rather more adequate provision was made for further purchases. Whiting was just as eager as Carter to obtain a good piece of sculpture. At first there was some success, although not precisely as hoped for. Two pieces turned up in the hands of Cairo dealers, and both were purchased after an exchange of photographs. One was an unusual funerary inscription in yellow quartzite (CMA 20.1977); it appeared to be of early Old-Kingdom date—about 2600 BC—and it was as such that Carter bought it. It soon became apparent—first it seems through the study of the piece by Mrs. Williams[7]—that it was almost 2,000 years later in date, still ancient Egyptian, but an archaizing piece of rare interest and quality. The determination of its date came from a study of its inscription, which Carter was not well qualified to handle. Almost by chance, Cleveland had acquired a real rarity. The second acquisition at this time was an unfinished recumbent lion (CMA 20.2001), possibly an artist's trial, an addition of great technical value to the collection.

Toward the end of 1919 there occurred a bizarre incident which illustrated only too well, if also rather painfully, what Carter had said about the scramble for antiquities. At last a number of good sculptures became available, and with commendable speed and skill he established claims on four pieces: a trial piece with a number of incised heads (CMA 20.1975), of great potential interest; a Deir el-Medina stela for the cult of King Tuthmosis III (CMA 20.2002); a limestone pair-statuette of a Theban official and his wife (CMA 20.2003); and a small, rather damaged scribal statuette (CMA 20.2004). In writing to Whiting on December 31, Carter was understandably enthusiastic. After discussing costs, he commented:

*This is not an unreasonable price when one considers their rarity, artistic merits, and the demand for such works by collectors and museums. So much do I feel it to be the case that I most strongly recommend their immediate purchase by your museum. I therefore have taken possession of them on your behalf lest they be snapped up as many European dealers are coming again to Egypt.*

In the same letter he announced that he had paid a large deposit on "a naophoros statuette of basalt, a fine and characteristic piece of Saite art." This acquisition caused much trouble. It was a figure of Horwedja (CMA 20.1978), an agricultural official in the region of Memphis, the great Egyptian capital city just south of present-day Cairo. Of graywacke (not basalt), the piece shows the subject kneeling and holding a small shrine containing a figure of Ptah, the principal Memphite deity. Originally assigned somewhat loosely to the Saite period (Dynasty XXVI), it has now been dated more precisely to Dynasty XXVII (about 500 BC).[8] By prompt action Carter had secured it for Cleveland. Unfortunately, James H. Breasted, Director of the Oriental Institute in the University of Chicago, thought that he had obtained a first refusal on it from Nicolas Tano, the Cairo dealer. Not used to being forestalled in this way, Breasted at once set about trying to prise the statuette from Carter, using vigorous and not wholly admirable methods.

As far as it can be judged, what happened involved a simple misunderstanding, compounded perhaps by Breasted's assumption that by showing an interest in the piece he was in effect reserving it. Sometime in December 1919, he visited Tano's shop, which lay opposite the old Shepheard's Hotel in the Ezbekiya district of Cairo. There he was shown the statuette of Horwedja and expressed an interest in it. He did not have the funds to buy the piece at the moment, so he went away and cabled America for authority and money to purchase. On receiving authority he went back to Tano's shop on December 29, only to find that Carter had carried off the statuette. At once Breasted wrote to Carter in Luxor to see if he could

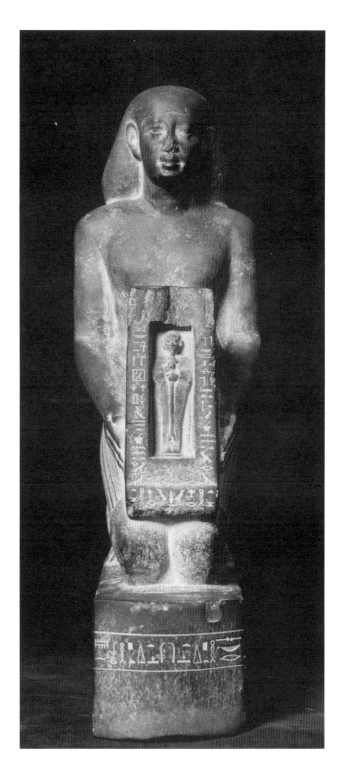

Carter's acquisition of this Dynasty XXVII *Horwedja* (CMA 20.1978) for the Museum was contested by James H. Breasted, Director of the Oriental Institute, University of Chicago.

get him to cede the piece to him.[9] He admits that Carter had tried to see him in Cairo before he left on a trip to Upper Egypt, but "the loss of the piece is a serious one for us at Chicago. Can we not therefore come to some agreement satisfactory to you, by which the piece may still go to Chicago, in accordance with my understanding with Tano...." In his reply of January 2, 1920, Carter states, "I certainly understood from Tano that there was no reserve upon the figure. He mentioned the fact of having shown the statuette to you and that among others was one of the reasons of my calling with Lansing [of the Metropolitan Museum] upon you." He goes on to explain that the purchase was for Cleveland. He would send Breasted's letter to Whiting to see if anything could be done.

And so began a long, unedifying series of letters between Breasted, Carter, Whiting, and others, which did not come to a conclusion until January 1921. It would be tedious even to summarize the principal exchanges; but it is still important to understand why feelings, especially on Breasted's part, ran so high. Carter, as agreed, wrote to Whiting on January 8, 1920, but his letter did not reach Cleveland for over a month. In the meanwhile Breasted had also written to Whiting and asked for a simple "yes" or "no" answer. In due course, after discussions with Trustees, Whiting cabled a terse "Regret no." Breasted had at first accepted Carter's explanation and had *magnanimously* absolved him of all blame in the matter (January 3). Later he began to modify his opinion when it seemed that Carter had not been in touch with Whiting—a mistaken assumption. This change of view comes out in a letter Breasted wrote to Charles Hutchinson, the President of the Art Institute of Chicago, for whom he had been acting in the business of the statuette. He complained of Carter's behavior at never having written to Cleveland about the problem:

*I have heard similar reports of Carter before. He has great influence among the native dealers and I have no doubt that by a policy of browbeating he forced the dealer to yield the statue to him on threat of future penalties. I ought to say, however, that he did attempt to see me when I happened to be out of Cairo ... and perhaps wished to find out more about the matter, and on discovering that I was out of town took possession of the monument. It would be very difficult to find such a work of art again. I think Cleveland is morally bound to deliver the monument to Chicago.*

The unfair imputations in this letter, which were repeated in a letter to Whiting, probably tipped the balance in the case toward the retention of the piece in Cleveland. Tano (who was scarcely a "native" dealer) was written to for confirmation of how the transaction was effected: "Now I beg to inform you that [object] was shewed at first to Professor Breasted but as he has not given me a definite reply, I ceded it to Mr. Howard Carter" (November 27, 1920). Henry Kent, the Secretary of the Metropolitan Museum, weighed in, probably conclusively, in Carter's support. On December 2 he wrote: "Also you should remember that he [Carter] is a *practical buyer*, which means more when dealing with the natives in Egypt than many would suppose." A day or two later (the letter is undated), he wrote again:

*I am still of the opinion which I expressed to you before Carter was engaged as your agent, that he is probably the most desirable ally you can have in Egypt. He is acknowledged to be the most skilful trader with the natives, he is a gentleman, and I doubt very much whether he would be found lacking in courtesy or fairness to men of his own class.*

Whiting was wholly taken by surprise to discover through talking to the Director of the Art Institute of Chicago, George William Eggers, that Breasted had been acting for that collection, and not for the Oriental Institute, as everyone had supposed. It introduced a new embarrassment in the matter because of the close association between the Cleveland Museum and the Art Institute. Whiting therefore sent copies of the relevant documents to Eggers in January 1921 and stated that Cleveland could hardly yield the statue to Chicago; apart from other considerations it would imply criticism of Carter. He added: "I should prefer that this correspondence be not taken up with Mr.

Breasted, since there seems to have been a little feeling between himself and Mr. Carter, but I do not insist on this limitation." On January 18 Eggers replied: "I have read over the correspondence which you have sent concerning the Egyptian statue. There does not appear to be anything for the Trustees of the Art Institute to do about the matter, and I shall let it rest where it is."

This strange episode, showing the great James Henry Breasted trying to elbow the relatively unimportant Howard Carter out of his way to occupy the moral high ground, is not very heroic. It is even less meritorious when the sculpture in question is coolly considered. The statue of Horwedja is a good, but rather run-of-the-mill example of Late-period work. For Cleveland in 1919 it was, however, a good acquisition, certainly filling one of the many gaps in the Egyptian collection as it then was. But it was not the outstanding masterpiece that Breasted made it out to be. One may suspect that he was particularly vexed not simply for the loss of the piece itself, but in a sense because he had been outmaneuvered by someone for whom he had probably never before given a thought. He was surely also vexed because he had been wrong-footed in not making it clear early in the business that he was acting as an agent for the Art Institute—though certainly without any expectation of personal financial advantage. There was, of course, no impropriety in this agency; he was almost certainly on the Board of the Art Institute and undoubtedly adviser for the Institute's own small Egyptian collection. Carter, on the other hand, may have moved a little too swiftly in clinching the deal with Tano; but in so doing he acted with the kind of professional expedition for which he had been engaged to act on behalf of the Cleveland Museum. Throughout his career, he was prone to take actions that might have been judged too hasty and even ill-considered, but in this case a sober assessment may find him innocent of serious misjudgment. And, as a comfortable coda to the whole disagreeable episode, it is good to find Breasted and Carter doing business together by the

end of 1920 in the most cordial terms, at least on paper.[10] It is, further, good to remember that in the troubles pursuing Carter after the discovery of the tomb of Tutankhamen, Breasted was among the group of well-wishers who worked hard to find a satisfactory solution to the political impasse.

Throughout 1920, while the Horwedja pantomime was enjoying its long run, Carter was engaged in various less dramatic activities connected with his Cleveland agency. Above all there was the problem of getting the material already acquired shipped to the United States. After several false starts, the consignment was at last on its way by mid-July, although it did not reach Cleveland until the very end of the year. He had no further purchases in mind after the excellent results of December 1919, which had yet to be paid for in part. But there were possibilities for the future. It is clear that Whiting had become committed to the development of the Egyptian collection and was beginning to stir up positive enthusiasm among several of the Cleveland Trustees. Carter had done well so far, and his success needed to be consolidated. Strongly supportive noises were also coming from Mrs. Williams: "Mr. Carter is a wonder in being able to hang on to material while he sends home photos and allows you time to put the deal through. The pieces are remarkable acquisitions considering their rarity—and will help your collection greatly."[11] In February also Carter wrote to Whiting about a large collection due to come on the market in the summer, "the management of which is to be put in my hands; I therefore trust to be able to procure good pieces for your museum should you wish it." This was to be the dispersal of the Amherst collection, but for the moment Whiting confused the matter with something else, which was potentially a source of considerable embarrassment for Carter.

On May 29 Whiting wrote to Carter:
*I presume you have already had a conference with Mr. Winlock* [of the Metropolitan Museum] *regarding the division in thirds of a certain collection which I presume is the matter you referred to in your letter to me. I have rea-*

*son to believe that if this is done and one of the thirds is allotted to this Museum we may have a friend who will take advantage of the opportunity for us.*

Carter responded on July 15, saying that Whiting's suggestion "is quite new to me, neither do I know what it refers to." To this denial Whiting on July 28 replied:

*Apparently it is an exceedingly important collection of material in gold as I remember it, which Mr. Lythgoe had some kind of option on and had in mind dividing it in three parts, and giving us one opportunity, the rest to go to England and the Metropolitan.*

In October Whiting returned to the subject: "the matter has been for some reason which he [Lythgoe] does not explain, temporarily withdrawn, so he is not free to discuss it for the time being." That in fact was the end of an affair in which Carter found himself unable to be completely frank, for it involved the purchase by the Metropolitan of the splendid treasure of the three princesses. It would not have done for Carter to make clear his own intermediary position in a most complicated transaction, although Cleveland was well aware that Carter did on occasion act also on behalf of the Metropolitan Museum. He could, however, write to Whiting on December 27: "The matter you mention concerning Mr. Lythgoe and Mr. Winlock of the Metro. Museum of Art, N.Y. has I think been closed." He would certainly have known that.

The experience of the Metropolitan Museum and other American Museums in acquiring excellent material from their excavations prompted Whiting to sound out Carter on the possibility of a Cleveland excavation in Egypt. Carter answered (July 15, 1920) very sensibly, bearing in mind the circumstances of the early 1920s:

*To have an excavation concession in Egypt would be of great interest; it would entail a large expence [sic], necessitate at least two Europeans and large native staff. Under the new regime the difficulties of obtaining concessions are becoming greater and the division of results more disheartening, as both Mr. Lythgoe and Winlock will tell you. Personally, owing to my other engagements, I should not be able to help you in that way further than to give advice upon the subject.*

So this option was dropped, and in due course the Cleveland Museum began contributing to the excavations of the Egyptian Exploration Society at El-Amarna through the generosity of a Trustee. Whiting wrote to Carter about it in January 1921, asking him to provide tips on the good material which might turn up in the excavation.

The best prospects for new acquisitions now lay in the sale of the Amherst collection. In the late nineteenth century the first Baron Amherst of Hackney had built up a fine Egyptian collection at Didlington Hall in Norfolk. Located only a few miles away from Swaffham where Howard Carter grew up, Didlington was where he had first encountered Egyptian antiquities. Through the patronage of Lord Amherst, Carter first went to Egypt in 1891, and he retained a close friendship with the Amherst family. A financial disaster struck Amherst in the early years of the twentieth century, obliging him to sell his remarkable library and parts of his Egyptian collection. Not long afterward, in 1909, he died, and in due course the remainder of the collection was put up for sale. Carter knew the collection intimately and helped to prepare the catalogue for the sale at Sotheby's, London, which took place over five days on June 13-17, 1921. As it was to be a public auction Carter had no opportunity to secure any preferential treatment for Cleveland; the best he could do was to send a proof copy of the catalogue in late December 1920. He marked desirable pieces, especially recommending seven: "Prices will be below dealers prices in Egypt and Europe."

Whiting, as ever, consulted Mrs. Williams about Carter's suggestions, which she fully supported. Cleveland should try to buy all he proposed, but he should be allowed leeway in case of failures. There was some difficulty over raising sufficient funds to back Carter, but by March the way was clear for part of the projected purchases, and further support was sent to London in May. In spite of being so well backed, Carter was unable to secure much of what he

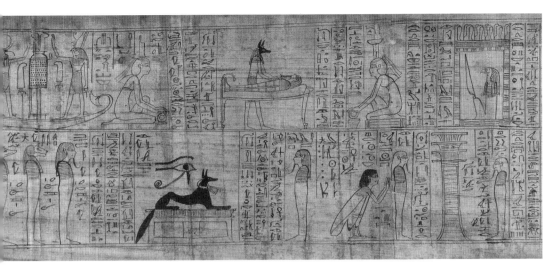

Carter was responsible for Cleveland's acquiring the Egyptian Dynasty XXI *Papyrus of Hori, Priest of Amen* (CMA 21.1032). A detail of this papyrus from the notable Amherst collection is shown here.

had earmarked for Cleveland. He wrote apologetically to Whiting on August 6, 1921, after trying without success to secure some of the lost pieces in post-auction negotiations: "[T]here was great competition among the European museums, private collectors and America.... [T]he prices of the principal and more valuable specimens soared up far beyond all expectations—in fact to almost prohibitive prices." He cited some examples among the pieces on the Cleveland list: the fine, most desirable quartzite block statue of Senwosret-Senbefni sold for £1,870 (about $9,300), Carter being the underbidder at £1,850. In this case the successful purchaser was William Randolph Hearst, a voracious and undiscriminating collector as far as Egyptian antiquities were concerned. This fine statue had been brought back from Egypt possibly by Napoleon as a gift for Josephine—a fact not known in 1921, but subsequently discovered by John D. Cooney, who much later managed to acquire it for The Brooklyn Museum.[12] If Carter had been successful, it would have been the crowning piece of his association with Cleveland. As it was, because of the high expectations, the purchases made at the Amherst sale were a little disappointing, although they were not insignificant acquisitions. Carter offered some compensation for his lack of success by purchasing for Cleveland by private treaty just after the sale a good Dynasty XXI religious papyrus, with

finely drawn vignettes, prepared for a Theban priestly official named Hori (CMA 21.1032).

These transactions in the summer of 1921 in effect marked the end of Howard Carter's active agency on behalf of the Cleveland Museum. It is almost certainly the case that the indifferent results of the Amherst sale, on which so much had been staked, dimmed Whiting's enthusiasm for Egyptian antiquities for some time. The substantial balance of funds held by Carter was recalled to Cleveland, and there was no positive response either to an independent initiative from Tano or to Carter's suggestion that certain pieces from the Earl of Carnarvon's excavations might be available—not at that time the outrageous proposal that it would seem to be today. Then, in the autumn, Carter was out of action for several months, undergoing a serious abdominal operation. For the time being there was nothing to be done, and on his return to Egypt early in 1922 to continue Lord Carnarvon's excavations in the Valley of the Kings, he had no incentive to look out for antiquities for Cleveland. Writing on December 14, 1921, to congratulate Carter on the successful outcome of the operation, Whiting added, "I sincerely hope that it will be possible for us to place further funds at your disposal later, but just at the moment it is not possible for us to make such arrangements."

Thereafter, other matters distracted Carter. In No-

vember 1922 he discovered the tomb of Tutankhamen and for the next ten years it engrossed his
time and energies. Whiting wrote soon after the discovery to offer his congratulations and took the opportunity to put in a claim for consideration if there
were to be a good division of the treasures of the
tomb. It was a faint hope, but a good try. And later in
the year he again wrote to Carter, recommending to
his possible good offices John L. Severance, one of
the Cleveland Museum's two Vice-Presidents. Mr.
and Mrs. Severance were to visit Egypt in November:
*You may not be in a position to be helpful or to give him
personal attention; but if it should be otherwise, and you
can in any way assist in making his visit to Egypt stimulating and interesting, I shall not only appreciate it for the
additional pleasure which it will give to Mr. and Mrs. Severance, but also for the greater intelligence with which he
will thereafter be able to consider the problems relating to
our Egyptian collection which may arise.*
The further hope he expressed, that Carter might be
able to buy again for Cleveland, particularly "some
life size (or nearly life size) portrait statues," would
never be realized.

The association between the Cleveland Museum
and Howard Carter had not lasted long. His efforts
for the Museum may not seem to have been dramatically effective, but within the limits of the funds made
available to him, he did not do badly. Some of his
purchases were unexpectedly good. He was, as he
maintained, economical: the statuette of Horwedja,
for example, he obtained for £E1,000, where Breasted
was expecting to pay £E1,200. Carter had, however,
other private agency commitments at the same time,
and it is not unlikely that he found the balancing of
the demands of his various clients a difficult and even
invidious business.

It is hard to know how Carter viewed his relationship with the Cleveland Museum, and with Frederic
Allen Whiting in particular. All their negotiations had
been conducted by letter, with no personal contact.
That would eventually come when it was too late to
establish a sympathetic working relationship. At the

This late Dynasty XVIII
*Seated Cat Amulet*
(CMA 73.29) once be-
longed to Howard
Carter.

end of May 1924, Carter visited Cleveland for a few
days in the course of his North American lecture
tour. He lectured twice on his Tutankhamen discoveries, on June 2 and 3 in the Masonic Hall. It is incon-
ceivable that he did not visit the Museum, to meet
Whiting and to see his acquisitions on display, although there seems to be no record of such a visit. It
was not, however, quite the last point of contact between him and the Museum. This was, appropriately,
posthumous, in good Egyptian tradition. In 1975 the
Museum purchased a small black hematite cat (CMA
73.29).[13] Originally belonging to Carter, it had passed
to his niece, Phyllis Walker, as part of his estate after
his death in 1939. Carter always admitted to being
more of a dog man than a cat man, but in this piece
he had recognized a splendid small-scale example of
animal sculpture, a genre in which the Egyptian artist
was preeminent, and with which Carter was by inclination and training especially in tune.

1. Many objects from this nucleus are published by C. R. Williams in *Journal of Egyptian Archaeology* 5 (1918): 166-178, 272-285. See also Henry W. Kent to Lucy Olcott Perkins [Mrs. Frederick Mason Perkins], January 22, 1913: "advising you to join the Adriatic party."

2. Howard Carter to Percy Newberry, July 5, 1918, letter 8/58 in the Newberry Correspondence in the Griffith Institute, the Ashmolean Museum, Oxford. I am grateful to the Committee of Management of the Griffith Institute for permission to quote from this letter.

Both Carter and Newberry were at the time engaged in war-work, Carter in intermittent duties with army intelligence services in Egypt, and Newberry with wartime censorship in London, on secondment from his professorship of Egyptology in Liverpool University. They were old friends, and had worked much together since 1891 when Newberry had first brought Carter to Egypt.

In 1918 $5.00 was worth approximately £1 sterling, and £1 sterling was the equivalent of £E 0.975 (i.e., Egyptian pounds). A 5-piastre note was roughly worth 25 U.S. cents.

3. Whiting to Carter, August 13, 1917. I am particularly grateful to Virginia Krumholz, Archivist of the Cleveland Museum, for providing me with an admirable calendar of relevant documents in the Museum archives, for preparing transcriptions of selected letters, and for being so hospitable on my visit to Cleveland in March 1990. The letters quoted here, unless otherwise noted, are from Howard Carter, file 445a-e, Director Whiting (I), CMA Archives.

4. Mrs. Grant Williams is better known in Egyptological circles as Caroline Ransom Williams. Born in Toledo, Ohio, she pursued Egyptological studies in Berlin under the great Adolf Erman and in Chicago with James Henry Breasted, the outstanding American Egyptologist of the first half of the twentieth century. Professionally she worked in the Metropolitan Museum, and at the time of the Carter initiative she was also the Curator of the very important Abbott Collection of Egyptian antiquities in the New-York Historical Society (now in The Brooklyn Museum). She was a knowledgeable scholar and an excellent judge of Egyptian antiquities. From the beginning she took more than a friendly interest in the Cleveland Museum's Egyptian collection, and she was naturally, and properly, the one to whom the Director would turn for advice and moral support.

5. Correspondence of the time is peppered with provisos about the likelihood of things not getting through because of enemy action, particularly by submarines. The sea-lanes to America from Europe and the Near East were especially hazardous.

6. See John D. Cooney, "Three Minor Masterpieces of Egyptian Art," *CMA Bulletin* 62, 1 (January 1975): 11-16.

7. In *CMA Bulletin* 12, 9 (November 1925): 145, 147 f. See also Bernard V. Bothmer in *Egyptian Sculpture of the Late Period*, exh. cat. (New York: The Brooklyn Museum of Art, 1960), 28, no. 24.

8. Bothmer, 1960, pp. 72 f.

9. Correspondence on this episode is held both in the Cleveland Museum and in the Oriental Institute of the University of Chicago. I am very grateful to the latter for permission to quote from letters in the Director's Office Correspondence, and particularly to John A. Larson, Museum Archivist of the Oriental Institute, for drawing my attention to the pertinent material and for being so helpful in many other ways. The quoted letters come from the files marked CA-CN 1919, and The Art Institute of Chicago 1920.

10. File CA-CN 1920, Director's Office Correspondence, Chicago Oriental Institute.

11. Williams to Whiting, February 21, 1920.

12. The statue's history is fully outlined by John D. Cooney in *Journal of Egyptian Archaeology* 35 (1949): 155 ff.

13. See Cooney, 1975, pp. 14-15. The imputation by Thomas Hoving in *Tutankhamun: The Untold Story* ([New York: Simon and Schuster, 1978], 356) that this cat was "presumably removed ... from the tomb [of Tutankhamen]" by Howard Carter is without foundation. Based, apparently, on a suspicion voiced by John D. Cooney, the idea rests essentially on the supposition that any small, pretty or exquisite piece in Carter's possession at the time of his death must *ipso facto* have come from that famous tomb.

William Mathewson Milliken (1889-1978) was appointed Director in August 1930, having been the Museum's Curator of Decorative Arts since 1919, and Curator of Paintings, 1925-1929.

This photograph of Milliken mimics Van Dyck's famous portrait of Charles I, now at Windsor Castle.

The Van Dyck portrait had had the practical purpose of giving the Italian sculptor Bernini multiple views from which to create a portrait bust of Charles I without ever having seen him in person.

# OVERVIEW: 1930-45

EVAN H. TURNER

On October 29, 1929, the stock market fell and the Great Depression began; Cleveland's spiraling prosperity of the past fifty or so years abruptly ended and the city faced painful retrenchment. The next fifteen years were not easy ones for the young Museum.

Finally, however, a staff was in place. Earlier, in 1926, after four years in Cleveland, Theodore Sizer had first taken a year's leave-of-absence and then returned East to pursue his penchant for teaching, at Yale. Happily, his improbable joint responsibilities for graphics and for Asia were then divided. Henry Sayles Francis became the Museum's Curator of Prints and Drawings in October 1927, and although he returned to the Fogg Museum at Harvard in 1929 for two years, he finally settled in Cleveland in 1931 where he remained for the next thirty-six years, becoming Curator of Paintings as well. Leona E. Prasse began her long career in the Print Department in 1925, also not retiring until 1967. Howard Hollis arrived in 1929, bringing the much-needed sense of direction for the growth of the Oriental Department. Gertrude Underhill, who had started in the Museum's Education Department in 1916, assumed responsibility for Textiles in 1924 and remained until 1947. Finally, and most important, William Milliken's leadership was firmly established when the Board appointed him Director in that pivotal first week of August 1930, even as he was in Frankfurt, acting on the Museum's brave decision to purchase six pieces of the Guelph Treasure.

The Depression soon had an impact upon the Museum, although the energies of the previous decade continued for another year or so. The entire Guelph Treasure, for example, came to America; it was seen at Cleveland by 77,000 eager visitors, many of whom had waited patiently in endless lines.[1] Nonetheless, concern about operating expenses was expressed as early as 1931. And in no time all salaries were cut back, some by as much as 15 percent, and budgets were planned literally to the penny.

Not too surprisingly, therefore, little was done with

Clevelanders queuing up at the Museum on January 11, 1931, to view the Guelph Treasure. In the middle ground at right are the dealers who brought this great medieval treasure from Europe. Left to right: Saemy Rosenberg (hands in pockets), Julius R. Goldschmidt, and Z. M. Hackenbroch (dark hair and moustache). Germany's crumbling economy forestalled government and private attempts to keep the Treasure—which was being sold by Duke Ernst August II—in Germany. (See also pages 88-91.)

exhibitions. The notable exception occurred in 1936, when the Museum celebrated its twentieth anniversary by mounting an exhibition of masterpieces to complement the city's Great Lakes Exposition, strung out downtown along the shores of Lake Erie, which celebrated the hundredth anniversary of Cleveland's incorporation. New Yorkers whose fortunes were established in Cleveland—John D. Rockefeller, Jr., Edward Harkness, Myron T. Herrick, Grace Rainey Rogers, and John Hay Whitney—enriched the exhibition by lending their treasures. The Museum also presented in 1936 the first much-publicized exhibition of Vincent van Gogh's works, which was the result of Leonard Hanna's involvement in funding exhibitions at the Museum of Modern Art in New York. Because of him, the Cleveland Museum presented such influential exhibitions as *Cubism and Abstract Art* in 1937, *Masters of Popular Painting* in 1939, and *Art of the American Indian* in 1942.

For the most part, during these lean years, the Museum concentrated its efforts on the collection. It did so, however, with a decidedly missionary vigor, as is evidenced in Milliken's message to the members: *Times of depression and unemployment have an effect upon cultural organizations.... Certainly the activities of an organization such as the Museum can be of incalculable value in times of increased leisure. The problem of leisure time and of its proper use is a fundamental one today. The members of the Museum perhaps do not realize what an invaluable part they are playing in solving this great social problem. They are making it possible* [through their membership dues], *at a time of greatly decreased budgets, to give the increased service demanded.*[2]

Without question, a major factor in the Museum's popularity throughout these years was the *May Show*, the Museum's annual exhibition of works created by Cleveland area artists. At the outset, in 1919, the Museum's *Bulletin* pointed out that: "The picturesque qualities of the city have not yet been adequately taken advantage of by many of our painters, etchers, and photographers. There is a wealth of material here which needs but the artist's eye to reveal it in its true

Organized by New York's Museum of Modern Art, the first exhibition of paintings and drawings by Van Gogh was shown in Cleveland, March 25-April 19, 1936.

Paintings Curator Henry Francis thought "that the importance of Van Gogh's contribution to painting distinctly merits the lavish acclaim which this presentation of his paintings has aroused."

The distinguished American photojournalist Margaret Bourke-White (1904-71) got her start in Cleveland. Working as a freelance photographer with a studio in the Terminal Tower, Bourke-White spent months trying to capture the flavor of the steel industry.

Such photographs as *Hot Pigs, Otis Steel Company, Cleveland, 1928* (CMA 72.244), won her a job with *Fortune* magazine. Her work appeared in the 1928 and 1929 *May Show*s.

The Armor Court has remained a perennial favorite with children, whether visiting with school groups, as shown here, or with families. During the 1930s the number of groups from public, private, and parochial schools of Greater Cleveland visiting the Museum peaked at 1,222 (35,267 students) in 1933.

Realizing that some schools found it difficult to visit the Museum, the Education Department attempted to go to them and to inform school principals, supervisors, and teachers about the constantly growing list of materials available for loan: lantern slides, color prints, casts of sculpture, and original works of art.

beauty...."[3] Milliken was closely identified with this exhibition; again and again during the 1930s he argued that the city should help its artists, particularly hurt by the hard times, by purchasing works from the exhibition. With justifiable pride, he could report in 1940 that during the first twenty-one years of the *May Show*, 4,020 works had been sold and Cleveland artists had received $192,899.73. He rightly recognized, however, that "the spiritual implications are even greater than the monetary ones."[4] The Museum's sense of responsibility for the well-being of the local artists was evident as well in its organizing tours of Cleveland-created paintings and watercolors which, in thirteen years, were shown in sixty-nine galleries in twenty-seven states.[5] The commitment was hardly passive!

The Museum's innovative educational programs during the 1930s represent some of its proudest moments. Thomas Munro accepted the Board's invitation to become responsible for those programs in the autumn of 1931; his appointment was seen also as a first step in forming a closer relationship with nearby Western Reserve University where, thanks to a grant from the Carnegie Corporation, he became Professor of Aesthetics in the Graduate School.[6] A succession of grants freed the Museum's education program from the frustrations of retrenchment and the program thrived. The Carnegie Corporation's on-going pro-

gram of funding the purchase of slides and photographs to teach art history meant that the Museum joined countless other organizations across America in enjoying the benefits of a venture that surely affected the nation's level of visual literacy during the years before World War II. However, of greater importance was Thomas Munro's research "on methods of discovering artistic ability in children and on the relation between the artistic ability and other factors in personality."[7] Supported by the Rockefeller-funded General Education Board, such work reflected the then-current interest in differential human development, a study which may not have stood the test of time but certainly aroused much comment then.

The Carnegie Corporation also generously supported the Museum's work with Cleveland's secondary schools. The Museum did not intend to train would-be artists; instead, by working closely with the collection, through lectures and the practice of drawing from works of art in the galleries, the Museum sought to promote a general awareness of the arts. When a particular talent was observed, the student was encouraged to pursue further study, often at the nearby Cleveland Institute of Art.[8] The programs nurtured under Munro's leadership were certainly original and stimulated much discussion among museum educators.

With the perspective of time it is easy to see that in

Leonard Colton Hanna, Jr. (1889-1957), iron ore, coal, and shipping executive, philanthropist, and a nephew of Marcus A. Hanna, graduated from Yale in 1913. He is shown here in a rare informal photograph.

Hanna first gave a work of art to the Museum at the age of 26. Contributing at least half of the money for the 1958 wing, he refused to have it named after him. Loathing publicity, he often kept his philanthropy secret.

*Time Magazine* in 1958 quoted him as saying, shortly before he died: "I've just done my share. Persons who gave $5 and $10 have done as much in proportion."

its frenetic effort to maintain operations, the Museum's greatest hardship during the Depression years was its recourse to using funds that had earlier been set aside for acquisitions. After the Guelph Treasure purchases, for example, the Huntington income was not used for acquisitions again until 1946 and thereafter only sparingly. This was especially disappointing because the Museum finally had a professional staff more than able to take advantage of the many tempting opportunities then emerging on the art market.

Nonetheless, during the 1930s virtually every department acquired one or two remarkable objects, although none displayed as much consistent method as the Print Department. That success owed a great deal to an avid collector, Ralph King. Dying within days of J. H. Wade, and therefore only briefly the acting President of the institution he so loved, King epitomized the enthusiastic commitment every museum desires. In 1919 he founded The Print Club,[9] whose infusion of acquisition funds enabled the department to be active in lean years; and most happily he strongly influenced early acquisition policies.

Other important donors of prints were emerging as well. In the Museum's lowest days Leonard C. Hanna, influenced by King, made the first of an awesome succession of gifts that would become the envy of the Museum world by giving a group of forty-three spectacular prints representing many different areas,

as well as a virtually complete group of lithographs by the Columbus-born artist George Bellows. The enthusiastic commitment of Mr. and Mrs. Lewis B. Williams was evident in their wide-ranging gifts, admirably chosen with the Museum's needs in mind. Quietly, too, Leona Prasse was already deeply involved in her own remarkable gathering, buying prints the Museum could not afford. Her gifts over the years, many made in honor of her parents, established her place among the most important donors in the department's history.

Thanks to the Wade Fund which expressed J. H. Wade's commitment to textiles, important works were acquired in this area even during the 1930s. And there were other committed collectors as well. Mrs. Wade's fine gathering of lace, presented earlier to the Museum by her children, was significantly increased by Mrs. John Sherwin's collection and the gifts from Mrs. Edward Harkness. With the establishment of the Textile Arts Club in 1934, the private collector and creative artist joined forces to sustain an appreciation of this art form in Cleveland.

During the 1930s the Museum's long-standing flirtation with Asian art became a firm if still modest commitment. One of the Museum's first gifts, received even before its building opened, was a Kangxi vase (CMA 14.535), presented by Ralph King, whose fascination with Asia had been enhanced by a trip

This 11th-century Indian bronze, *Nataraja: Siva as King of Dance* (CMA 30.331), is as popular as it is art historically important. It is among the notable Asian acquisitions made while Howard C. Hollis was in charge of the Department. He left in June 1947 to accept an appointment as Head of Arts and Monuments in Tokyo under the U.S. Government of Occupation.

around the world; King redirected his efforts elsewhere, however, when Worcester R. Warner in 1915 committed the then-impressive sum of $50,000 for the purchase of Asian art. Although the Museum's first Curator, J. Arthur MacLean, was a specialist in Asian art, he was also responsible for all the other areas until 1919. As a result Warner became deeply involved in spending the gift himself, with decidedly uneven results. Advisor Langdon Warner (no relation) was much more of a scholar than a connoisseur and Theodore Sizer, who was appointed in the autumn of 1922 as Curator of Oriental Art and of Prints, was far more experienced in the graphic arts, so that true method in collecting Asian material only occurred with Howard C. Hollis's appointment in 1929. While sadly his acquisitions were few in number, they exemplify his fine abilities. Within a very few years he had acquired such diverse treasures as the superb Chou bronze staff head inlaid with silver (CMA 30.730), an eleventh-century South Indian *Nataraja: Siva as King of Dance* (CMA 30.331), a Cham Siva of about 1300 (CMA 35.147), and a grand pair of Muromachi horse screens (CMA 34.373-74)—each, even today, among the Museum's finest Asian treasures. To crown these, in 1938 Hollis made the purchase of the extraordinary Eastern Chou Cranes and Serpents drum stand (CMA 38.9).

In 1938 and 1939 the Museum again suffered a setback from a third period of the Depression, and as late as 1941 the Director referred to the need for a "most rigid economy."[10] The world was falling apart and America had just entered World War II. Various staff members left to join the war effort, whether in the armed services or in local industry, which was thriving once again. Understandably, the Board greeted warmly Mrs. Robert Hornung's suggestion that much-needed volunteer activities should be coordinated under a newly created Junior Council.[11] But after twelve difficult years the clouds were about to break. As occurred in 1930 and later in 1957, 1942 marked a turning point in the Museum's history.

The Museum first enjoyed in 1942 the benefits of

Goya's *Portrait of Don Juan Antonio Cuervo* (CMA 43.90) was the first purchase made with income from the Mr. and Mrs. William H. Marlatt Fund. According to the terms of Julia Morgan Marlatt's will, the Museum received over $1.8 million from this unexpected gift.

Although frequent visitors to the Museum, apparently no one except the Director knew the couple, who were members in the $10 category.

Milliken, however, did recall talking "with them fifty, sixty times or more … on a Sunday afternoon…. I never thought of them as potential donors. I was only glad that they seemed so pleased in the service the Museum gave."

Mrs. Marlatt specified that the fund be used to purchase paintings, but none by local artists. Milliken speculated that he had "perhaps over played [his] hand" in stressing the impor-

tance of helping local artists.

The Museum also inherited the paintings, etchings, rare books, and manuscripts in their home on Fairmount Boulevard in Cleveland Heights. An ardent bibliophile, Marlatt had been a senior partner in the law firm Treadway and Marlatt.

Leonard Hanna's recently created fund "for the purchase of pictures of outstanding importance."[12] Within four years the Hanna Fund made possible the acquisition of Renoir's *Mlle Romaine Lacaux* (CMA 42.1065), Gauguin's *L'appel* (CMA 43.392), Picasso's greatest masterpiece of the Blue Period, *La Vie* (CMA 45.24), the grand Degas *Frieze of Dancers Adjusting Their Slippers* (CMA 46.83), and Van Gogh's *The Road Menders at Arles* (CMA 47.209), as well as two early seventh-century Cambodian figures (CMA 42.56 and 42.63): an awesome gathering that had an impact upon the Museum's image almost equaling that of the Guelph Treasure acquisitions.

Some years before, the Museum had been astonished to learn that Julia Morgan Marlatt, apparently influenced by the much-publicized generosity of Andrew Mellon at the National Gallery, had decreed that her estate should establish the Museum's first fund restricted to the purchase of paintings. At the end of 1942, three years after her death, the money became available. The first acquisition, Goya's *Portrait of Don Juan Antonio Cuervo* (CMA 43.90), was most appropriate for this important bequest.

Also in 1942 John L. Severance's earlier bequest of his collection was finally delivered even as the promise of his handsome acquisition fund loomed.[13] In that

Picasso's *La Vie* (CMA 45.24): While paying a routine visit to the New York dealer Germain Seligman in 1945, Milliken was astonished to learn that Picasso's famous painting *La Vie* was on the market. He immediately telephoned Leonard C. Hanna, who was fortunately in his New York apartment.

After rushing over "armed with photographs," Milliken reported "there wasn't a moment's

hesitation. [Hanna said] 'I'll get my overcoat and we'll go immediately.' When he saw it, he wanted to decide then and there. 'No, Leonard, we must call Henry Francis first and get his reaction.' I called … 'Henry, Leonard and I are at Germain Seligman's and there is a picture here which interests us … *La Vie* of Picasso.' He literally exploded over the phone. 'But, that's impossible. It's in the Rhode Island

School of Design.' I answered "Yes, I know. It was, but it's here now…. I let him talk with Mr. Hanna and there was no question from Leonard's expression as he listened to his reaction. The picture quickly made its way to Cleveland."

John Long Severance (1863-1936) is captured here by the Cleveland photographer James J. Meli. Severance's Cleveland residence, Longwood, stood on the site of the present Severance Center in Cleveland Heights. His sister Elisabeth and her husband (Francis F. Prentiss) lived just across Mayfield Road at Glenallen.

Milliken thought that the "friendly rivalry [in collecting] between brother and sister ... brought the Museum great dividends. If Mr. Severance bought a Rembrandt, Mrs. Prentiss bought what she considered a better Rembrandt. If Mrs. Prentiss bought a Hobbema, Mr. Severance countered by what seemed to him a

finer painting by that artist. The same competition developed in the realm of French furniture and prints, tapestries and Chinese ceramics as well."

The collectors had privately let Milliken know that the Museum would receive their treasures by bequest or gift so that their efforts would not be duplicated.

same remarkable year, Grace Rainey Rogers gave an important gathering of eighteenth-century French objects and, as was intimated then, subsequently bequeathed the Museum a third of her residual estate.

Even though gas rationing meant an abrupt decline in attendance, the Museum could face the future with decided anticipation as 1942 drew to a close. Admittedly it would be another year or so before the treasures would be moved from their wartime exhibition in the  lower reaches of the building to their customary places and the sandbags removed, but the end was in sight. With the death of Elisabeth Severance Prentiss (formerly Mrs. Dudley Allen) in 1944, the Museum gained another important group of objects. She

emulated her brother in bequeathing major funds to establish an endowment as well, but with a remarkable modesty she decreed that the income should be used for operations, rather than acquisitions.

With her death the first generation, who had done so much to define the Museum, was largely gone. The example of their unflagging commitment, however, had cemented a solid base for the Museum's future growth.

Grace Rainey Rogers gave an entire room in the Louis XVI style in 1942 in memory of her father, the Cleveland industrialist William J. Rainey.

Mrs. Rogers had assembled the room in her New York City apartment with the help of the Metropolitan's Curators.

She consulted Milliken in 1941 about a portrait of her father. That visit resulted in the gift of this engaging room. Mrs. Rogers made no conditions on her gift, merely hoping "that the things could be kept together." This "proposed no difficulty as they were all of one period," according to Milliken.

Although the room has since been dismantled, its contents remain on exhibition, including the seven painted panels set into a modern *boiserie*. The Metropolitan Museum, the Museum of Modern Art, and Cleveland were named her residual legatees.

Inscriptions on the
*Portable Altar of
Countess Gertrude
and First and Second
Crosses of Countess
Gertrude* date their
creation in Brunswick
to about 1040 (CMA
31.461-.462, 31.55).

Milliken considered
these three objects to
be "among the hand-
ful of basic monu-
ments in the history
of early German gold-
smith work."
　Since Mrs. E. B.
Greene, along with
her husband and

daughter, happened
to be on the same
steamer to Europe
as Milliken when he
first went to see the
Guelph Treasure, it is
not surprising that she
contributed toward
the purchase of the
one of the crosses.

The Guelph Treasure represents the finest
expression of German art and spiritual
values of the Middle Ages. Although once
numbering 140 items—crosses, portable
altars, reliquaries, pyxes, and manuscripts made from
precious metals, gems, and enamels—only 85 pieces
remained when the treasure was dispersed in the
1930s to public and private collections in Europe and
America. Its name derives from the family name of
Henry the Lion, a powerful German duke of the mid-
12th century, the heir of the Brunons and a forebear
of the House of Brunswick-Lüneburg (Hanover). By
continuing the family's tradition of giving fine objects
to the Treasury of the Cathedral of St. Blaise, in his
capital city of Brunswick, Henry the Lion became a
major patron of the arts. His activities were vital in
shaping the remarkable cache of the Ottonian, Romanesque, and Gothic periods that comprise the
*Welfenschatz* or Guelph Treasure.

　Milliken recalled receiving the sale catalogue for
the Guelph Treasure and poring over it. With Whit-

The *Monstrance with the Paten of St. Bernward* (CMA 30.505) was created "by the Master of the Oswald Reliquary, so-called from the Reliquary in the Cathedral Treasure of Hildesheim, at the end of 14th century."

Milliken maintained that its association with St. Bernward "unquestionably had brought about the effective mounting of the Paten in the Monstrance made for it in the 14th century. The marriage of Romanesque and Gothic elements has been achieved with dignity and rare elegance. Under a piece of rock crystal inserted in the pointed top is a fragment of the True Cross, one of the most revered elements in the entire Treasure, a piece unquestionably brought from the Holy Land or from Constantinople by Duke Henry the Lion when he returned from the Crusades in 1175."

ing's encouragement, the young Curator discussed the opportunity with various Trustees. After obtaining the approval of the Accessions Committee and the consent of the entire Board, the Huntington Trust was successfully approached for "a very considerable sum ... by far larger than had ever been appropriated for purchase before."

Arriving in Frankfurt and personally viewing the Treasure in no way abated Milliken's enthusiasm: "The thrill of seeing such objects, the knowledge that it was possible for Cleveland to acquire some of them, was tremendous.... The unbelievable thing was that there were no other buyers clamoring at the door." Faced with little or no competition, he agonized over what to select: "Would it not be better to secure the maximum of pieces available, never sacrificing the precious element of quality? Would it be better to think of unique objects of varying types and of different epochs?"

Milliken could not help being amazed that no other purchasers came forward even when the Treasure was next shown in Berlin and then in New York City: "Perhaps it was due in part to the absorption of the American museums in painting and sculpture.... Yet almost no comparable objects such as these pieces from the Guelph Treasure could ever come on the market again. Here was the paradox, the greatest objects of their kind and no takers except the Cleveland Museum."

During its three weeks on view in Cleveland 89,000 visitors saw the Treasure: "the whole city was interested in it and talking about it."

The gilt-silver *Arm Reliquary,* made in Hildesheim during the third quarter of the 12th century (CMA 30.739), is "a pure creation of the spirit," according to Milliken. "In some extraordinary fashion the artist had incorporated in the simple gesture of a hand, a profound and moving otherworldliness. It was pure flame; in it was the spiritual essence which is the wellspring of all religion."

Milliken considered the ivory, carved in Liége about 1000, that forms part of this *Reliquary in the Form of a Book,* "the most beautiful ivory that I knew" (CMA 30.741).

Its frame, made in Brunswick, dates to the second half of the 14th century.

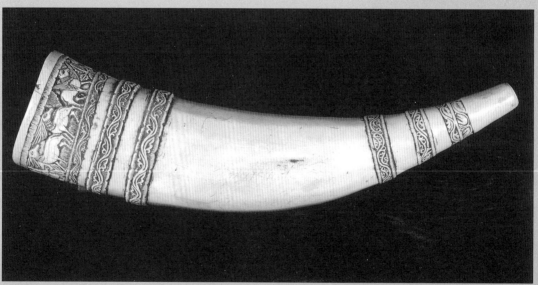

The 12th-century Sicilian ivory *"The Horn of St. Blasius"* (CMA 30.740) was named after the patron saint of the Cathedral and of the Ducal family.

Milliken wrote, "What did it matter that the horn was 12th century and that St. Blasius died in the 8th century? It had been associated for long years with St. Blasius and it would continue to be associated with him."

The silver-gilt and crystal *Monstrance with Relic of St. Sebastian* (CMA 31.65), probably made in Brunswick during the second half of the 15th century, was the gift of Julius F. Goldschmidt, Z. M. Hackenbroch, and J. Rosenbaum, the dealers who handled the sale of the Treasure.

Milliken noted that its "late Gothic flamboyance represents well the characteristics of that period. Because all of the pieces bought by the Museum represented the earlier centuries, this gift, the ninth object from the Treasure, supplemented the others in a most gracious and generous way."

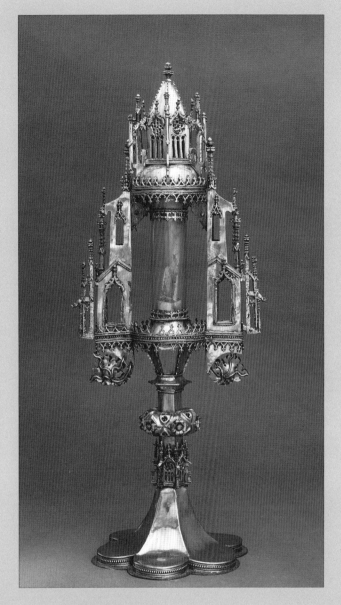

The cloisonné enamel on copper *Medallion with the Bust of Christ,* made in Weserraum in the late 8th century (CMA 30.504), represents Christ "in half figure upon the rainbow, flanked by the Greek letters *Alpha* and *Omega,* and two strange fishlike motives which may refer to *Ixthus,* the Greek word for *fish,* the initial letters of the words in Greek referring to the Christ."

In this view of the *John L. Severance Collection* show the Reynolds portrait *The Ladies Amabel and Mary Jemima Yorke* looks on as a splendid group of French furniture holds the center stage.

Milliken was quoted as saying that "in the field of furniture the [Severance] collection was untouched by other American museums." Smaller galleries displayed the Severance collection of Chinese porcelain and his superb prints, which included works by Rembrandt, Van Dyck, Whistler, and Meryon. At the close of the special exhibition, the objects were distributed in the galleries as Severance wished.

The Severance home, Longwood, stood at the center of a 180-acre estate at Mayfield and Taylor Roads in Cleveland Heights. A journalist for the *Cleveland News* found the library (shown here) "a feast for tired eyes." Besides Turner's *Burning of the Houses of Parliament* (CMA 42.647) on the far left wall, there was a landscape by Hobbema (CMA 42.641). Sir Thomas Lawrence's *Daughters of Colonel Thomas Carteret Hardy* (CMA 42.642) hung over the fireplace. Chinese porcelains tastefully filled any voids; a gilt-bronze *Pair of Fire Dogs,* by Jacques Caffieri (CMA 42.799-.800), decorated the hearth.

Although John Long Severance had died in 1936, it was 1942 before his estate was settled due to the effects of the Depression on the assets. Called "one of the great private collections in the country, not so much in quantity as in quality," the Museum was permitted to select "everything of merit" which it wished from the collection under terms that neither bound it to keep the pieces permanently nor to place them on continuous exhibition.

When the Severance bequest was shown in 1942, William Milliken wrote in the *Bulletin*: "In their lifetime Mr. and Mrs. Severance were among the greatest donors to the Museum. The great Collection of Arms and Armor was given by them at the opening of the Museum in 1916. Important ivories, rare watches,

and other fine things came as his gift at other times, and in 1930 he presented a unique series of Romanesque capitals in memory of his wife, Elisabeth DeWitt Severance, who predeceased him." President of the Museum for over ten years, Severance had "a profound influence upon the growth of the Museum collection, as well as upon the development of those Museum policies which had to do with its service to the community. He believed that a museum collection must be founded on the highest level of quality. He and Mrs. Severance carried out the same thought in the selection of their own private collection, and when he left it to the Museum with penetrating liberality, he did not hedge his gift about with restrictions which would hamper in any way its greatest use."

John Long Severance is perhaps best known for making possible Severance Hall, the home of the Cleveland Orchestra, dedicated to his late wife, Elisabeth DeWitt Severance. His father was Louis H. Severance, a pioneer Cleveland oil man; his grandfather Dr. David Long began to practice medicine in Cleveland in 1810.

A graduate of Oberlin, John Severance had an active career in business and banking. He was a Museum Trustee from 1915, and President from June 18, 1926, until his death on January 16, 1936.

William G. Mather was quoted in the *Cleveland News*: "The death of John L. Severance seems to me an almost inexpressible loss to the community. His many friends will deeply mourn his loss, for his high character and lovable nature commanded both respect and affection."

With respect to Elisabeth Severance Prentiss the *Cleveland Plain Dealer* quoted William Milliken: "Her interest [in the Museum] ... goes back to its opening day and in all those years she never failed for one moment in her devotion. Now the beautiful things that she loved and with which she lived long years memorialize a life which in its beauty and usefulness was truly 'a work of art.'"

In 1928 Mrs. Prentiss received a medal from the Cleveland Chamber of Commerce because of her far-reaching influence in materially helping to improve life in Cleveland. Among those improvements was the Dudley P. Allen Medical Library, founded in 1926, in memory of her first husband, Dr. Dudley P. Allen, a founder, officer, and benefactor of the Cleveland Medical Library Association. In 1938 she was named President of St. Luke's Hospital Association, succeeding her late husband the industrialist and philanthropist Francis Fleury Prentiss, who had also been a Museum Trustee. The Cleveland Health Museum and the Y.W.C.A. numbered among the other recipients of her generosity. She also established the Elisabeth Severance Prentiss Foundation for the improvement of public health. Naturally, she and her second husband contributed toward Severance Hall, the home of the Cleveland Orchestra.

*Dido Showing Aeneas the Plans for the Fortification of Carthage* (CMA 15.82) is the fourth in the Dido and Aeneas Series of tapestries, woven in Antwerp in the mid-17th century, that were given to the Museum by Elisabeth Severance (Mrs. Francis F.) Prentiss in memory of her first husband, Dr. Dudley P. Allen.

Gracing the walls of the Armor Court, the tapestries complemented the collection of armor given by her brother and his wife also in time for the Museum's opening.

OBJECT LESSONS **95**

Reminiscing about the Museum's 25th anniversary celebration, Milliken wrote: "One will always remember Mrs. Francis F. Prentiss, grand dame, with her beauty, heightened by her wonderful evening gown and her dazzling jewels."

A *Chest of Drawers with Panels of Oriental Lacquer* by René Dubois (CMA 44.113) is just one of the objects bequeathed to the Museum by Mrs. Prentiss. Others include paintings, furniture, sculpture, an impressive array of Chinese porcelains, and a small group of etchings by Rembrandt, Dürer, and Masson. Mrs. Prentiss made a similar bequest of objects to the Dudley P. Allen Memorial Art Museum of Oberlin College, which she had founded in memory of her first husband.

OVERVIEW: 1945-58

EVAN H. TURNER

The building fund established in 1939 by Mrs. Edward B. Greene[14] in memory of her parents, the J. H. Wades, influenced other donors by the end of the war, notably Leonard C. Hanna, Jr. Mrs. Greene had had the vision to respond to a need identified by William Milliken even as the Depression began[15]—a need that only became more pressing as time passed.

Exhibitions came to figure significantly in the programs of most American museums after World War II, and Museum visitors multiplied accordingly. The great local success of the much-publicized *Masterpieces from the Berlin Museums* (comprised of the paintings temporarily stored in the United States after being discovered by advancing American troops) meant that the Museum's attendance soared to a new high in 1948, with 600,841 visitors. Also, more gallery space was needed as once again the collection was augmented with the energy that had been evident in the 1920s, though happily with better planning. The Annual Report for 1951 proudly declared that among America's museums, Cleveland's acquisitions funds were second only to those of New York's Metropolitan Museum.[16] And as the numbers of objects increased, so too, it would seem, did their scale; in 1951, for example, the Museum celebrated its thirty-fifth anniversary with a fine group of Venetian acquisitions, among them the splendid Tintoretto *Baptism of Christ* (CMA 50.400), which became the largest painting then in the collection. Who could doubt, therefore, that the need for space was finally coming to a head?

Curiously, however, the impetus for action came from an unexpected source. In the autumn of 1950 the American museum world was swept by anxiety about a possible World War III.[17] An architect was needed to consider emergency measures, even as the need to repoint the 1916 building and the surrounding terraces of the Fine Arts Garden could no longer be denied. After much discussion, J. Byers Hays of Hays & Ruth was retained to respond to these needs and, incidentally, to make initial studies for a new

Detail of the Chinese handscroll *Streams and Mountains Without End,* late Northern Song dynasty, early 12th century. Gift of the Hanna Fund. CMA 53.126

addition that could be built incrementally. The Museum's new President, Harold T. Clark,[18] cautiously insisted upon the Museum's right to withdraw from such planning efforts at any point, but from Hanna, William Milliken enjoyed staunch support not unlike that he had enjoyed thirty years earlier with J. H. Wade. The Director's enthusiasm was infectious as he reported at length on his tours with Hays to study the many new museum buildings then being constructed across America. Thus, in 1952, with the $1,467,725.85[19] quietly accumulated during the previous eleven years firmly in hand, the Museum felt itself prepared to launch an ambitious if still discreet fund-raising effort.

In the years after World War II, not only did the Museum benefit from the immense generosity of Leonard Hanna, but the staff also had the all too rare pleasure of sharing their unbridled delight with the donor who was making it all possible. The acquisitions multiplied. In 1953—to cite the example of one year, albeit a major one—his fund enabled the Museum to purchase Poussin's *The Return to Nazareth* (CMA 53.156) from the Liechtenstein collection, Monet's early yet bold painting *Spring Flowers* (CMA 53.155), and Vuillard's *Under the Trees* (CMA 53.212), one of the rare complete sets of Jean Duvet's *Apocalypse* (CMA 53.231), and the masterly Northern Song handscroll *Streams and Mountains Without End* (CMA

53.126). There was sculpture as well, the extraordinary Mayan *Stone Head* from Copan (CMA 53.154), acquired from Harvard's Peabody Museum, and the most important Greek sculpture ever acquired by the Museum, the Archaic torso of a youth (CMA 53.125). And if that was not enough, in the same year Hanna offered to match every gift made to the Museum's Building and Endowment Fund, on a one-to-one basis, up to $1,500,000.

He was equally considerate of the staff and its needs. His annual commitment to the Museum's Library advanced the steady growth of those holdings so essential in developing a considerable research facility. In the summer of 1953 he also funded the first European trip for the Museum's new Curator of Oriental Art, who was responsible for the Egyptian and classical collections, too.[20] The name of that Curator, Sherman Lee, had first appeared in the 1946 Board Minutes in a report from Japan. At the request of the War Department, Howard Hollis had been given a leave-of-absence in 1945 to serve in Tokyo as Chief of the Arts and Monuments Division. A year later, in requesting a year's extension, he wrote that he and his associate, Sherman Lee, believed that—as Hollis expressed it—"we are putting in our time as valuably as we possibly could and that what we learn here will ultimately be of great benefit to our Museums."[21] When the Museum's President wrote Lee seven years

While visiting the United States in the summer of 1949, Albert Schweitzer made a special trip to Cleveland to see the Museum's P. J. McMyler Memorial organ. He is shown here with with the Cleveland organ builder, Walter Holtkamp, Sr., who had recently rebuilt the organ, first installed in 1922.

later confirming the new appointment in Cleveland, he prophetically expressed "every confidence that the new relationship with you will prove to be so mutually satisfactory that both parties will want to have it long continue."[22]

Two other curatorial appointments had a quite an impact upon developing standards. Dorothy Shepherd's arrival in 1947 introduced new scholarship to the Textile Department. Her methods of analyzing the construction of textiles as a means of establishing their origins had a profound impact upon the profession and also led to remarkably original acquisitions. Walter Blodgett became the Curator of Musical Arts at the end of 1942 and remained so for thirty-three years. His enthusiasm and enterprise in bringing major musical groups to the Museum led to a succession of programs that can only be a source of marvel today. The organ, built by the Skinner Organ Company of Dorchester, Massachusetts, which had been given earlier in memory of P. J. McMyler, was rebuilt by Walter Holtkamp, Sr., of Cleveland in time for the Museum resoundingly to celebrate the 200th anniversary of Bach's birth. Led by Charles E. Roseman, Jr., the Musart Society was founded in 1946 to ensure that such programs continued.

The variety of material collected during these years reflects the consistency and range of William Milliken's taste. A wave of German sculptures (for ex-

ample, masterpieces by Tilmann Riemenschneider [CMA 46.82, 59.42-.43], Veit Stoss [CMA 39.64], and Hans Leinburger [CMA 38.293]) succeeded the earlier French sculpture. The beloved precious medieval metal works had almost disappeared from the market—or when they did appear, commanded astronomical prices amid heavy competition from other buyers. Such realities may well have redirected the Museum's interest toward pre-Columbian art, although it would seem that this effort was also influenced by the presence of a new dealer, John Wise, and such enthusiastic donors as Liberty Holden's granddaughter, Mrs. Henry R. Norweb, and most remarkably, a Spanish-language teacher in the Cleveland Public School System, Helen Humphreys. Increased means may have led to greater breadth in the choice of paintings, with fewer of the gold ground pictures favored at the outset.

In 1955, however, everything changed. All efforts were concentrated upon the construction of a major new addition to the Museum building. Arguing that it was for the proper care of the objects acquired with the Severance, Wade, and Marlatt funds, the Museum sought permission—and the courts acceded—to allocate three years of the income from these funds toward building the new wing. The staff chaffed, not too surprisingly given the remarkable temptations then appearing on the market. But even with these

*St. Jerome and the Lion* by Tilmann Riemenschneider, German (about 1460-1531). Purchase from the J. H. Wade Fund. CMA 46.82

funds, costs mounted as construction continued; twice the Huntington Trustees and Hanna Fund matched each other and made further allocations: $866,500 each in 1956 and $250,000 in 1957. In 1956, for the first time since the 1918 worldwide influenza epidemic, the Museum closed its doors, this time for nine months, to achieve the linkage of the old and the new—the collection was entirely reinstalled. No one was more excited than Leonard C. Hanna, who had managed to participate in the cornerstone ceremonies. Unfortunately, however, he did not live to see the enlarged museum that owed so much to his vision.

Even as Clevelanders poured into their newly reopened, enlarged Museum, the city learned that Hanna had bequeathed his fortune with a generosity having no equal in the museum world at that time, thereby assuring both the Museum's future well-being and the growth of its collection.

1. It was fortunate that the Treasure came to Cleveland because seeing the material first hand persuaded the Museum's Trustees to return a Byzantine Romanesque altar for credit and to raise an additional $265,000 to purchase the traveling altar and the two accompanying crosses created originally for Countess Gertrude in about 1040. The gravity of the decision was evident in its being the sole matter for discussion at the Board's January 16, 1931, meeting. Board Minutes, pp. 1091-1093.

2. William Milliken, *CMA Bulletin* 19, 1 (January 1932): 3-4; proof of the Museum's success in responding to the challenge is the then all-time high of 400,468 visitors in 1933. In his Annual Report for 1934 the Director referred to the Museum's similar experience during the depression of 1920-21. *CMA Bulletin* 22, 2, pt. 2 (February 1935): 3.

3. *CMA Bulletin* 6, 5 (June 1919): 84. The point was well taken. The artists' fascination with the city is repeatedly evident in the frequent appearance of Cleveland subjects, particularly in the early years of the *May Show*. No one exemplifies this better than Margaret Bourke-White, who first displayed six photographs as early as 1928 and won a first prize for *Romance of Steel. CMA Bulletin* 15, 5 (May 1928): 119.

4. *CMA Bulletin* 27, 5 (May 1940): 55.

5. Louise H. Burchfield, "Traveling Shows," *CMA Bulletin* 28, 4 (April 1941): 51.

6. Board Minutes, January 21, 1932, p. 1159.

7. Report of Curator of Education, January 6, 1936, CMA Archives.

8. In reporting on its progress at the December 19, 1939, meeting, the Department proudly identified a dozen remarkable students, including two who later became distinguished employees of the Museum: the Conservator Joseph Alvarez and the Museum Designer William E. Ward.

9. King believed that it was in the Museum's best interest to encourage those who did not have the means to buy paintings to acquire prints. Certainly his own collecting activities provided a fine example for all. He was persuaded by Whiting to become the first Curator of Prints in 1920 while the Museum sought a young curator who, as was agreed, would be trained by King and Boston's English-born Curator, FitzRoy Carrington.

10. William M. Milliken "Report for the Year 1941," *CMA Bulletin* 29, 3 (March 1942): 24.

11. Board Minutes, August 5, 1942, p. 2001. The Junior Council was renamed the Women's Council in 1986 .

12. Board Minutes, May 27, 1942, p. 1987. In 1939, as a memorial to his mother, he had presented the Coralie Walker Hanna Collection essentially comprising the furniture and other decorative arts which had graced her Renaissance palazzo, which is today part of the Western Reserve Historical Society. A major influence in the creation of the Fine Arts Garden, she had also given the *Fountain of the Waters* by Chester Beach.

13. John L. Severance had been an exemplary Board member, always making it clear that his collection would come to the Museum, urging that the Museum's limited funds should be spent in other areas. Although he died in 1936, the complexities of settling the estate during the Depression, as well as his commitment to build Cleveland's concert hall as a memorial to his wife, delayed the settlement. Finally settled in 1946 the Museum received about $2,100,000 to establish an acquisitions fund.

14. Mrs. Greene's husband was a member of the Museum's Accessions Committee for thirty-one years and, emulating his father-in-law, created a collection of European and American portrait miniatures for the Museum: The Edward B. Greene Collection of Portrait Miniatures.

15. "Report of the Director for the Year 1930," Fifteenth Annual Report of The Cleveland Museum of Art, 1930, *CMA Bulletin* 18, 2, pt. 2 (February 1931): 21.

16. Board Minutes, Eighth Annual Meeting of the Advisory Council of The Cleveland Museum of Art, in Joint Session with the Trustees, December 5, 1951, p. 4 (Minute Book, p. 3227).

17. As reported to the Board of Trustees at the September 29, 1950, meeting (Minute Book, p. 2967), the President and Director attended a meeting for some seventeen museums organized by the Metropolitan Museum of Art to discuss issues and policies for the salvation of collections in a post-atomic world.

18. He had been serving as Museum counsel as early as 1928 and succeeded William Gwinn Mather as President in 1949. Clark was Leonard C. Hanna's lawyer and unquestionably played an important role in Hanna's pivotal decisions that made the Cleveland Museum we know today. Personally, he was deeply committed to the importance of the Extensions Division and established a fund to acquire objects for its touring exhibitions.

19. The Annual Meeting, December 3, 1952, Board Minutes. The Museum had finally received its third of the residual estate of Grace Rainey Rogers in 1950 and that, without doubt, provided the needed impetus to launch a campaign.

20. For the previous twenty-five years these collections had been under the supervision of a remarkable linguist, Sylvia Wunderlich, who was also Editor of the *Bulletin.*

21. Board Minutes, November 25, 1946, p. 2396. Sherman Lee was on leave-of-absence from the Detroit Institute of Arts, where he was Curator of Far Eastern Art; he returned to the States in 1948 to become Assistant Director at the Seattle Art Museum.

22. Board Minutes, August 12, 1952, p. 3353. Besides being named Curator of Oriental Art, Lee was "In Charge of Classical and Egyptian Arts."

# DIRECTORSHIP OF
# WILLIAM M. MILLIKEN

HENRY HAWLEY

Henry Hawley is the Museum's Chief Curator of Later Western Art.

The factor that perhaps most clearly differentiates The Cleveland Museum of Art from similar institutions is that, from its foundation, it has been a cooperative venture, with material and intellectual contributions coming from varied sources. It had no single founder, and its Directors have prided themselves on working closely with Trustees and staff. Its greatest financial benefactor was only a Vice-President of its Board, and it has been a long-standing policy that individual collections would not be isolated when exhibited. But if any single individual left the imprint of his personality on the institution, it was William Mathewson Milliken, by virtue of his early and extended association with the Museum and the pivotal roles he played during most of that time.

The son of British-born parents, William Milliken grew up in comfortable circumstances in Stamford, Connecticut, and graduated from Lawrenceville School and Princeton University. At the latter, he was a member of the class of 1911, but because of illness, he was not granted his degree in that year. Instead, he remained through the fall term, finally graduating in March 1912. There is some indication that, though this illness was described as typhoid fever, it—as well as earlier and later bouts—was at least partly psychological in nature. In a letter written to him in his youth, his half-brother Hugh spoke of William's being typically nervous, and throughout his life he was known for wide swings of mood openly demonstrated, for instance, by weeping. It has been suggested by some with special knowledge that his outbursts may not always have been involuntary, being instead the product of consciously invoked drama. The positive aspects of his mercurial temperament—his intense enthusiasms—were often found endearing and bound him closely to many of his professional associates.

In his last two years at Princeton, Milliken took several courses in the history of art and architecture, and though he resented the forced postponement of his graduation, he realized that in the long run it permitted him to prepare himself better for what proved to be his future career. Immediately after graduation, Milliken made a fruitless attempt to follow in his father's footsteps and become a textile merchant in New York. In this course of action, however, he found neither significant financial reward nor a sense of personal satisfaction. Soon after leaving Princeton he had gone to see the Director of the Metropolitan Museum of Art, Edward Robinson, about an appointment there, but was offered only an unpaid position, which Milliken refused. Two years later, chastened by his experiences in the world of business, he applied again, and when a similar offer was made, he accepted it. Beginning in the fall of 1914 he worked for six months in the museum's cataloguing department, before becoming an Assistant in the Decorative Arts Department under its absent Curator, William Valentiner. Valentiner had returned to Germany with the outbreak of war, and Milliken found himself a member of a much-depleted department. In 1916 he was made Assistant Curator of Decorative Arts, but when the United States entered World War I the next year, he resigned and enlisted in the army, winning a commission as a second lieutenant in the Air Service as a Ground Officer. Stationed first in America and then in England, he was discharged at the end of hostilities on December 24, 1918.

To his great displeasure, William Milliken found upon his return to New York that the personnel of the Decorative Arts Department of the Metropolitan had been augmented in his absence and there was no longer a place for him there. Quickly he discovered an opening at The Cleveland Museum of Art, was chosen by the Director, Frederic Allen Whiting, to fill it, and on February 1, 1919, took up duties there as Curator of Decorative Arts, beginning an association that lasted almost forty years.

In *The Bulletin of The Cleveland Museum of Art* for January-February, 1919, appears an article titled "French Gothic Sculpture in the Museum," signed *W. M. M.* Several of the pieces illustrated therein bear accessions numbers indicating that they were

William M. Milliken was photographed with Mrs. Paul Moore of New Jersey (she was Leonard C. Hanna's half-sister) at Cleveland's Union Club. They were attending a dinner for out-of-town guests and patrons hosted by Harold T. Clark, the Museum's President, celebrating the Museum's 1958 wing.

purchased in 1919. Presumably Milliken had a role in choosing them, for they represent a kind of material not previously acquired. Perhaps his opinion had been sought on them even before his appointment became official on February 1. In the March *Bulletin* there is another notice by Milliken, this time entitled "Eighteenth Century French Art." It reports on a temporary exhibition, much of the contents of which were lent by Captain and Mrs. Harry Payne Bingham and by New York dealers. Thus, soon after his arrival in Cleveland, Milliken had become active in two areas of collecting that remained of major interest to him throughout his association with the Museum.

The next few years seem to have been relatively quiet ones for Milliken. He organized an exhibition of oriental rugs for the Museum and described them in the *Bulletin*. He also concerned himself with the Museum's collection of lace, an enthusiasm which he shared with several local collectors. A few purchases of late Gothic and Renaissance sculpture were made, but acquisitions with which he was actively concerned remained relatively minor.

There seems to have been a rather important change in this situation about 1922, when Milliken acquired some small German ivory reliefs from a portable altar representing Christ and the Apostles, dating to the second half of the eleventh century.[1] It is interesting to note that J. H. Wade, the Trustee who at this moment was perhaps most personally engaged in collecting activities, visited the Metropolitan Museum while the ivories were still under consideration for purchase to compare them with ones in New York. He came away favorably impressed, and Milliken's stock seems to have risen as a result. These were the first of a series of medieval objects of small size and often precious materials that were to constitute Milliken's most significant personal contribution to the enrichment of the Museum holdings. In 1923 there was the Spitzer enamel cross, in 1924 the silver gilt and enamel *Table Fountain*, in 1925 the Strogonoff ivory plaque, and an enamel reliquary in 1926.[2] This facet of Milliken's collecting activities

According to William Milliken, the purchase of the French 14th-century *Table Fountain* (CMA 24.859) ranks as one of the most remarkable that the Museum has ever made.

Table fountains have "many a literary and historical association," but "only this one in silver gilt has survived." He had first seen it at a dealer's in Paris still encrusted with "the remains of the ball of earth which had so miraculously preserved it were still about it...." It had been excavated from the gardens of a palace in Constantinople, where it was probably buried "when the Eastern Empire was tottering to its fall." The Louvre had rejected it due to uncertainty over how it would look when cleaned.

Milliken lovingly described the fountain: "a beautiful piece of Gothic design in silver gilt late 14th century in date. The central stem holds three levels, the upper, a tiny crenellated terrace with minute spouting animals. The second and third levels, progressively larger, have balustrades each decorated with panels of translucent enamel with subjects which have to do with music or drinking. Fantastic figures bend down to drink or to play musical instruments, recalling their appeal to the senses—the pleasant sounds of the tinkle of bells and of falling wine or water.

"There are tiny animals on the second level who spout upwards and turn minute paddle wheels with silvery bells attached. On the lower terrace, instead, there are tiny nude figures who spout to turn slightly larger paddle wheels and ring their bells as well. What happiness and gaiety it invokes...."

Milliken was quite fa-
miliar with this mag-
nificent Limoges Cross
(CMA 23.1051) by the
so-called Master of the
Royal Plantagenet
Workshop, as it had
been often repro-
duced and belonged
to the famous 19th-
century Spitzer collec-
tion: "But one can
never be quite ready
when one sees for the
first time something
well known in repro-
duction and in litera-
ture. One can never
quite expect the
power which a great
work of art exerts, the
impelling force, the
impact which comes
from the seeing and

the feeling.... It is the
give and take be-
tween the object and
the viewer, the re-
sponse to the genius
which brought the
piece into being,
which makes that
genius live anew."
  Knowledge of the
technique enhances
this experience, how-
ever: "recognition of
what champlevé
enamel is, is therefore
of interest, the way
the ground of the
copper plate was dug
out, filled with pow-
dered glass, each
portion mixed with
the particular metallic
oxide which with
firing would bring
the desired color."

  Further, "the simple
fact that in the Spitz-
er Cross the figures
are enameled and
the background left
plain and gilded,"
helps date the piece
to about 1190. But
"what matters is
not how the artist
worked, it is what he
did. Mediocrity and
genius use the same
technical means."

culminated in 1930 and 1931 with the purchase of
eight objects from the Guelph Treasure.

  In 1922 Milliken also persuaded Director Whiting
to allot him a discretionary fund for the purchase of
French furniture. In so doing Milliken cited the difficulty of having furniture shipped to Cleveland to be
presented to the Board's Accessions Committee.
Although several significant purchases were made,
Milliken seems to have then viewed French furniture
more as an adjunct for galleries hung with paintings
and tapestries rather than as important objects for
their own sake.

  In his unpublished history of the Museum collection, William Milliken tells us that in 1923 he was
made acting Curator of Paintings as well as Curator
of Decorative Arts. He officially held both titles from
1925 to 1930. During his first years virtually all the
paintings purchased by the Museum were early
American portraits, bought on the recommendation
of a non-resident Curator of Colonial Art, Lawrence
Park. Beginning in the summer of 1920 and continuing for about fifteen years, the Museum mounted an
annual exhibition of American paintings. They were
mostly lent by New York dealers and mostly of fairly
recent vintage. William Milliken seems to have played
the major role in choosing these exhibitions, and
from 1922 through the rest of the decade, purchases
were made from these shows. Again, Milliken seems
to have enjoyed primary responsibility for the
choices, which were often excellent indeed—Bellow's
*Stag at Sharkey's* in 1922, Homer's *Early Morning After a Storm at Sea* in 1924, Eakins's *Biglin Brothers
Turning the Stake* in 1927, and Ryder's *The Race Track,
or Death on a Pale Horse* in 1928.[3] By the time of their
Cleveland acquisition, these artists had made significant reputations and were already represented in several public art collections, but the particular works
chosen for Cleveland have exceptional distinction. A
few pictures by somewhat younger artists—Rockwell
Kent and Maurice Prendergast, for example—were
also bought, and though slightly less distinguished,
they also proved to be interesting acquisitions.[4] Iron-

ically, Milliken's connoisseurship in the field of American paintings seems to have been of a more consistently high order than in any other. Elsewhere he made mistakes; for example, buying a sculpture by the notorious Italian forger Alceo Dossena in the 1920s. Fortunately, in this case his error was discovered before the Dossena scandal became widely known, and Milliken was able to return the piece to the dealer, thus avoiding any monetary loss to the Museum.[5]

In its earliest years, the Museum had acquired some pieces of American furniture on the recommendation of Henry W. Kent, Secretary of the Metropolitan Museum of Art, who was acting as an adviser primarily on the planning and construction of the Museum building. He suggested that American period rooms be installed, a project favored by Whiting, but this idea never got beyond the planning stages. Accompanying the *Inaugural Exhibition* of 1916 was a large collection of American silver, much of it lent by Hollis French, a consulting engineer for the Museum building. He left most of his collection on loan here for the next twenty-five years, making a gift of it in 1940. In the early 1920s J. H. Wade bought some American silver, mostly from Tiffany's, and immediately gave it to the Museum.[6] These pieces were published by Park in the *Bulletin*, but it is not apparent whether he participated in their selection. In any case, Milliken seems to have had little interest in collecting early American decorative arts. During his entire career at the Museum, with the exception of the Wade gifts, only three such objects were purchased, all silver, and one came from an old friend of Milliken who needed money during the Depression.[7] It should also be noted that Helen Foote, who served as Assistant, then Associate Curator of Decorative Arts through most of Milliken's years as Director, was particularly interested in American silver, and her enthusiasm may have inspired these purchases.

Despite his having been named Curator of Paintings in 1925, this field seems to have always played a secondary part in Milliken's designs for developing

Milliken supervising work on a so-called South Kensington display case. During the 1920s the Museum manufactured such dust-proof, almost air-tight cases for other museums; for example, supplying them for the Art Institute of Chicago's new wing.
In answer to one inquiry, however, Whiting noted that Cleveland was "not a case factory...."

*Initial S with Madonna and Child* by Silvestro dei Gherarducci, Italian (1339-99). Gift of J. H. Wade. CMA 24.1012

*Miniature: Two Female Saints* by Niccoló di ser Sozzo Tegliacci, Italian (active 1334-36). Gift from J. H. Wade. CMA 24.430

the Museum collection. When paintings were purchased, they were generally acquired with endowment funds so specified, or with moneys clearly intended for that purpose. Nevertheless, some outstanding acquisitions were made. Most adventuresome, perhaps, were those in the field of modern French painting— a Toulouse-Lautrec portrait and two Redons—all still somewhat advanced for most tastes in the 1920s.[8] Curiously enough, William Milliken attributed the Museum's reluctance at this time to purchase paintings from general sources of revenue to Wade's opinion that all varieties of art should be bought and to the lack of large funds. But Wade himself owned important paintings—many of which came to the Museum—and his last gift on the eve of his death in 1926 was Poussin's *Landscape with Nymphs and Satyrs.*[9] A group called The Friends of The Cleveland Museum of Art, which Wade had been instrumental in forming, presented in his memory that year El Greco's *The Holy Family with Mary Magdalene.*[10] Through the decade this group continued giving pictures to the Museum, among them important works by the Master of the Fröndenberg Altarpiece and Bernardo Strozzi, but the Depression seems to have ended its activities.[11]

Related to the paintings collection, although categorized by the Museum as decorative arts, were the fragments of illuminated manuscripts collected by William Milliken with avidity from the mid-1920s onward. He recorded that, because of the relatively small cost of these pieces, it was possible for the Museum to provide stylistic variety in works of aesthetic merit without making the sizable financial commitment that paintings of comparable date and style would have incurred.

The year 1930 marks a watershed both in the career of William M. Milliken and in the history of The Cleveland Museum of Art. Three important events occurred: Whiting left Cleveland to become Director of the American Federation of Arts and Milliken was chosen to be his successor; the first of the Guelph Treasure objects were purchased; and the Depression began. Each of these events profoundly influenced the Museum's future. During the previous decade, William Milliken had played an important role in developing the collection of European and American art, but as Director he was in a position to influence all aspects of the Museum's acquisitions.

Shortly after becoming a widow in 1924, Milliken's mother, Mary Spedding Milliken, came to live in Cleveland. Thereafter, their lives were closely entwined. They both lived at the Wade Park Manor, though in separate apartments, and they traveled to Europe together each summer on the extended pleasure and study trips that had become an important aspect of Milliken's annual round of activities. Italy—especially Venice—Germany and Austria, and Paris were included almost every year, with occasional visits to Spain, Britain, Holland, and Switzerland. While they were in Venice in 1932, Mrs. Milliken died. He had been very close to her, and her death seems to have left an emotional void in his life that was never again filled by an individual. Instead, the Museum took her place, and its staff became his family. He identified himself with the institution, and it with him. Many staff members and Trustees responded to this bonding by granting to William Milliken and the Museum a personal commitment of unusual strength and endurance.

The only other Museum staff member who was in serious contention with Milliken to succeed as Director upon Whiting's resignation was Rossiter Howard, who had come to Cleveland in 1921 to head the Education Department. By 1930 he was also Curator of Classical Art (1924-1930) and Assistant Director (1925-1930). In a letter congratulating Milliken on his appointment, Howard wrote, "Of course I should have been glad of the place myself ... at least glad of the election...."[12] Shortly after Milliken's appointment as Director, Howard resigned. In a similar vein Whiting wrote to Milliken: "you are fortunate in having the confidence and devotion of Mr. Severance...."[13] The latter was by this date President of the Museum's Board of Trustees, and the relationship to which

Whiting refers was probably instrumental in securing Milliken's promotion. Perhaps the most interesting of all his congratulatory messages was one received from another, younger Trustee, Leonard Hanna. There we read:

*We may at times disagree on certain matters—Lord knows we always have in the past—but this is a healthy condition to have existing anyway, and if it doesn't lead to any more trouble in the future than it has in the past, everything will be fine, and I see no reason it shouldn't, do you?[14]*

There must not have been, for Hanna remained a Trustee until his death in 1957, and proved to be the Museum's single greatest benefactor. He was the biggest fish, and it is to Milliken's great credit that Hanna remained a staunch supporter of the Museum over a very long period of time.

On a number of occasions, Milliken commented upon Whiting's pioneering work in establishing the Museum's Education Department and in instituting close community ties. Clearly he wished to continue these activities during his directorship, but his decision to shift emphasis somewhat from the education of children to an older age group was manifest in his choice of Dr. Thomas Munro to succeed Howard as head of Education. It was understood that though appointed and paid by the Museum, Munro would also serve as a member of the faculty of Western Reserve University, thus cementing more tightly an already existing relationship between the Museum and the University.

Another field in which William Milliken chose as Director to maintain but slightly modify existing programs was that of the Museum's relationship to artists of the region. He had arrived in Cleveland in 1919, the year of the inauguration of the *Annual Exhibition of Work by Cleveland Artists and Craftsmen* (now better known as the *May Show*), and though it seems to have been Whiting's conception, Milliken was involved in its administration from the beginning. On a number of occasions he remarked on the need for local patronage for the arts, and the *May Show* was the primary vehicle for pursuing this goal. His

Milliken previewing the 25th *Annual Exhibition of Work by Cleveland Artists and Craftsmen* on April 30, 1943, with Elisabeth Severance Prentiss.

In the *Bulletin* he noted: "The war has struck hard at the cultural life of Cleveland, as it has struck at cultural life through the world. Many artists are in the armed forces, others are devoting their energies to war industries; all are profoundly affected by the dislocations in normal living. What is encouraging, however, is that even a disaster of world-wide character cannot quench entirely, must not quench even if it circumscribes, the creative efforts of the individual. It is for freeing of the creative spirit that the Allied World is fighting today."

point of view is well summarized in a 1939 radio talk: *Cleveland has won country-wide recognition of its interest in its artists.... There are three elements which have made Cleveland's position what it is. First, the artists, who by their loyal work have made the Cleveland annual exhibitions what they are; second, the public, who by their purchases, interest, and other encouragement have made the artists' work an economic possibility; and third, the Museum which, by its prestige and standing in the city, has thrown all the weight of its influence into fostering Cleveland's creative efforts.*[15]

Despite the fact that the *May Show* was a juried exhibition with mostly out-of-town jurors, a significant core of the artists whose work he admired were represented year after year. But it was not the only means for encouraging the patronage of local artists. Each year some *May Show* entries would be held over and included in the annual exhibition of American painting, permitting direct comparisons between local and national production. Selections from the *May Show* were also sent as exhibitions to smaller museums, and the Cleveland Museum was often involved with the national exhibitions of ceramics organized by the Syracuse Museum of Art. With the Depression came several schemes for federal patronage of the arts, and Milliken was actively involved in their administration on a local and regional level. For a few artists whose work he particularly admired, he did

even more; for instance, he wrote in support of a scholarship for Clarence Carter's son at Hawken School, a local private school of high reputation. As with the Museum staff, Milliken was much beloved by the charmed circle of Cleveland artists who benefitted from his goodwill. Not everyone made it, but many of the most talented did, and without his help, many of them would probably not have been able to survive the difficult Depression years in their chosen profession of visual artist.

Like such revered collector-predecessors as J. Pierpont Morgan, William Milliken's tastes in art were broadly eclectic and encompassed examples of almost every variety of the visual arts, with the possible exception of certain aspects of the decorative arts of the last half of the nineteenth and the beginning of the twentieth centuries. He does seem to have had a particular liking for small, intricately worked three-dimensional objects. Not surprisingly, in light of what we know of his personality, Milliken emphasized the importance of emotional responses to works of art. He admired the writings of Walter Pater—the author of *Studies in the History of the Renaissance* (1873), a landmark of the aesthetic movement in England—which exhibit a similar bias. In most cases, Milliken's method of evaluating possible acquisitions by relying upon his initial emotional response seems to have served him well, and he made comparatively few mistakes in dealing with the kind of material he found most appealing. There were factors that could lead him astray, however. He had a particular fondness for mother and child images, and he could at times be too impressed by an object's provenance, especially if it involved royalty. But perhaps the greatest weakness of his methodology was his apparent failure to go beyond emotional responses to rational analyses. In a few cases, notably the x-ray examination of the Dossena forgery, he did employ scientific methods, but these seem to have been exceptional. Of course, intellectualizing about works of art is by no means always beneficial, but in several instances careful examination, including the few scientific procedures then available, might have been helpful, especially concerning questions of condition.

The purchase of objects from the Guelph Treasure in 1930 and 1931 capped Milliken's major collecting activity of the preceding decade, with its emphasis upon precious objects of the Middle Ages. Certainly he considered it his greatest accomplishment as a collector for the Museum. In a wonderfully enthusiastic letter dated the day after he first examined pieces from the treasure, he wrote:

*We were able to make a killing and had the first pick and made the first purchase.... It is incredible and if I only had two million dollars instead of 200,000 we could have made the Cleveland Museum immediately world renowned. As it is this will mean a tremendous increase in prestige. Six pieces from the Guelph Treasure!!!*[16]

He decided on six pieces, but had to pass up several others, among them the Gertrude Altar and Crosses that he was later able to purchase when the treasure was exhibited in its entirety in Cleveland in 1931.[17] What was arguably the single most important piece from the Guelph Treasure, however, the Dome Reliquary, escaped his grasp. It was the most expensive. But if he had acquired nothing else, he could have had it in the end since it cost less than the total spent for the pieces bought. He chose instead eight objects of historical variety and intrinsic importance, and never mentioned the reliquary he had missed.

The purchases from the Guelph Treasure also pointed the way toward the future—not the immediate future, for the Depression meant that little was acquired during the 1930s, but the years after 1940, when funds for acquisitions again flowed freely. One then finds, especially with European decorative arts, a persistent pattern in Milliken's collecting. He would buy for the Museum clusters of related objects, either all at the same time or within a short span of years, and then make no further acquisitions in that field. It happened with Venetian and Central European glass, with Italian majolica, with French ceramics, and with Byzantine metalwork. He often stated his objection to museums collecting art in series, like filling in the blank spaces of a postage stamp album. Certainly if care is not exercised it can be very difficult to maintain high standards with such a mode of collecting. To some degree, Milliken's alternative was the product of the market. Certain sorts of materials were readily available at quite reasonable prices in the years just after World War II, and since his tastes, measured by those of his day, were often retardataire, he was only too happy to take advantage of a situation that many of his contemporaries ignored. Another relevant factor seems to have been his great enthusiasm for particular objects, which perhaps built on itself. Having discovered one piece that excited his acquisitive instincts, he would search for others of similar ilk. This factor of enthusiasm, along with his ability to communicate such feelings, seems to have played an important part in his museum career. It probably helped him win the directorship, at a moment when the Board of Trustees was headed by a great collector, John L. Severance, and counted among its members several other men with similar interests.[18] It also helped him in acquiring the objects from the Guelph Treasure, for he was able not only to persuade the Trustees to allot considerable purchase sums, but also to obtain several sizable donations from private patrons toward that end.

The 1930s must have been a difficult decade for William Milliken. On the surface, the life of the Museum

The *Exhibition of Machine Art* was shown at the Museum, December 6, 1934-January 13, 1935. Among the educational programs accompanying the show were gallery talks and lectures by Charlotte Bates, Clayton Bachtel, and Milton Fox. The Cleveland architect W. Richard Rychtarik spoke on The Aesthetic of the Cog Wheel and Margaret Bourke-White on Art in Industry. Thomas Munro gave a radio talk about the show; a display of prints of industrial subjects complemented this first exhibition from New York's Museum of Modern Art to be shown at the Cleveland Museum.

went on as it always had, but there was a constant struggle for operating funds and the building of the collection came to an almost complete halt for about five years. Although salaries were cut, few people actualy lost their jobs. Attendance rose because many people were looking for cheap ways to spend excessive leisure time. Milliken and curatorial staff members continued to make extended journeys abroad, but it is not evident who paid for them. New activities were introduced, particularly ones related to government patronage of the arts. Several times Milliken commented that the Museum's staff was being called upon increasingly to supply services for the public when their own resources were being reduced. Special exhibitions were perhaps curtailed to some degree, but they did continue to be mounted. In 1936, for example, there was an important exhibition of the work of Vincent van Gogh organized by the Museum of Modern Art and then shown in Cleveland. Later in the year there was a large international loan exhi-

bition of modern and Old Master pictures celebrating the Museum's twentieth anniversary and organized along with The Great Lakes Exposition held in Cleveland. A major undertaking, this anniversary exhibition was rather hastily organized. Perhaps overextended with these activities, William Milliken suffered from several physical ailments—and probably from some psychological problems as well—that required an extended period of rest and inactivity during the opening months of 1937.

In the late 1930s a general improvement in the United States economy was reflected in the Museum's revenues. Salaries were returned to their pre-Depression levels and money was once again available for purchases. Several important ones—for example, the Andrea del Sarto[19]—were made at this time.

During the 1930s Milliken received indications that all was not well in Europe. Since he enjoyed traveling in Italy and Germany, and admired the art produced in both countries, at first he was inclined to overlook

The Great Lakes Exposition, held in Cleveland in 1936-37, was a cooperative community effort to restore the region's prosperity. Devoted to the commerce, industry, arts and science, and culture of the Great Lakes States and neighboring Canadian provinces, it also marked Cleveland's centennial of incorporation as a city. For its part the Museum put on a spectacular exhibition spread out over its entire second floor, celebrating its own twentieth anniversary. Milliken called it "one of the greatest exhibitions ever held in America—the brilliant exhibition of old and modern masters which was the Official Art Exhibit of The Great Lakes Exposition."

A 25¢ admission fee was charged for non-member adults (including clubs and conventions); 10¢ for 12- to 16-year-olds. Elementary and secondary school classes, and accompanying teachers, were admitted free. Charges were made for illustrated lectures;

group tours by qualified docents could be arranged in advance at $1.00 per hour. The illustrated catalogue sold for $1.00.

Gallery IX, illustrated here, was devoted to French 19th-century painting and sculpture. Paul Gauguin's *Ia Orana Maria* on loan from the Adolph Lewisohn Collection can be seen in the center of the wall, while his *Te Raau Rahi* (later given to the Museum by Barbara Ginn Greisinger) is just around the corner. Amedeo Modigliani's *The Woman with the Necklace* from Mr. and Mrs. Charles H. Worcester can be seen through the doorway. Such loans from private collectors—including Walter C. Arensberg's *Nude Descending a Staircase* by Duchamp—were shown interspersed with the Museum's holdings and objects lent by museums, including the Louvre, as well as by dealers in New York and Europe.

their political shortcomings, especially those of Italy. He advocated an open-minded attitude toward her expansionist tendencies in the mid-1930s. By that time, he was feeling distinctly uncomfortable with Hitler's regime, being aware of colleagues who had been ousted from positions in German museums because they were Jews or because they did not support the Nazi movement. In 1935 he received a letter from a colleague in Berlin, Hans Huth, reporting:

*Sooner than I thought of, I am forced to write to you and to beg a favour. On account of the new laws I almost surely shall have to abandon my place which until now I was able to keep as I have participated in the war* [World War I]. *I am protestant but not "Vollarier" in the sense of the law. The only possible chance seems to me, to look for a position in U.S.A.... Now I would be very grateful indeed if you might think about it if you know anything that would fit for me somewhere.*[20]

In reply, Milliken wrote a sympathetic but not very encouraging letter. Fortunately, Huth did find a position as Curator of Decorative Arts at the Art Institute of Chicago. Whether Milliken helped him in securing that post is unknown, but they did remain on cordial terms throughout their careers. Many art dealers, including several who had negotiated the sale of pieces from the Guelph Treasure, had left Germany. When traveling there Milliken was aware of the repressive government. Still he continued to go every year until 1939, when at the end of the summer he had difficulty retaining his long-held booking on an Italian liner sailing from Genoa to New York. After much cajoling, he and his automobile were allowed on board, but it was by then obvious that for the immediate future, things were going to be very different in Europe.

In other respects, too, 1939 seems to represent another turning point in the Museum's history. The first of a series of important gifts and bequests of money and works of art were received. From Leonard C. Hanna, Jr., came the gift of The Coralie Walker Hanna Memorial Collection, comprised chiefly of Italian Renaissance furniture and northern European

late Gothic tapestries.[21] More surprising, since completely unexpected, was the announcement of a sizable monetary bequest from Julia Morgan Marlatt that established the Mr. and Mrs. William H. Marlatt Fund for the purchase of paintings. This trickle of new resources became a torrent during the war years.

In 1940 the Museum received the bequest of James Parmelee, consisting of 524 items, including a few very good early Italian paintings, European sculptures from the seventeenth to the twentieth centuries, British watercolors, Old Master and modern prints and drawings, Far Eastern ceramics, Japanese prints, Egyptian antiquities, and textiles: a varied collection, much of it of considerable distinction. Also in 1940 a small but important group of objects was given by the heirs of Samuel Mather, as he had requested. In 1941 a number of gifts were made in honor of the Museum's twenty-fifth anniversary. Of much greater significance was the establishment in that year of the Hanna Fund, which was used for the acquisition of a great variety of works of art during the next decade. In 1942 two important donations were received. First, there was the contents of the music room of Grace Rainey Rogers, who although a native of Cleveland had lived for many years in New York.[22] She made a monetary bequest, too, with which further objects were purchased from her estate after her death in 1943. Then, toward the end of the year, the bequest of John L. Severance, who had been President of the Museum from 1926 until his death in 1936, was received by the Museum. Its distribution had been delayed until the economic situation improved, because the effects of the Depression would have much reduced his estate if it had been settled too quickly. Not only did the Museum receive over 250 objects of quite varied date and provenance—a few of them unquestioned masterpieces—but also a sizable monetary bequest to be used for future purchases of works of art as well as operating funds. After a relatively quiet year, another important bequest was received in 1944, that of Elisabeth Severance Prentiss. Her collecting activities were similar to those of her brother, John L.

Severance, and though only about half as large, her bequest paralleled his in terms of the variety of objects included. Unfortunately, her taste was not as sure and a number of pieces, especially Old Master paintings, turned out to be less significant than she had thought. She also left a bequest to be used for operating funds.

Despite the important gifts and bequests received during the early 1940s, this period was not an entirely easy one for the Museum. Both attendance and membership declined early in the decade, but then began to recover when the allies' eventual triumph became obvious. Several areas of collecting previously neglected at Cleveland were opened up; most notable perhaps was that of the ancient art of the Americas. Although many of the usual channels of supply for works of art were closed by the war, the Museum was nevertheless able to make some very important acquisitions, for example, Gauguin's *L'Appel* and Picasso's *La Vie*, both bought by the Hanna Fund and with the enthusiastic concurrence of Leonard C. Hanna, Jr.[23] By 1945 it was obvious that The Cleveland Museum of Art was in a position to play a far more important role in America's collecting and exhibition of the visual arts than it had heretofore.

Although the Museum was the chief focus of William Milliken's existence, it was by no means his only interest on either a personal or professional level. Mention has already been made of his European travels, and except for World War II and its immediate aftermath, it was his custom to spend at least two— and after his retirement six—months abroad each year, with extended stays in Venice and during later years in Greece and Salzburg as well.[24] During the war, he substituted trips to the western United States for these European jaunts and began also making annual winter visits to Sun Valley, Idaho, for skiing. Over the years he developed a wide circle of acquaintances in those places, besides the many people in Cleveland with whom he maintained social ties by virtue of his position at the Museum, as well as more personal relationships based on shared interests and

Among the many splendid acquisitions made possible by the Hanna Fund is *L'Appel (The Call)* (CMA 43.392) by Paul Gauguin, French (1848-1903).

In his autobiography, Milliken singled out Sun Valley, Idaho: "The glory of the snow, the purity, the immaculateness of high mountains, their silences, their loneliness, the poetry of uncluttered space was a balm to the soul of a city man. The sense that man could somehow ... control speed, could move with surety through the frosted forests of this enchanted world made one catch one's breath. At 85 I was still skiing."

William G. Mather (1857-1951) and Elizabeth Ring Mather (1891-1957) vacationing in Hot Springs, Virginia, in 1931.

After graduating from Trinity College, Mather went to work for his father, Samuel Mather, working his way up in the Cleveland-Cliffs Iron Company to Chairman of the Board.

Named a Trustee in 1919, Mather was elected Museum President on the death of John L. Severance in 1936 and served until he was named honorary President in 1949. As a member of the Museum's Accessions Committee from 1914 to 1949, he gave continuity to its purchase program.

Milliken found that "Mather ... had the widest culture, an instinctive love and understanding of fine things and above all the blessed quality of being emotionally moved by works of art." Among his many gifts to the Museum are the French 16th-century *Heads of a Man and Woman* by an artist in the circle of Michel Colombe (CMA 21.1003-.1004).

Mrs. Mather served on so many civic boards that she did not always permit her name to be used. A skilled gardener, she was a founder and first President of the Cleveland Garden Center. Besides organizing the horticultural hall for the Great Lakes Exposition, she sponsored free gardens for the needy during the Depression. Interested in the preservation and improvement of greater Cleveland, she largely financed the development of a master plan for rebuilding University Circle.

long association. In 1946 he was a founder of Ten Thirty Gallery, the chief objective of which was "To provide a permanent sales outlet for the creative artists of Cleveland...."[25] He served as its president in 1949. Although this project survived for less than a decade, it was intended to expand upon the services offered to local artists by the *May Show*, and was thus allied to one of Milliken's long-cherished goals.

Professionally, he began to widen his contacts as early as 1932, when he became a member of the Internationaler Verband von Museumsbeamten, a rather secretive German-based international organization of art experts concerned primarily with the detection of forgeries. The rapidly deteriorating European political situation made his association with this group quite brief, but after the war he became actively involved with the International Council of Museums (ICOM), an organization affiliated with the United Nations Educational, Scientific, and Cultural Organization (UNESCO). Milliken served as its First Vice-President from 1956 to 1958.

National and international recognition for his accomplishments as Director of The Cleveland Museum of Art also began in the 1930s, with awards made by Hungary in 1937, Italy in 1938, and Sweden in 1939. These were followed after the war with honors bestowed by France, Germany, and Spain. Milliken seems to have particularly appreciated his rank as Officer in the French Republic's Legion of Honor awarded in 1955. In 1946 Milliken received what was perhaps the most important of the seven honorary degrees granted to him by American colleges and universities, a doctorate from Yale. Theodore Sizer, who had been a colleague in Cleveland in the 1920s before being appointed to the Yale faculty, seems to have been largely responsible for initiating this award. On the national level Milliken served as President of the Association of Art Museum Directors from 1946 to 1949 and of the American Association of Museums from 1953 to 1957. Locally, he was active in many organizations, chiefly in capacities at least tangentially related to the visual arts—for example, as a member of the Memorials Committee of the Church of the Covenant and as a member of the Board of Directors of Karamu House, a settlement house emphasizing the arts, primarily for the benefit of African Americans. Even a brief review of his only partially preserved correspondence indicates that William Milliken, while Director of The Cleveland Museum of Art, was a very busy man with a wide variety of interests. The Museum, however, always remained the central axis around which all else revolved.

If the Museum was the core of his life, Milliken seems clearly to have assumed that the primary purpose of his directorship was his leadership in the augmentation of its collection, and the decade from the end of World War II until the start of construction of a major expansion of the Museum's building in May 1955 constitutes the golden age of such activities. Money was more readily available than ever before, both from endowed purchase funds—particularly the Wade, Severance, and Marlatt bequests—and from the Hanna Fund; in the case of the latter this was true especially for the purchase of late nineteenth- and early twentieth-century art, but also for other areas.

In several respects purchases in these years differ from those of the 1920s and early 1930s. Ambitions rose to match the funds available. Some American paintings were acquired, but they no longer assumed the important role that they had enjoyed twenty years earlier. Certain fields—for example, ancient art of the Americas and medieval Islamic art—that had previously been almost totally ignored were now actively cultivated. European objects of the Middle Ages were still acquired, but probably in large measure because of their scarcity on the market, they no longer dominated decorative arts purchases. Instead, Renaissance bronzes, ceramics, and glass were of greater importance, as were eighteenth-century objects, particularly French ceramics and furniture. Archaeological material—most of it probably of recent, though surreptitious, discovery—loomed larger, and fields such as ancient sculpture and Byzantine metalwork were significantly enriched. But the field experiencing the

most obvious changes was that of European painting. Not only was the Marlatt Fund specifically designated for the purchase of paintings, but also, beginning in 1942 and gradually increasing in amount, Hanna Fund monies were available. Although not limited to the purchase of European paintings, they did represent a field in which Leonard Hanna was personally interested and his influence played a significant part in deciding how money was spent. It is a bit difficult to be sure precisely how the responsibilities were delegated when Old Master pictures were bought. Milliken and Henry Francis, the Curator of Paintings and Prints and Drawings, seem to have worked quite closely together. During the war years and until 1947, most purchases of works of art were made in New York, through dealers or at auction. In 1947 William Milliken again resumed his prewar pattern of spending several months in Europe most years. He would usually go to Venice in the late summer and then to Paris in the early fall, with occasional side trips to Switzerland, Austria, Germany, and England. He seems quickly to have established a routine involving considerable social contact with dealers, particularly with Alessandro Brass in Venice and with the Mallon family and Caesar de Hauke in France. He had known Alessandro's late father, Italico Brass, in the 1920s, and had made some significant purchases for the Museum through him at that time. After the war, pictures of relatively high price were bought from Alessandro Brass almost every year between 1947 and 1955. Some were quite acceptable, but others presented problems of attribution or condition. It must be noted, however, that the condition of paintings being considered for purchase does not seem to have been as thoroughly examined then as it is today. Reliance was placed upon the evidence of the eye, rather than examinations using ultra-violet light or a microscope. Of course, all collectors, whether public or private, make errors, but the odd thing about this situation was that only a few Old Master paintings were purchased by Cleveland from any other European dealer during this period, although it

Paintings Curator Henry Sayles Francis (center) discussing the arrangement of the Edward B. Greene collection of portrait miniatures for the June 1951 exhibition with Preparator Frederick Hollendonner (left) and Milliken.

The son-in-law of J. H. Wade, Greene had formed his collection of European and American works with the express purpose of giving it to the Museum. Milliken pointed out the Museum's good fortune in receiving it because of: "the consistent high quality which marks the entire group; the representative character of the whole; and, above all, the generous and farsighted way in which the collection was brought together."

Associate Paintings Curator Louise H. Burchfield noted: "The painters of these little portraits bear comparison with the greatest painters of their time. Their luxurious art reflects the realities of the past and tells the story of the fashions and romance of our ancestors' social life."

The portrait *Thomas Hobbes* (CMA 49.548) is the work of the miniature painter Samuel Cooper, English (1609-72).

Horace Walpole observed that Cooper was the first to give the miniature the strength and freedom of oil paintings. Although profoundly influenced by Van Dyck, Cooper was better at representing individual character in disregard of visual conventions.

was a time when much material was coming onto the market because of the socioeconomic disruptions of World War II. London was a major marketplace for works of art, especially paintings from English collections, but Milliken seldom went there and seems to have positively avoided doing so. Such behavior was perhaps appropriate before the war, when the Cleveland Museum was a minor player in the international art world and it may have been useful to cultivate only a few dealers, but the situation had changed considerably by the 1940s. With the new funds available, a much wider range of choices might have been found had they been sought, and with more from which to choose, the pitfalls of some of the Alessandro Brass purchases might, in turn, have been avoided.

Besides supplying the wherewithal for purchases, Leonard Hanna and his fund made another important contribution to the life of the Museum in the postwar period. Although he maintained a country house in a distant Cleveland suburb, Hanna lived much of the year in New York City, where he had a wide circle of friends interested in the arts. He himself was a collector of note, specializing in French painting of around 1900. As early as 1936 he underwrote the exhibition in Cleveland of the works of Van Gogh organized by the Museum of Modern Art in New York. In the 1940s and 1950s almost every year witnessed an important exhibition of the art of a European modernist planned in New York and then shown in Cleveland, with the Hanna Fund paying the cost of at least the midwestern venue. Degas, Bonnard, Braque, Toulouse-Lautrec, Modigliani, Soutine, Ensor, Feininger, Matisse, Kandinsky, Rouault, Vuillard, Lipshitz—the list is impressive, and these exhibitions seem to have been well received by the Cleveland public. Hanna probably made personal as well as monetary contributions that facilitated this alliance. Other traveling shows also stopped in Cleveland; the most popular was the *Masterpieces from the Berlin Museums*, shown in 1948. Comparatively few large-scale exhibitions were organized by the Cleveland Museum, and the few that were

*Masterpieces from the Berlin Museums* was exhibited in cooperation with the Department of the Army and the United States of America. It traveled to several cities besides Cleveland.

Museum attendance during this show reached 151,240 which helped set a new annual attendance record of 600,744 people.

The cache of paintings had been discovered by advancing American forces and had been sent to the States for safekeeping. Before returning them to Berlin, this exhibition was circulated, the proceeds to go to the German Children's Relief Fund.

realized—such as *Art of the Americas* in 1945-46 and the *Exhibition of Gold* in 1947-48—were on broadly based, popular themes with little to offer in the way of new historical or critical insights. Sherman Lee's *Chinese Landscape Painting* of 1954 pointed the way toward new goals, but it was the exception. At one point Milliken declared that he saw nothing wrong with making available shows that had originated elsewhere, and certainly there was not, when they were of the quality of those supplied by the Museum of Modern Art. In even making this statement, however, a certain defensiveness is evident; something about the situation must have been troubling.

For some time it had been apparent that with the expansion of its collection and activities, The Cleve-

land Museum of Art had outgrown its original building. As early as 1939 a fund had been established to remedy this situation, but it grew slowly, probably more slowly than the postwar inflation of building costs. By the mid-1950s it was clear that something had to be done. Again the Hanna Fund led the way, with generous grants for construction costs made with the proviso that matching sums be found. The Museum's membership rose to this bait admirably, and funds to cover anticipated expenses were raised without recourse to a public campaign. Building costs proved higher than expected, and in the end, the Trustees decided to commit acquisition funds to the building project for a limited period of time. Thus, few art purchases were made in 1956 and 1957. In the

As early as 1937 Mrs. Edward B. Greene began making contributions toward a building fund, recognizing that the Museum was outgrowing its original quarters. Her example led to substantial contributions from various individuals, the Hanna Fund, the Elisabeth Severance Prentiss Fund, and from the Trustees of the Grace Rainey Rogers Trust. The Court of Common Pleas ruled that the income from three purchase funds (the Marlatt, Severance, and Wade) for three years could also be put toward a new addition. A grant from the John Huntington Art and Polytechnic Trust helped, too; but most heartening and exciting were the spontaneous gifts, large and small, which came from so many of the Museum members in response to the Hanna Fund challenge.

latter year the entire Museum was closed to permit some alterations of the 1916 building and the subsequent reinstallation of the entire collection.

Leonard Hanna died in 1957, and when the new Museum opened in April of 1958, it included as a temporary exhibition works bequeathed from his private collection, as well as a large sampling of the literally thousands of pieces given by him or purchased through the Hanna Fund over the years. William Milliken's last great task as Director was that of supervising the installation of this exhibition and of the Museum's permanent collection in its new setting. His retirement immediately followed the opening of the new facilities. The building and its contents at that moment, better than any verbalization, represented William Milliken's contribution to The Cleveland Museum of Art. He was undoubtedly one of the most successful American art museum directors of his generation. If he cleared no new pathways, he certainly followed his own, often unfashionable course while maintaining a wide base of support from his staff and the community.

In 1952, when he had reached the age of sixty-three, Milliken was informed that the Trustees had decided that henceforth sixty-five would be the mandatory retirement time for Directors of the Cleveland Museum of Art. He said that he had presumed that he would remain in charge until he was seventy, and in the end he was permitted to stay on until the new building had been completed and installed, but that occurred short of his seventieth birthday. For several years it had been apparent that Milliken would be succeeded in the directorship by Sherman E. Lee, who had been appointed Curator of Oriental Art in 1952. In letters to friends, Milliken commented on his satisfaction with this arrangement, though there is some indication that in the end, with Leonard Hanna's death and the concomitant increase in the Museum's resources, he was sorry not to stay on longer and supervise the spending of those expanded purchase funds.[26] But that was not to be.

Immediately after his return from Europe in the

autumn of 1957, William Milliken was honored at a surprise party given by the Junior Council, the women's support group of the Museum. In a long letter to a friend, he described in detail the event that obviously touched him deeply:

*They had a piper with kilts who piped me in and the nine Chairmen of the Junior Council received with me. It was a most beautiful dinner with a lot of jokes which kept it from being unbearable emotionally. At the dinner I was given the Order of the Golden Pickle* [a reference to the Pickle Society, composed of persons who had purchased works from the May Shows] *which was a wonderful joke and when anything got tense one of my friends popped up, first, with a bath towel embroidered as a crying towel, then a rubber sponge tied with tartan* [a reference to Milliken's Scottish origins], *then a golden bucket tied with a tartan bow, then a mop tied with tartan. They gave me no chance to do anything but laugh.*[27]

This party and William's reaction to it demonstrate the wonderful rapport that existed between the Museum's Director and the segment of the Cleveland community most involved with his administration.

Before retiring, Milliken stated that he planned henceforth to devote much of his time to research and writing about art. Although conversant with the major European languages, familiar with the literature of European art history, widely traveled and knowledgeable about much of the world's art treasures, and a frequently contributor to various publications—particularly the Museum's *Bulletin*—William Milliken was not really a scholar. There is little in his writings or lectures on art that is truly original in conception or information. It is not surprising, therefore, that though writing occupied much of his retirement time, it was not essentially art historical in nature, consisting instead of memoirs and travel books in a rather old-fashioned, consciously belle-lettristic style. Several of these works were published, while others remain in unedited, but otherwise completed, form.[28] Though the author and his responses to the world

Cornerstone laying ceremonies July 14, 1956. Left to right: Severance A. Millikin, Garretson Wade, Mrs. William G. Mather, Mrs. R. Henry Norweb, and Leonard C. Hanna.

about him form their common subjects, these publications remain oddly impersonal. He obviously intended to entertain as well as to inform his readers, but his writing reveals little beyond superficialities about his life and personality.

At least the external aspects of Milliken's life after his retirement are clear. With some yearly variations, he followed a routine with considerable constancy. Although he retained the apartment in Cleveland that he had long occupied, he usually spent roughly six months in Europe, going in the spring first to Greece and then to Venice. In the summer he was regularly a paying guest at a Schloss near Salzburg. Paris was his base of operations in the early fall, and then he would return to Cleveland and remain through the holidays. At least during the first years of retirement there were skiing trips in mid-winter. In this early period his routine activities were frequently interrupted by specific professional assignments of considerable interest but limited duration—such as advising the National Gallery of Victoria in Melbourne, Australia, or organizing an exhibition for the Seattle Worlds Fair. Although it was a life that many would have considered idyllic, it must also have been a rather lonely existence, one beset with considerable frustration. As the end of a long life approaches, with the ultimate and most drastic of changes unavoidably in

view, any further alterations of circumstance often seem to become difficult to bear. This was the case for William Milliken in his relationship with the institution that had been such an important factor in his personal identity for most of his adult life. After his retirement, the Museum continued to grow and change. Each year he returned to Cleveland to find in his beloved Museum less and less of what had been in large measure his creation. Toward the end of his life William Milliken seems to have become an increasingly frustrated man, no longer able to control, but also unable to relinquish, his Museum.

One of Milliken's first important medieval purchases for Cleveland was made in 1922 from the connoisseur and dealer Emile Rey, New York partner of Arnold Seligman, Rey and Company. According to Milliken, Rey "was ... associated closely with J. P. Morgan in the heroic days of collecting in America ... as well [as] with Henry Walters and other famous collectors. Many of the objects in the Metropolitan Museum of Art had come from or through his firm...."

In describing his first view of the *Plaques from a Portable Altar* (CMA 22.307-.309), Milliken wrote: "Mr. Rey showed a series of four reliefs in morse ivory—ivory from the tusk of a walrus—the material as such, [was] unfamiliar. The pieces were immensely intriguing. Monumental in scale, even if tiny in size, the Christ in the Mandorla could have been enlarged and would have graced the tympanum of a great cathedral. What was the basis on which to judge them? Was there a criterion?

"Many years before, with not the faintest idea that life would ever be passed in museums, my family and I were crossing the ocean. A conversation of my mother and two older brothers with the then Director of the Metropolitan Museum of Art, Sir Casper Purdon Clark, turned on the joys and trials of collecting. Sir Casper said something which supplied that criterion. 'There are three kinds of objects to buy; those of which you are sure at first sight; those about which you have a moment of doubt; and those which seem possibly wrong. Buy only in the first category and then check with every means in your power to be sure that you are right....'

"These morse ivories had overwhelmed me. I had a veritable *Uberraschung*, a word which expresses perfectly the emotion when a work of art sweeps you off your feet. The ivories did that in no uncertain fashion. Somehow they must come to Cleveland. How was the question? Yet they would and must....

"Unsure of the material from which they were made, Sir Casper Purdon Clark's words came back, as they have many times since. There was no element of doubt as to their authenticity. That was certain, but they were still a puzzle. Emile Rey set certain questions at rest. A comparison with similar pieces in the British Museum answered all other doubts."

Milliken discussed the ivories with J. H. Wade, who checked the information, even going to New York City: "He firmly backed the recommendation to buy with the statement that there was nothing as fine of this type in the Metropolitan.... They were bought and labeled 'Gift of J. H. Wade,' bought from a fund he had just established."

1. *Plaques from a Portable Altar*, Walrus ivory, Germany, Lower Rhine Valley, second half 11th century (CMA 22.307-.309).

2. *Cross*, champlevé enamel and gilding on copper, by the Master of the Royal Plantagenet Workshop, French, Limoges, ca. 1190 (CMA 23.1051); *Table Fountain*, silver gilt and translucent enamel, France, late 14th century (CMA 24.859); *Madonna and Child Enthroned with Angels*, ivory, Byzantium, 11th century (CMA 25.1293); *Disk Reliquary*, champlevé enamel and gilding on copper, by the Circle of Godefroid de Claire, Valley of the Meuse, ca. 1160 (CMA 26.428).

3. *Stag at Sharkey's* by George Wesley Bellows (CMA 1133.22); *Early Morning After a Storm at Sea* by Winslow Homer (CMA 24.195); *Biglin Brothers Turning the Stake* by Thomas Eakins (CMA 1984.27); and *The Race Track, or Death on a Pale Horse* by Albert Pinkham Ryder (CMA 28.8).

4. *Maine Coast* by Rockwell Kent (CMA 1132.22) and *On the Beach, No. 3* by Maurice Prendergast (CMA 1653.26).

5. Milliken, "Stories Behind the Museum Collections," pp. 31-34, CMA Ingalls Library. A more complete history of Cleveland's Dossenas is included in David Sox, *Unmasking the Forger* (London and Sydney: Unwin Hyman, 1987).

6. *Beaker* by John Aitken (CMA 19.867); *Cream Pitcher* by Zachariah Brigden (CMA 20.253); *Tankard* by John Burt (CMA 19.862); *Cream Jug* by John Germon (CMA 19.865); *Mug* by Thomas Hamersley (CMA 19.861); *Creamer* by William Haverstick (CMA 19.864); *Teaspoons* by William Haverstick (CMA 19.872-.875); *Tea Pot* by Jacob Hurd (CMA 20.225); *Beaker* by Isaac Hutton (CMA 19.868); *Porringer* by William Jones (CMA 20.119); *Creamer* by John McMullin (CMA 19.866); *Sugar Tongs* by Otto Parisien (CMA 19.869); *Cream Jug* by Paul Revere, Jr. (CMA 21.38); *Spout Cup* by Moody Russell (CMA 21.954); *Pitcher* by Joseph Shoemaker (CMA 24.748); *Creamer* by William Simpkins (CMA 21.955); and *Sugar Tongs* (CMA 19.870). *CMA Bulletin* 7, 4 (April 1920): 44-45; ibid., 7, 9 (September 1920): 96-97; ibid., 7, 8 (October 1920): 119-120, repr. 127.

7. *Teapot* by John David (CMA 46.424); *Tankard* by Samuel Vernon (CMA 34.378); and *Tankard* by Edward Winslow (CMA 52.264).

8. *Monsieur Boileau at the Café* by Henri de Toulouse-Lautrec (CMA 394.25); *Orpheus* by Odilon Redon (CMA 26.25); and *Portrait of Mlle Violette Heymann* by Odilon Redon (CMA 1976.26).

9. *Landscape with Nymphs and Satyrs* by Nicolas Poussin (CMA 26.26).

10. *The Holy Family with Mary Magdalene* by El Greco (Domenico Theotocópuli) (CMA 26.247).

11. *Coronation of the Virgin* by the Master of the Fröndenberg Altarpiece (CMA 29.920) and *Minerva* by Bernardo Strozzi (CMA 29.133).

12. Rossiter Howard to Milliken, August 20, 1930, William M. Milliken papers, Container 1, Folder 1, Western Reserve Historical Society.

13. Whiting to Milliken, August 20, 1930, William M. Mil-liken papers, Container 1, Folder 1, Western Reserve Historical Society.

14. L. C. Hanna to Milliken, August 26, 1930, William M. Milliken papers, Container 1, Folder 1, Western Reserve Historical Society.

15. Typescript, Radio Talk, WTAM, May 7, 1939, Milliken papers, Radio Talks, 1932-49, Archives of American Art.

16. Milliken to Rossiter Howard, August 8, 1930, William M. Milliken papers, CMA Archives.

17. *Medallion with the Bust of Christ* (CMA 30.504); *Reliquary in the Form of a Book* (CMA 30.741); (1) *Paten of St. Bernward*, (2) *Monstrance* (CMA 30.505); *Arm Reliquary* (CMA 30.739); *The Horn of St. Blasius* (CMA 30.740). The sixth object initially chosen by Milliken from the Guelph Treasure, a portable altar, was subsequently returned in part payment for the following pieces: *Portable Altar of Countess Gertrude*; *First and Second Crosses of Countess Gertrude* (CMA 31.462, 31.55, 31.461). One additional item from the Guelph Treasure, *Monstrance with Relic of St. Sebastian* (CMA 31.65), came to the Museum as a gift from the dealers involved in the sale of Guelph Treasure objects.

18. Among the Trustees in 1930 who were enthusiastic collectors were William Gwinn Mather, Leonard C. Hanna, Jr., Ralph M. Coe, Henry G. Dalton, Edward B. Greene, and Samuel Mather.

19. *The Sacrifice of Isaac* by Andrea del Sarto (CMA 37.577).

20. Hans Huth to Milliken, October 6, 1935, William M. Milliken papers, Archives of American Art.

21. CMA 39.92-.195.

22. William M. Milliken, "The Rousseau de la Rottière Room, The Gift of Grace Rainey Rogers," *CMA Bulletin* 29, 4 (April 1942): 45-66.

23. *L'Appel (The Call)* by Paul Gauguin (CMA 43.392) and *La Vie* by Pablo Picasso (CMA 45.24).

24. *Unfamiliar Venice* (Cleveland: Case Western Reserve University Press, 1967). There also exists in the William M. Milliken papers, Folder 5, Western Reserve Historical Society, a group of essays in typescript entitled "Greece: Many-Blossomed Spring."

25. The Ten Thirty Gallery was located at 1515 Euclid Avenue in downtown Cleveland. Documents pertaining to this venture are to be found among the William M. Milliken papers, Archives of American Art.

26. See, for example, his exchange of letters with Harold C. Parsons in 1957, William M. Milliken papers, Archives of American Art.

27. Copy of Milliken to Mme Paul Mallon, October 24, 1957, William M. Milliken papers, Archives of American Art.

28. Besides those already cited, see *A Time Remembered* (Cleveland: Western Reserve Historical Society, 1957) and *Born Under the Sign of Libra* (Cleveland: Western Reserve Historical Society, 1977).

This *Mochica Gold Mask* from Peru, dating to AD 100-500 (CMA 56.85), is an example of the 46 objects Miss Humphreys gave to the Museum in honor of her parents over a 25-year period.

Helen Humphreys (left) is shown here in 1933 with her father, Henry Humphreys, and a friend, Arline Preston. The women had met at Bryn Mawr College.

A mong other donors of pre-Columbian material, Milliken found Helen Humphreys, a Cleveland high school Spanish teacher, to be "extraordinary." Wanting to establish a memorial to her parents, Helen Humphreys, according to Milliken, "turned to the Pre-Columbian arts of the Spanish colonies. Gold fascinated her, but ... she sought objects which would inspire the imagination of children, and the bizarre and often comic detail of a piece interested and intrigued her.... For twenty years or more, she contributed regularly, it was her salary as a teacher, and as the sum contributed reached the required figure, one piece after another became a part of the memorial. Her gifts are a major part of this section of the Museum's collection."

The Holdens at the wedding of their daughter Gertrude to Thomas A. McGinley, September 15, 1906.

Left to right: Liberty E. Holden, Delia Holden White, Delia Bulkley Holden, an unknown man and

woman, perhaps the groom and his mother. Emery May Holden is holding the bride's train.

This Mayan incised shell from Guatemala, dating to AD 600-800 (CMA 65.550), is one of the 85 pre-Columbian

objects that Mr. and Mrs. Norweb gave to the Museum.

irector Milliken found that "Chance and good fortune ... play important parts in the development of a Museum.... [if] you keep quality as your guide even in the most un-familiar fields, and you have faith in those whom you trust." This philosophy proved itself when simultane-ous, unforseen visits to the Director by John Wise, a well-known dealer in pre-Columbian art, and Emery May Holden Norweb (1895-1984), a granddaughter of the Liberty E. Holdens, led to their introduction. Milliken thought that this encounter marked "the beginning of Mrs. Norweb's interest in developing that side of the Museum's collection. Her husband [R. Henry Norweb] had been First Secretary of the American Embassy in Mexico City, later Ambassador to Peru and Ambassador in other South American

capitals as well as Portugal. I did not know then that Mrs. Norweb owned quite a number of pieces of Pre-Columbian origin."

On another occasion Mrs. Norweb offered to show him her pre-Columbian textiles. Following a delight-ful dinner, "a mysterious trunk" was opened. "A most remarkable treasure emerged from it, each piece finer than the one before. They had come from ... the Paracas necropolis in Peru ... and dated in the Pre-Columbian period.... I was transfixed, beside myself with excitement." Milliken noted that when the tex-tiles were later given, "they became a keystone of the Museum's collection in this field."

Named a Trustee in 1941, Mrs. Norweb was elected President in 1962. In an 1970 interview with *Plain Dealer* columnist Wilma Salisbury, Mrs. Nor-

This *Ceremonial Cloth,* (detail) created about the first-third century AD in Peru (CMA 40.530), is one of the 25 pre-Columbian textiles given by the Norwebs.

web remarked: "Then in 1962 when I was asked to become president, I thought the foundation of the museum had probably collapsed. We were really moving with the times then—abstraction, French impressionist, and a woman president!" In a memorial tribute, Sherman E. Lee wrote: "Her quick and delighted positive reaction to the pair of Japanese screens of Iris by Watanabe Shiko (CMA 54.603), which she gave in 1954, both amazed and delighted me. She really *knew* a great deal about them: their subject and their previous owners, the Matsukata family. Her stay in Japan had provided her not only with the experience of the 1923 earthquake, but with the opportunity to sharpen her eye for Japanese art."

Besides her many contributions to this Museum, she was actively associated with the Holden Arbore-

tum, the Cleveland Museum of Natural History, the Cleveland Play House, the Garden Club of Greater Cleveland, and the Ohio Arts Council.

Mrs. Norweb's major collecting efforts, however, centered on numismatics. Having collected coins since the age of eight, she owned Anglo-Saxon, British, American, and Latin American coins from 50 BC through the 1980s. In 1969 she gave a fine collection of English gold coins to the Museum. Active in the American Numismatic Society and the British Numismatic Association, she was a fellow of the Royal Numismatic Society, London.

# THOMAS MUNRO: MUSEUM EDUCATION 1931-67

NEIL HARRIS

Neil Harris is a Professor of History at the University of Chicago.

homas Munro's 1931 arrival in Cleveland as Curator of Education brought to the Museum of Art the most accomplished and certainly most prolific aesthetic philosopher among American museum educators. In the more than thirty years that Munro spent at the Museum he extended its already existing reputation for educational innovation, strengthened its ties to academic research, and provided it with a prestigious and prominent representative of an important philosophical movement. In its turn the Cleveland Museum became an effective setting for Munro to test his ideas and expand his horizons. The character of the collection and its urban location encouraged his progress and helped shape his intellectual goals.

Munro's impact and enthusiasms merit attention today, for they not only exemplify a period in the history of the American art museum, they embody a mood, a temper, a way of thinking about art itself that was a shaping force for many institutions. As the subject of museum education grows more central (if more contested), the need to recover its complex history grows with it. Thanks to the recent work of several scholars, it is now possible to see Munro's work within an existing community of discourse.[1]

Thomas Munro's background proved to be a particularly useful blend of academic training and practical experience.[2] Although only in his early thirties when Director Milliken invited him to Cleveland, he had crowded into the previous half dozen years a college education, teaching experience, museum work, foreign travel, and an impressive publication record. After undergraduate study at Amherst, Munro moved to Columbia University to work with his personal hero, John Dewey, America's greatest educational philosopher. Devoted to Dewey's ideas, Munro also became an admirer of another of the era's major philosophers, George Santayana. Basically a naturalist, Munro was animated by twin commitments to empirical observation and idealistic reform, eschewing final judgments about quality but insisting that provisional rulings were always possible and demonstrable.

After spending several years studying philosophy at Columbia, Munro, on John Dewey's recommendation, went to work in 1923 for that redoubtable popularizer of modern art: Dr. Albert Barnes. His wealth established by development and distribution of the wonder potion, Argyrol, Barnes was at work assembling an extraordinary collection of paintings in suburban Philadelphia.[3] Although it included Impressionist masterpieces by artists like Renoir, the collection also featured major works by such controversial contemporary painters as Henri Matisse, Amedeo Modigliani, Chaim Soutine, and Jules Pascin. Local connoisseurs had begun by treating this taste with suspicion and ridicule; they ended with expressions of admiration and envy. But the prickly demeanor which was the special possession of Albert Barnes produced a string of quarrels and confrontations.

More than just a collector, Barnes was also an impassioned crusader for the modernist cause and an admirer of Dewey. The Barnes Foundation held classes, sponsored lectures, and commissioned books. Munro taught there and in several universities, subsidized by the Foundation. It was also with Barnes's help that Munro published *Primitive Negro Sculpture* in 1926, a text written with Paul Guillaume, in both French and English. But that same year, after Barnes found him insufficiently loyal to his personal cause, Munro left his employment. A couple of years later Munro followed up his first art book with *Scientific Method in Aesthetics.*

During the 1920s Munro also lectured on fine arts at New York University, on philosophy at Rutgers, and taught at The People's Institute in New York where he came in close contact with Philip Youtz, a museum reformer who would eventually direct the Brooklyn Museum. The young Munro was seized with a passion to extend and legitimatize a systematic approach to the study of aesthetics. In his brief introduction to *Scientific Method in Aesthetics*, Youtz told readers that the embryo science of aesthetics "has hardly yet been born. Here we can watch the scientific mind impartially approaching a new material,"

The June 1931 *Bulletin* announced the appointment of Thomas Munro as Curator of Education: "After graduate work in philosophy and psychology and social science under John Dewey [at Columbia University], he was appointed University Scholar in Philosophy at Columbia, 1916-1918. From 1918-1924 he was Lecturer and Instructor in Philosophy and Economics, Columbia University. From there Mr. Munro became Associate Educational Director of the Barnes Foundation and Visiting Professor of Modern Art at the University of Pennsylvania. Since 1927, Mr. Munro has been connected with Rutgers University as Professor Philosophy and has been in charge of the Department of Art. He has also been Lecturer on Fine Arts at the University of New York."

"The Museum is fortunate to be able to add such a distinguished member to its staff."

Among Munro's innovations in the 1930s were: an expanded program of summer classes for young people and teenagers (with an emphasis on sketching outdoors); increased correlation of educational activities to special exhibitions (including sending exhibition announcements to schools, inviting them to schedule class visits accordingly); a special campaign to interest high school students in art; the introduction of marionettes into classes; and scheduling films and live performances to inspire the creation of imaginative pictures. Story hours and moving pictures were made regular weekly events.

he wrote breathlessly. "One enters the art laboratory to witness the birth of a new science, which will be contemporary with our lifetime...." No one could say, he admitted, "whether this child will live...."[4]

Youtz's mixture of enthusiasm and anxiety caught Munro's tone, and Munro would spend the next several decades tirelessly organizing American aesthetic philosophers into a professional association (which he would head as well as editing its journal) and promoting similar efforts at organization throughout the world. He was convinced that careful analytical methods could define the nature of artistic communication across a broad series of cultures and set of forms. "What aesthetics needs in its terms now is more narrow, sharp precision, to make them more effective tools of communication," he announced in one of his first books.[5] Aesthetics is "not a purely evaluative, normative subject," he wrote years later, in 1945. "It has a descriptive function also," investigating the varieties of art and "the causal factors which help to explain their development."[6] Fond of biological metaphors and evolutionary analogies, Munro spent four decades in pursuit of developing a more objective study of art and in frankly "boosting" the cause of aesthetics wherever he could.[7]

But any careful evaluation of his philosophical arguments or his contributions to American aesthetics must be left to another time. It is the relationship be-

tween his scholarly interests and his museum career that must be examined here. Besides his writing, teaching at Western Reserve University, participating in international meetings, and professional leadership, Munro's primary concern was the educational program developing at the Museum. He periodically recounted its progress in Museum reports and bulletins, described his approach to other museum professionals at conventions and in journals, and successfully gained the financial support of foundations and philanthropists for a number of his projects.

There were several aspects to the diverse programs Munro supervised at the Museum. One set focused on children. Young people offered special challenges. They constituted the source for future artists as well as future museum visitors; their openness, lack of prejudice, and emotional needs made the art museum a natural site for part of their education. "America's contribution to museum practice is widely recognized as being in the realm of work with children," Lawrence Vail Coleman wrote in 1939. "Every student of museums from abroad comments on this development, and carries away the influence of our educational pioneering in the last century...."[8]

Cleveland had long demonstrated a special interest in programs for children. As Munro himself pointed out in a summary essay on the Museum's educational work, school contacts were made even before the museum building opened its doors in 1916.[9] Soon there-after a teacher was appointed to work with visiting classes and to travel to schools with slide talks and exhibits. Cleveland became the first American art mu-seum to permit children to draw in the main galleries, and drawing classes of various kinds remained a cen-terpiece of its educational program. On weekends and during summer vacations, special classes were organ-ized for children with apparent artistic talent. Admis-sion was controlled by testing; indeed the program contained a research experiment, always an interest of Munro, aimed at recognizing and grading the creative abilities of children. He wrote, after working at the Museum a few years, that it would be "highly desir-able to have a measure of *aesthetic age* analogous to mental age, by which we could determine whether a child was normal, advanced, or retarded in those characteristics most active in the production and ap-preciation of art."[10] Whenever he could, Munro sought empirical tests for generalization, striving to attach to aesthetic judgments the prestige of science.[11]

As Thomas Munro himself pointed out, however, since most children were destined to become neither artists nor art historians, the program's emphasis lay not on isolating the extremely talented but on pro-viding the majority of youngsters with contextual ap-preciation, linking up art forms with the history, the literature, and even the recreation children got else-where. Using language that resonated with his own philosophical assumptions, Munro wrote that chil-dren visiting the Museum were helped to "perceive and understand as clearly as possible the form and meaning of the works of art they see; to develop criti-cal standards and intelligent modes of appraisal," the aim being "a diversity of experiences in art ... rather than ... narrow specialization."[12]

Convinced that knowledge and discipline aided rather than constrained development of artistic skill, and suspicious of claims that children's spontaneous effusions were inevitably more effective than the re-sults of instruction, Munro's Education Department reflected his own intellectual bias. Studying basic

growth processes, Munro wrote in 1941, "does not necessarily mean letting children take the lead in di-recting their own studies or letting them do at each moment what they wish to do. Teachers who possess a scientific understanding of personality development should be better able than the child himself to under-stand what the child needs and fundamentally de-sires...."[13] In the mid-1920s Munro had visited the famous children's art classes of Franz Cizek in Vienna and reported back his disappointment at the repeti-tive, formulaic quality of the art produced. He blamed this on the effort to isolate children from ex-isting works of art in an attempt to keep their sensi-bilities pure and untainted. In his view free expression in itself offered nothing but vague aspirations of per-sonal fulfillment; it was a dead end. "A broad study of traditions is thoroughly compatible with individual experiment," Munro noted, "and in fact makes origi-nal choice and reorganization almost unavoidable."[14]

The power of a museum setting and the impor-tance of popularizing its aesthetic varieties were very broadly defined, for the Cleveland Museum offered music study as well as art courses centered on its own wide-ranging collection. In both, children were di-vided by age and moved through the material period by period. "The aim is to develop intelligent, dis-criminating listeners," Munro explained.[15] Along with the art there was also folk dancing for children in the Museum. As a student of aesthetics Munro examined music, literature, drama, dance, and architecture, as well as the visual arts, always emphasizing breadth and scope.

But while the programs for young people in Cleve-land were important and innovative, and were di-rected according to a set of carefully worked out principles, other aspects of the Museum also attracted Munro's enthusiastic interest. Not merely an aes-thetic philosopher, he also championed certain prin-ciples that were even better expressed by an appeal to the adult audience, and to teachers.

The years of Munro's tenure at Cleveland, particu-larly its first half, in the 1930s and 1940s, represented

In May 1950, John Kashuk and Dave Black worked on a 6-by-12 foot mural montage entitled *Museum Treasures,* a feature of the second annual Junior May Show held in the 10th-floor gallery of the Higbee Company in downtown Cleveland. The show exhibited more than 125 works by art pupils in the Museum's free gallery classes, special and outdoor sketch groups, and sessions for members' children.

a special moment in the history of American art consciousness. A series of events, some of them inside the art world and some outside, were challenging traditional definitions and assessments of quality. His position at Cleveland enabled Munro to exploit and channel these energies, using educational programs aimed at adults to popularize his values. These activities were not unique, for great art museums in New York, Chicago, Detroit, Philadelphia, and elsewhere in America were also engaged in what may be seen, in retrospect, as broad campaigns of cultural promotion. But in Cleveland Munro's prominence and enthusiasm for the new values helped dramatize the effort.

What was the purpose of the adult programs? From the most general standpoint it was, of course, simply to enhance the viewing experience, to give visitors information, advice, and guidance about encountering art with the help of professionally trained lecturers and enthusiastic curators. The more satisfying the encounter, the more often visitors would return, the more rapidly news of a museum's hospitality would spread, and the more willingly would the community support the institution. A paying membership, which was the heart of the mixed system that sustained major urban art museums, needed some specific benefits in return for their annual dues, and the educational program—which included printed bulletins with explanatory articles, concerts, tours, classes, and lectures—was one method of doing this.

There was more at stake, however, than simply enticing visitors. By coordinating policies for exhibitions, collecting, and promotion, museum administrators could encourage more specific attitudes among their audiences. During Munro's tenure in Cleveland the areas of contest could be divided into four large sectors. The first, and perhaps most important, was a campaign on behalf of the newer, nonrepresentational forms of art. The clamorous and contentious receptions given the Armory Show exhibition in New York, Chicago, and Boston, just before World War I, suggest the scale of popular American debates about modernism.[16] Before the great reputa-

tions of artists like Pablo Picasso, Constantin Brancusi, Georges Braque, Piet Mondrian, Henri Matisse,
and others had been fixed in this country, skepticism,
befuddlement, and considerable hostility greeted their
graphic and sculptural art. Despite some gains during
the 1920s (and the infiltration of popular art forms
like photography and advertising), modernism provoked strong counter reactions in any number of
places during the Depression. It continued to attract
ridicule from the popular press.[17]

   Many in the museum world leapt to modernism's
defense. Albert Barnes, that vigorous crusader for
the new sensibility, was not alone. Collectors, curators, some critics, and museum administrators—
increasingly sympathetic to modernism—saw to it that
important and sometimes expensive works of art entered museum collections during this period, while
modernist painters, sculptors, and printmakers won
important prizes and competitions. But they confronted considerable skepticism among the larger public.

   The gap between museum valuation and popular

Although the Mu-
seum's programs for
children tend to
receive the most
publicity and produce
the most appealing
photographs, a rich
variety of adult pro-
graming has been the
norm in Cleveland.
   In 1956, for ex-
ample, members'
courses included such
hands-on experiences

as a clay workshop
with Fern Giorgi,
drawing and painting
for amateurs with
Paul B. Travis, studio
drawing and painting
with Price A. Cham-
berlain (shown here),
the art of enameling
with Jo Natko, a seri-
graph workshop with
William E. Ward (who
also taught composi-
tion for color pho-

tography), and flower
arranging with Mar-
garet F. Marcus.
   The emphasis was
on a comparative
study of works of art
in the Museum collec-
tion and on introduc-
ing the beginner to
various media and
techniques, "adapted
to the interests and
needs of the amateur
artist."

approval attracted the concern of some educators. A new form of elitism was being generated—a connoisseurship attached to art that excited derision and discomfort, as opposed to the reverence that clung to traditionally accepted masterpieces. In either case deliberate vagueness could result, along with a vocabulary of explanation and justification that did little to encourage broader public visitation and more discriminating judgments.

Personally sympathetic to many aspects of modernism, Munro also committed himself to combating the derision or hostility that modernism provoked. As an aesthetic philosopher whose mission was to develop a morphology of forms that transcended different periods and various media, he concerned himself with fashioning a set of commentaries to help people understand the logic and character of the new art. As he wrote in a 1933 essay, no one insisted that a mature visitor "who would rather look and enjoy by himself ... be educated against his will." But there were many people, Munro continued, who found "that art does not always speak for itself, fully and distinctly." This was particularly true given the "recent tendency of museums to acquire examples of exotic, primitive, and modernistic art," leading visitors to seek "some clue to their understanding and appraisal."[18] Capable instructors, offering just the right sort of information and guidance, could initiate novices into the mysteries of modernism.

They could also, as Munro's list of new collecting arenas suggested, open the American public to a second subject of interest: the art of non-western traditions, ranging from China and Japan to Meso-America and the Middle East. Munro's first book, after all, had treated African art and he collected tribal art and artifacts himself.[19] During the inter-war years American museums had begun to benefit from the broader horizons of private collectors and the scholarship of anthropologists as well as art historians. Cleveland would develop notable strengths in non-Western areas and, like museums in many metropolitan areas, embraced the arts of many media,

many centuries, and many cultures. Unlike great European cities, with institutions individually dedicated to modernism, to decorative or applied arts, or to oriental art, the American metropolis tended to concentrate all types of art into a single museum.[20] New York, boasting a Museum of Modern Art, a Whitney, and a Guggenheim, as well as a Metropolitan, constituted something of an exception here, one that has shaped some popular perceptions of art museums' hostility to contemporary or American art during the middle third of this century.

But by accommodating such widely varied art in this period, museums in Chicago, Philadelphia, Cleveland, and Detroit confronted basic educational challenges, less among their connoisseur collectors than among visitors new to these artistic conventions. Again Munro's interest in morphology—his concern with explaining how certain compositional methods and relationships transcended individual art traditions—formed a useful platform on which to build programs of instruction and appreciation.[21]

A third challenge to the educational work of art museums involved the traditional hierarchy of the visual arts. As an aesthetician convinced that no single art form had a monopoly on value or dignity, Munro helped to expand the institution's subject matter. "By discounting the snobbery of the 'fine arts,' we shall be readier to appreciate the creative elements that often occur in less genteel arts.... Creative originality in art is not limited to any particular arts," he wrote in 1941.[22] During the 1930s the Cleveland Museum hosted showings of classic films, acknowledging their historical and aesthetic significance. Lectures on photography and presentation of industrial and commercial art forms were also welcomed. Only a comprehensive museum could mingle examples from many media and, by simply presenting them, award them the legitimacy coming from an association with a great collection.

Fourth and finally, Munro, like many other art museum curators, used his institutional position to attack the view that aesthetic judgments were simply whims of individual preference, heedless of informed commentary, precise vocabularies, or learned wisdom. Condemning narrow and prejudiced opinions was one thing; abandoning authority was another. In seeking to become more inclusive—by medium, period, geography, form of representation—art museums were neither proclaiming an end to expertise nor surrendering their claims to detect merit. Convincing lay audiences that expert judgment deserved respect, while simultaneously encouraging independence and self-reliance in personal responses to art works, was no easy chore; it stimulated many of Munro's best energies. "Life is too short to keep raising the same aesthetic or moral issues time after time," he wrote.[23] Munro's task was to create a persuasion marrying authority and independence. It was an old dilemma in a society refusing to abandon an attachment to egalitarian ideals even while accepting the restrictions that accompanied professionalization and meritocracy. In a series of impressively large books and extended scholarly essays Munro pursued his task; and at the same time he administered his department and served as an organizing master for aestheticians throughout the world.

Much has changed since Munro's departure from Cleveland. The evolutionary naturalism that formed his philosophical vocabulary, his hopes for broad and convincing aesthetic syntheses, his secular humanism and cultural relativism no longer dominate the scholarly agenda of his colleagues. Vocabularies have changed considerably in the last few decades, for aestheticians as for everyone else. But in a stubborn way Munro's interests and concerns remain with us. Quite recently they have gained new credibility with the cultivation of systematic modes of institutional self-inquiry.[24] Many in the museum world today realize their need for reliable information about the tastes, preferences, and reactions of their visitors; they face the task of defending or revising existing hierarchies and gallery arrangements. Challenges to canonical choice and reassertions of the value of vernacular, craft, and popular arts form one set of trials; a con-

cern with pornography, blasphemy, and subversion within contemporary art constitutes another. In both these areas the status of the museum as a legitimizer of standards has been a source of concern and, occasionally, angry debate.

These are matters Munro would have found fascinating if worrisome. He was provoked by the challenge of handling the largest, most difficult questions about artistic quality and impact, and determined to develop empirically valid, objective measurements to test his conclusions. His ambition and his sense of rigor formed an effective combination. At Cleveland Munro served not simply as the curator of a set of educational programs but as a philosopher in residence. The issues that he raised continue to make curators and administrators uncomfortable. Without in any way seeking to play the role of an adversary or perennial critic—he was professionally averse to confrontation or conflict—Munro nonetheless was an energetic participant in shaping the American art museum's approach to interpretation and display. As such, he exemplified an alternative vision, one that has been newly rediscovered by some of today's expanding education departments as they try to analyze the character of gallery encounters and to improve the services that museums offer to their large and diverse publics. However one may characterize Thomas Munro's specific conclusions or wish to qualify the almost imperial extent of his attempts at historical and cultural coverage, the enterprise that he launched over half a century ago continues to have central importance. His quest has not yet been fully described or understood.

1. The most extensive recent study of art museum education is Terry Zeller, "The Historical and Philosophical Foundations of Art Museum Education in America," in *Museum Education: History, Theory, and Practice*, ed. Nancy Berry and Susan Mayer (Washington, DC: National Art Education Association, 1989), 10-89.

2. For a review of Munro's career and a consideration of his intellectual contributions, see Max Rieser, "Thomas Munro's Position in American Aesthetics," *Journal of Aesthetics and Art Criticism* 23 (Fall 1964): 13-20. In this same issue, pp. 7-11, can be found a bibliography of Munro's publications. A far more personal testament, containing much information about Munro's years in Cleveland, can be found in Eleanor Munro, *Memoirs of a Modernist's Daughter* (New York: Viking, 1988).

3. The most recent study of Barnes is Howard Greenfield, *The Devil and Dr. Barnes: Portrait of an American Art Collector* (New York: Viking, 1987). For Munro's work with Barnes, see pp. 113-143.

4. Philip Youtz, introduction to Munro's *Scientific Method in Aesthetics* (New York: Norton, 1928), x.

5. Ibid., p. 46. Munro also confessed that "among all the branches of philosophy" aesthetics "is probably the least influential and the least animated..." (p. 13).

6. Thomas Munro, "Society and Solitude in Aesthetics," *Journal of Aesthetics and Art Criticism* 3 (September 1945): 36-37.

7. For passages typical of Munro's affectionate, even parental sense of pride in the developing "science" of aesthetics, see the opening paragraphs of "Aesthetics and Philosophy in American Colleges," Thomas Munro, *Art Education, Its Philosophy and Psychology: Selected Essays* (New York: Liberal Arts Press, 1956), 321. This essay was originally published in the *Journal of Aesthetics and Art Criticism* 4 (March 1946).

8. Laurence Vail Coleman, *The Museum in America*, 3 vols. (Washington: American Association of Museums, 1939), 2: 341.

9. Thomas Munro, "Educational Work at the Cleveland Museum of Art," *Museum Journal* 40 (September 1940): 165. The article itself provides an excellent summary of the educational programs of the Cleveland Museum. See also Carl Wittke, *The First Fifty Years: The Cleveland Museum of Art, 1916-1966* (Cleveland: The John Huntington Art and Polytechnic Trust and The Cleveland Museum of Art, 1966), 61-71; and Zeller, "Historical and Philosophical Foundations of Art Museum Education," 52-56. For an example of the educational work done in Cleveland before Munro's arrival, see Marguerite Bloomberg, "An Experiment in Museum Instruction" (*Publications of the AAM*, n.s. 8, Washington, DC, 1929).

10. Thomas Munro, "The Psychological Approach to Art and Art Education," in *Art in American Life and Education: Fortieth Yearbook of the National Society for the Study of Education*, ed. Guy Montrose Whipple (Bloomington, IL: Public School Publishing, 1941), 277.

11. Munro warned, however, about the dangers of improperly designed tests, or over-generalization from them. See "Art Tests and Research in Art Education," in *Art Education, Its Philosophy and Psychology*, 191-208. This essay was originally published in *Western Arts Association Bulletin* 17 (December 1, 1933). Another essay in *Art Education* ("Children's Art Abilities: Studies at the Cleveland Museum of Art," 209-236) summarizes the tests and their findings. It was originally published in the *Journal of Experimental Education* 11 (December 1942). Much of Munro's testing experiments was supported by the General Education Board and the Brush Foundation of Cleveland.

12. Munro, "Educational Work at the Cleveland Museum of Art," 169.

13. Munro, "The Psychological Approach to Art and Art Education," 275.

14. Thomas Munro, "Franz Cizek and the Free Expression Method," in *Art Education, Its Philosophy and Psychology*, 241.

15. Munro, "Educational Work at the Cleveland Museum of Art," 170.

16. For the Armory Show and its impact see Milton W. Brown, *The Story of the Armory Show* (New York: Joseph A. Hirshhorn Foundation, 1963); and many of the essays in Sue Ann Prince, ed., *The Old Guard and the Avant-Garde: Modernism in Chicago, 1910-1940* (Chicago, 1990).

17. The best account of the angry debate about modernism is George H. Roeder, Jr., *Forum of Uncertainty: Confrontations with Modern Painting in Twentieth-Century American Thought* (Ann Arbor, MI: UMI Research Press, 1980).

18. Thomas Munro, "The Educational Functions of an Art Museum," *CMA Bulletin* 20, 9 (November 1933): 142-143. This essay was reprinted in Munro, *Art Education, Its Philosophy and Psychology*, 132-137.

19. Eleanor Munro points out that her father's first published book was actually *American Economic Life and the Means of Its Improvement*, whose byline he shared with Columbia University Professor Rexford Tugwell. See *Memoirs of a Modernist's Daughter*, p. 73. For some reminiscences of Thomas Munro's collecting see ibid., pp. 87-88.

20. For a comment on this tendency, shortly before Munro joined the Cleveland Museum, see Frank Jewett Mather, Jr., "Smaller and Better Museums: A Commentary and a Suggestion," *Atlantic Monthly* 144 (December 1929): 768-773. See also Fiske Kimball, "The Modern Museum of Art," *Architectural Record* 66 (December 1929): 559-580; and Florence Paul Berger, "Should the Size of Museums Be Limited?" *Museum Work* 4 (September-October 1921): 76-78.

21. For Munro's views on the importance of broadening public knowledge of varied art traditions, see his essay, "Art and International Understanding," in *Art Education, Its Philosophy and Psychology*, 151-168. This was published originally in the 1949 *Yearbook of the Eastern Arts Association*.

22. Thomas Munro, "Creative Ability in Art, and Its Educational Fostering," in *Art in American Life and Education*, p. 294.

23. Thomas Munro, "Aesthetic Ability: Powers of Art Appreciation and Evaluation," *Art Education, Its Philosophy and Psychology*, 132. This essay appeared originally in 1941 in *Art in American Life and Education*.

24. For some comments on the history of this interest and some recent developments, see Neil Harris, "Polling for Opinions," *Museum News* 69 (September-October 1990): 46-53. These new interests are exemplified by several projects sponsored by the Getty Trust. They are described in the *J. Paul Getty Trust Bulletin* 5 (Spring-Summer 1990).

After being initially installed over the dome of the rotunda, the McMyler Memorial Organ was placed over the loggia at the west end of the Garden Court, when it turned out that its softer tones could not penetrate the thick glass and brick walls.

It is shown here as it appeared in 1946, shortly after being rebuilt by Walter Holtkamp, Sr., making it one of the finest organs in the world.

Walter Blodgett played the last scheduled concert in the Garden Court in December 1968. While the 1971 wing was under construction and the organ was being rebuilt in the new auditorium, no concerts were given.

Only two years after the Museum's dedication, the Board of Trustees approved Frederic Whiting's proposal to include music among the regular programming. The Museum's superior acoustic properties were observed in listening to the canaries singing in the Garden Court. The desire in 1921 of P. J. McMyler's wife and daughters to create a memorial made possible the installation of a concert organ—the first in the country in a museum gallery—the purchase of a grand piano, and the establishment of a Department of Musical Arts. The noted educator and editor Thomas Whitney Surrette of Concord, Massachusetts, held the first appointment.

Frequent recitals by the Curator and some of the world's greatest organists and occasional chamber music concerts were presented, supplemented by music literature and appreciation classes, and lectures by prominent musicians. Surrette was succeeded first by composer Douglas Moore, who had been his full-time assistant since October 1921, and then by Arthur W. Quimby, an accomplished organist and a thorough musician, who had in turn served as his predecessor's assistant.

By the time Walter Blodgett became Curator in 1942, classes had largely been abandoned because music education was well served by other institutions, so Blodgett emphasized performance. Besides playing regular recitals on the organ (which was thoughtfully rebuilt by Cleveland's Walter Holtkamp, Sr., in collaboration with Blodgett and noted musicologists and organists, and featured pioneering modifications to accomodate the revival of interest in the music of Johann Sebastian Bach and his contemporary baroque masters), he brought in a wide range of musicians to perform in the Museum's 300-seat Lecture Hall—some were well known and others were new, young talents. To help stimulate the local appreciation of contemporary music, all were encouraged to perform new music. This philosophy naturally grew into the May Festival of Contemporary Music (paralleling the Museum's annual *May Show*), featuring performances

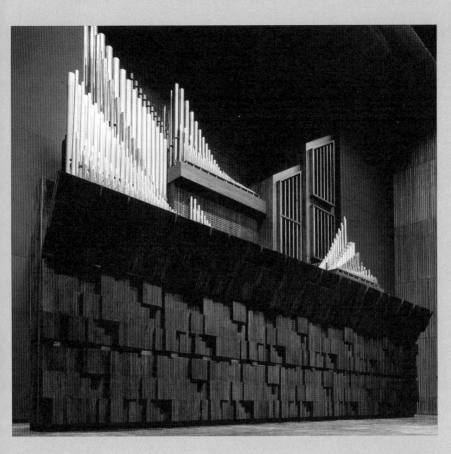

The McMyler Memorial Organ has been substantially rebuilt four times since its first installation in 1922, most recently by Walter Holtkamp, Jr., when it was moved to its new quarters in the Ernest L. and Louise M. Gartner Auditorium in the 1971 wing.

It is of American Classic design, with 62 stops, 79-1/2 ranks, and about 4,015 pipes; the key and stop action are both electric.

of new music by local and outside soloists and ensembles at many area institutions. All concerts were free to the public.

Blodgett retired in 1974, having supervised the Department's move into its new quarters in the 1971 wing. He was succeeded by Czechoslovakian-born organist Karel Paukert. Today, the Curator gives some 30 organ recitals each season and serves as artistic director for a year-round series of some 40 chamber music concerts. The varied programs include western music from medieval and Renaissance works to the very latest contemporary creations, and extend into non-western and dance forms. Lectures and other educational programs often complement the performances. From 1977 through 1985 the Department also sponsored a biennial festival of new music, called *AKI* (the Japanese word for autumn). With the exception of the eight Gala Subscription Series concerts each season, the Department's events remain free and open to the public, whether offered in the 765-seat Gartner Auditorium, built in 1971, or in the galleries or outdoor garden court. Many of the free concerts are supported by the generous annual contributions of members of The Musart Society.

With regard to the genesis of Gartner Auditorium, Milliken remembered casually meeting Ernest L. Gartner returning from New York in the train's club car and having a pleasant chat about the Museum." Years later, after retiring, Milliken learned that Gartner "had set up an Irrevocable Trust ... in his name and that of his wife for the benefit of the Cleveland Museum's music department. He had moved away from Cleveland but although living in Wilmington he wished to designate this very considerable [close to $2 million] fund for the benefit of Cleveland. Again a Clevelander showed his profound loyalty to his native city."

*Objects of Craft: North and South America* was installed at Karamu House in 1955. The annual report for 1955 mentions that the Division of Circulating Exhib- its, as it was then known, provided 843 exhibits designed for cases (such as this display) and 18 wall installations, plus many individually placed paintings and framed prints. A newly acquired station wagon must have helped immensely.

The Extensions Division of the Department of Education and Public Programs continues one of the Museum's earliest activities —sending traveling exhibitions to area schools, community centers, and libraries. The Division's Exhibitions Specialists develop custom displays for individual school curriculum needs as well as larger, thematic exhibitions designed to reach a broader adult public, using works of art for educational purposes beyond the walls of a museum.

The Division maintains its own collection of art objects, which range in date from ancient to contemporary, come from many areas of the world, and represent virtually all media. Such objects must meet the same criteria as those for the Museum collection and have educational significance. Acquisitions with monies from The Harold T. Clark Educational Extension Fund and gifts have brought the collection to its present size of well over 18,000 objects. Special support materials include explanatory models such as a Japanese folding screen and displays illustrating a particular artistic process.

Over 100 local schools (in 35 school districts) each receive five displays from the Extensions collection yearly. The subjects are carefully integrated with classroom needs through consultation with school administrators and classroom teachers. Extension staff specialists plan, design, package, deliver, and

George Brewster, Joseph Finizia, and Richard Boggess (left to right) prepare to make an exhibition change in the late 1960s at one of the six outreach galleries that are supplied with four different displays a year.

*The Order of Things: A History of the Column* opened at the Cleveland Clinic Foundation (South Lobby) and traveled to various civic, cultural, and educational facilities during 1989. It received support from TRW, Inc., the Women's Council of The Cleveland Museum of Art, and the Herman R. Marshall Memorial Fund. Its installation at the Ashtabula Art Center is shown here.

install as well as monitor the exhibits during their minimum six-week stay. Between 1916 and 1990 the Division has put together 32,500 such displays.

Since 1916 various regional community galleries have received over 1,000 thematic exhibitions aimed at an adult audience. Occasionally such shows include materials borrowed from other galleries, dealers, private collectors, and even museums; sometimes they premiere at the Museum in the educational level gallery. Descriptive wall copy and accompanying illustrated brochures, as well as lectures and demonstrations, further the exhibits' educational aims.

Finally, the Division also puts together modular displays with varying themes. These self-contained units—which include freestanding panels, pedestals, display cases, and audio-visual equipment—can be set up virtually anywhere. Such displays are valuable in introducing the public to works of art and in encouraging them to visit the Museum. The Extensions Division now serves a radius on the Northcoast from Ashtabula (east) to Lorain (west), and as far south as Wayne County.

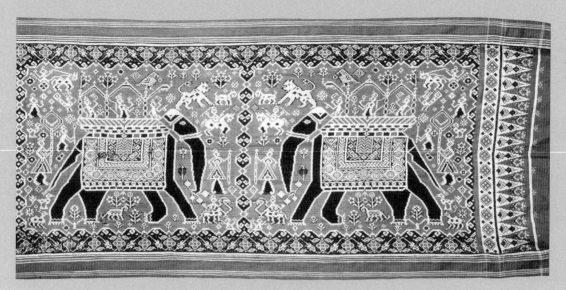

*Patolu* (detail), 19th
century, India,
Bujarat. Gift of The
Textile Arts Club. CMA
90.92

The Textile Arts Club was organized on November 12, 1934, when Textiles Curator Gertrude Underhill called together 47 interested people. They hoped "to revive, encourage, and maintain interest in the textile arts, to enlarge the textile collection of The Cleveland Museum of Art, and to further educational courses, classes, and lectures." Textiles were defined as "laces, embroideries, woven and printed fabrics of all kinds, tapestries, and rugs."

Since then, the Club (renamed the Textile Art Alliance in 1985) has more than met its goals. Its 45 gifts to the Museum date from the 5th through the 20th centuries and embrace western, Asian, and Islamic cultures. Club programs extend from workshops on the latest techniques and experimental styles in fiber art to discussions about historical subjects. All lectures and workshops are open to the public.

Annual exhibitions of members' work are another tradition that has evolved from *Cleveland Textiles* of the 1950s, which emphasized crafts, to the juried *Focus: Fiber* shows beginning in 1967. Fund-raising events have included the sale of members' work and demonstration of techniques, silent auctions, a special workshop, and a studio tour. Proceeds go toward acquisitions for the Museum collection.

*Silk Fragment with Falcon and Dog,* last third of the 14th century, Italy. Gift of the Textile Arts Club. CMA **44.458**

# YEAR OF THE OLD
# MASTER PRINT: 1949

LOUISE S. RICHARDS

Louise Richards retired
as Chief Curator of
Prints and Drawings at
the end of 1986, after
thirty years on the
Museum staff.

arly in the summer of 1929 Curator Henry
Sayles Francis was sent to Europe armed
with $5,000 to spend for the Museum's col-
lection of prints and drawings. In June he
wrote to Leona E. Prasse in the Department of Prints
and Drawings back in Cleveland: "It is a drawing year
and prices are already soaring so I indulged heavily,
on the advice of several people as well as my own inclination.... Prints are disappointing!"[1] It was indeed a
drawing year. From that European trip the collection
was enlarged by twenty-four drawings by, among
others, Cambiaso, Castiglione, Gainsborough, Van
Goyen, Molyn, Rowlandson, Tempesta, and Tiepolo.[2] Drawings by Jacopo da Empoli and Géricault
had been acquired earlier that year, a Watteau drawing the year before.[3] The nucleus of a strong drawing
collection for Cleveland was in place. But while the
drawing collection had been propelled sharply forward, the print collection had to wait another twenty
years before its opportune moment arrived. When it
came, in 1949, it was more sudden, rich, and dazzling
than even that early "drawing year."

If great prints of the quality to which the Museum
aspired were difficult to find abroad in 1929, they
were even scarcer on the market at home, frustrating
the aim of The Print Club of Cleveland which had
urged and supported the formation of a print collection since the Museum's early years.[4] Then as now,
Old Master prints of average quality by the most prolific printmakers (from whose plates and blocks posthumous impressions were liberally printed) were
abundant. Rare prints and fresh, early impressions,
however, seemed to have been absorbed long since by
established print rooms, libraries, and private collections in Europe. Not that the Cleveland collection
had been completely neglected, for the first significant purchase in fifteenth-century engravings had
been made in 1924. This was the matched set from
the Strogonoff collection of the series of so-called
Tarocchi prints, which is to this day one of the great
treasures of the Cleveland print room.[5] It is true that
the defeat of Germany and its allies in 1918 and the

*Samson Rending the Lion*, engraving, 1460-1467, by the Master E. S., German (active 1450?-1470s). Grace Rainey Rogers Fund. CMA 48.456

economic ruin that followed forced long-cherished art treasures to the auction block in just those years when the Cleveland collection was being formed. With the dissolution of the Austro-Hungarian empire the Austrian state appropriated the collection made in the late eighteenth and early nineteenth centuries by Archduke Albert Casimir, for which he had built the Albertina Museum in Vienna, and the settlement made by the Austrian state allowed the then-reigning Archduke Friedrich to keep any works purchased for the Albertina during his reign. These were eventually sold privately and at auction between 1922 and 1956. Similarly much of the collection that had been amassed in Dresden in the early nineteenth century by Friedrich August II, King of Saxony (to rival the collection that his cousin Archduke Albert was amassing in the Albertina), was dispersed by his heirs in sales between 1928 and 1937. Works from the collections of Graf Yorck von Wartenburg and from the princely house of Gotha were sold at auction together in 1932 in Leipzig, but many of the prints from these sales disappeared into European private collections until the cataclysmic events of 1939 to 1945 brought them to the trans-Atlantic market.

In the meantime the Cleveland Museum was well aware of the Old Master prints sold in Europe in the 1930s, but funds were shrinking with the onset of the Great Depression. "We are poorer than Job's turkey just now," wrote Director Milliken to a New York art dealer in 1932.[6] In 1933 the Museum's funds were impounded for a time, as were bank funds nationwide, and in 1935 the Museum purchased no prints or drawings at all. It was then that the Print Club proved its value. The Club and its members gave forty-some Old Master prints (and many more nineteenth-century and modern prints) to the collection from 1930 to 1936, but its most significant contribution in this decade was to purchase the engraving *Venus Reclining in a Landscape* by Giulio Campagnola for Cleveland's collection.[7] It had been the death of Count Gregory Sergeievitch Strogonoff at his villa in Rome that had brought his set of Tarocchi engravings to the market; it was the poverty of the struggling Soviet regime that brought treasures from the state-owned Hermitage Museum in Leningrad to sale in 1931, among them the Giulio Campagnola *Venus*. Passionately coveting this jewel for Cleveland, Leona Prasse lobbied Milliken and Francis, and all three appealed to the Print Club for assistance. They knew that Campagnola's engraving was the finest impression by far of the subject and unsurpassed among the artist's existing prints. Convinced of the engraving's importance for the collection, the Print Club provided the money. It was the first time, but by no means the last, that the Club strained its resources to purchase a major work for the Museum.

Eventually, as Museum funds recovered from the straitened circumstances of the Depression and war, works of art flowed across the Atlantic from war-ravaged Europe. Just twenty years after Curator Francis's "drawing year," Director Milliken stated in his annual report for 1949:

*The after-war dispersal of several of the greatest princely collections in Europe has brought never-to-be repeated opportunities for the development of the Print Department. Special emphasis has been laid, therefore, on purchases in this field.*[8]

For the first time rare print masterpieces were available in appreciable numbers in the United States, and the Museum began to build an Old Master print collection of high quality and hitherto unachievable rarity. Whereas only one engraving by the Master ES, a fifteenth-century German printmaker, had been purchased for the collection in 1923 and a second fourteen years later, in the three years 1948 to 1950 seven engravings by this artist (four of which had once belonged to King Friedrich August II) entered the Cleveland collection.[9]

A harbinger of this trend was the purchase in 1940 of a large engraving by Lucantonio degli Uberti, a fifteenth-century Italian printmaker.[10] Loosely modeled on a fresco painting of the Last Supper by the Italian artist Perugino, it was printed from two plates on two separate pieces of paper. Because of the un-

*The Assumption of the Virgin (after Sandro Botticelli),* engraving on 2 sheets of paper, about 1490-1495, attributed to Francesco Rosselli, Italian (1445-1513). Purchase from the J. H. Wade Fund. CMA 49.32

*Equestrian Portrait of the Emperor Maximilian I,* woodcut printed in black and white ink on blue tinted paper, 1508, by Hans Burgkmair, German (1473-1531). John L. Severance Fund. CMA 50.72

usually large size of the print and its resulting fragility, only two impressions from the left half have survived and only one of the right, making the Cleveland impression the only existing print of the complete design. It came from the princely house of Gotha, had been sold at auction in Germany in 1932, and was offered on the New York art market that same year—in the depths of the Depression—where it caught the eye of Henry Francis. So it was especially satisfying when it reappeared on the market eight years later and was acquired for Cleveland.

The 1932 auction in which the Gotha prints were sold featured the collection started by Graf Ludwig Yorck von Wartenburg in the early nineteenth century. Among several prints from the Wartenburg collection acquired for the Cleveland Museum in the postwar period, the most important is a landscape etching by Albrecht Altdorfer—one of his few etchings that celebrate the beauty of the Danube region in the earliest portrayals of pure landscape in European art.[11] It had been withheld from the 1932 auction along with a few other important prints in the collection, but these also had to be sold in 1948. In the 1950s the Museum purchased several prints formerly in the collection of the princes of Waldburg Wolfegg in Wuerttemberg; of them the outstanding acquisition was a series of forty woodcuts, also by Altdorfer, of *The Fall and Redemption of Man.*[12] Printed several small woodcuts to the page, the set from Waldburg Wolfegg is one of only two extant proof sets in which the pages were not later cut apart into separate prints. Besides the prints now in The Cleveland Museum of Art from the noble houses of Friedrich August II, Waldburg Wolfegg, Gotha, and Yorck von Wartenburg, there are one or more prints formerly in the Albertina and from the old world collections of the ducs d'Arenberg and Baron Adalbert von Lanna. Many of these works had belonged in the interim to European private collectors who resold them in the postwar period.

Though these were major additions to Cleveland's print collection they are overshadowed nevertheless

*The Three Crosses,* etching, drypoint, and engraving, 1653-1660, by Rembrandt van Rijn, Dutch (1606-1669). Bequest of Ralph King and Purchase from the J. H. Wade Fund. CMA 59.241

by the sheer number and quality of the Old Master prints that became available when the Liechtenstein print collection was offered for sale in 1948. The reigning Prince Franz Joseph of Liechtenstein, as a collateral member of the Hapsburg family, maintained a palace in Vienna as well as his residence in Liechtenstein. His collection, which dated back to at least the seventeenth century, was not only large but had remained virtually intact even through the troubled years of the early twentieth century. When the Nazis came to power in Austria, he moved to Vaduz in his neutral principality of Liechtenstein, taking with him the portion of his painting collection that had been housed in his palace in Vienna. After the war the Liechtenstein drawings were sold privately while the prints were consigned to the venerable firm of P. & D. Colnaghi in London.

However, any of the choicest and rarest prints from this collection were brought to America by the art dealer Richard H. Zinser. Born in Stuttgart in 1885,

Zinser was court jeweller to Prince Maximilian von Waldburg of Wuerttemberg. In the late 1930s, when life in Germany became untenable, he sold his own private collection and moved to New York, where he became a private dealer in works of art of many kinds but concentrated especially on prints. In 1948 Zinser was introduced to the Prince of Liechtenstein by a member of the Wuerttemberg family, who was at that time a Benedictine monk living in the United States, and through this relationship he was able to bring a choice selection of Liechtenstein prints to his American clients.[13] Himself a connoisseur, Zinser appreciated the quality of the Museum collection and quickly established a dealer-client relationship with Cleveland that would continue for more than thirty years. The Cleveland Museum's purchases of Liechtenstein prints in 1949, the year signaled in Director Milliken's annual report, were spectacular. First was the large engraving of *The Assumption of the Virgin* by Rosselli after a drawing by Botticelli, larger than the

*Last Supper* by Lucantonio purchased in 1940, and as Director Milliken wrote, "the single most important print ever to come to the Museum."[14] Two smaller fifteenth-century Italian engravings, one of them unique, were added; and finally the Liechtenstein purchases of 1949 climaxed in the monumental, perfectly preserved six-part woodcut of the *Bird's-Eye View of Venice* made in 1500 by Jacopo de' Barbari.[15]

Some forty more prints from the Liechtenstein collection were acquired by the Museum in the years that followed, among them the unique trial proof on blue painted paper of the *Equestrian Portrait of the Emperor Maximilian I* by Hans Burgkmair; two chiaroscuro woodcuts by Hans Wechtlin, startlingly fresh in color and condition; the Titian-designed woodcut of *The Submersion of Pharaoh's Army in the Red Sea*, another enormous project, printed from twelve blocks on twelve sheets of paper; Dürer's *Knight, Death, and the Devil*; and Rembrandt's etching of *The Three Crosses.*[16] No later year quite matched 1949 in the number of extraordinary prints added to the collection—eight other Old Master prints were purchased besides the four from the Liechtenstein collection—but a pattern had been set that was to

continue over the next decade and a half.[17] The last great masterpiece from Liechtenstein acquired from Zinser for Cleveland was Antonio Pollaiuolo's *Battle of the Nudes*, a landmark in the development of European engraving that the Museum had coveted for many years.[18] The Liechtenstein impression, the only extant example of the first state before the plate was re-engraved, was purchased in 1967, placing the capstone on the Old Master print collection.

In 1967 Henry Sayles Francis and Leona E. Prasse retired. From the drawing year of 1929 through the print year of 1949, the drawing collection had also continued to grow and had also benefitted from purchases made in the postwar years, especially from 1952 through the 1960s when drawings by Dürer, Rubens, and Rembrandt were acquired. When the two Curators retired, their professional legacy to the Department of Prints and Drawings was the collection they had selected and nurtured over forty years—a collection that at their leaving had achieved a stature of acknowledged quality and significance.

*Battle of The Nudes,*
engraving, about
1470-1475, by Anto-
nio Pollaiuolo, Italian
(1431/2-1498). Pur-
chase from the J. H.
Wade Fund. CMA
67.127

1. Francis to Prasse, June 17, 1929, CMA curatorial files. Francis came to the Museum in October 1927 as Curator of Prints and Drawings. He resigned in October 1929 to become Assistant to the Directors of the Fogg Art Museum, Harvard University. In October 1931 he returned to the Cleveland Museum as Curator of Paintings, Prints and Drawings.

2. *Temptation of St. Anthony* by Luca Cambiaso (CMA 29.540), *Tobit Burying the Dead* by Benedetto Castiglione (CMA 29.535), *Scene with a Road Winding through a Wood* by Thomas Gainsborough, (CMA 29.547), *Landscape with a Cottage and Figures* by Jan Josephsz van Goyen (CMA 29.548), *August: Landscape with Wagons* by Pieter Molyn (CMA 29.541), *Watering Horses* by Thomas Rowlandson (CMA 29.539), *Battle Scene with a Fort* by Antonio Tempesta (CMA 29.545), *Head of a Young Man* by Giovanni Battista Tiepolo (CMA 29.558), and *Flight into Egypt: The Holy Family Embarking in a Small Boat* by Giovanni Battista Tiepolo (CMA 29.443). Purchased from the Vicomte Bernard d'Hendecourt auction sale at Sotheby's, London, this latter Tiepolo was by far the costliest of the drawings Francis found, but it did not diminish the allotment for European purchases because, as Francis wrote to Prasse: "The Tiepolo was paid for by those sweet people, the Trustees!" (undated list accompanying letter of June 17, CMA curatorial files).

3. *Madonna and Child* by Jacopo da Empoli (CMA 29.10), *Fighting Horses* by Théodore Géricault (CMA 29.13), and *The Romancer* by Jean Antoine Watteau (CMA 28.661).

4. Founded December 19, 1919, The Print Club was the first organization formed to encourage a specific part of the collection; its aim was to aid The Cleveland Museum of Art "to acquire a print collection of high excellence." Continuously active since 1919, its name was formally changed to The Print Club of Cleveland in 1950.

5. *Tarocchi Cards* by the Master of the E-series Tarocchi (CMA 24.432-.481).

6. Milliken to Paul M. Byk of Arnold Seligmann, Rey & Co., October 26, 1932, CMA Archives.

7. *Venus Reclining in a Landscape* (after Giorgione) by Giulio Campagnola (CMA 31.205).

8. *CMA Bulletin* 37, 6 (June 1950): 130.

9. *The Apostles: St. Bartholomew* (CMA 23.327), *The Evangelists: St. Luke* (CMA 37.567), *Madonna Enthroned with Eight Angels* (CMA 48.170), *Madonna and Child in a Garden between SS. Barbara and Dorothy* (CMA 48.455), *St. Michael* (CMA 48.457), *Samson Rending the Lion* (CMA 48.456), *The Martyrdom of St. Sebastian* (CMA 49.7), *The Small Playing Cards: Playing Card with King and Helmet* (CMA 49.564), *John the Baptist Surrounded by the Evangelists and Four Fathers of the Latin Church* (CMA 50.585).

10. *The Last Supper (after Perugino)* by Lucantonio degli Uberti (CMA 40.473-a).

11. *Landscape with Two Pines* by Albrecht Altdorfer (CMA 53.627).

12. *The Fall and Redemption of Man* by Albrecht Altdorfer (CMA 52.38-.77).

13. One of Zinser's letters illustrates connections between the families—as well as Zinser's inimitable epistolary style: "In the last days in London I received the sad news from Prince Maximilian von Waldburg's sudden death—I was with the prince in good spirit at Bad Ragaz [Switzerland] from where we visited his Cousin old Prince Liechtenstein in Vaduz Castle—but the prince had a stroke late in September and must have died a few days later in Chur Hospital. The Funeral was at the Family's Gravevault at Castel Wolfegg [near Ravensburg] in presence of the members of the Ducal family of Wuerttemberg and his princely Austrian friends on September 30th, his age 88 and in perfect health. Whenever one of these fine old gentlemen passes away you feel that there is no place anymore for these magnanimous hearts in a world of the worst plunder, in which we have to carry on!" Zinser to Francis, October 19, 1950, CMA curatorial files.

14. *CMA Bulletin* 37, 6 (June 1950): 130; *The Assumption of the Virgin (after Sandro Botticelli)* by Francesco Rosselli (CMA 49.32).

15. *St. Jerome in Penitence* (CMA 49.33), *The Prophets: Jeremiah* (CMA 49.416), and *Bird's-Eye View of Venice* by Jacopo de' Barbari (CMA 49.565-.570).

16. *Equestrian Portrait of the Emperor Maximilian I* by Hans Burgkmair (CMA 50.72); *The Knight and Lansquenet* (CMA 50.241) and *Pyramus and Thisbe* by Hans Wechtlin (CMA 50.396); *The Submersion of Pharaoh's Army in the Red Sea* by Titian (CMA 52.296-.307); *Knight, Death, and the Devil* by Albrecht Dürer (CMA 65.231); and *The Three Crosses* by Rembrandt van Rijn (CMA 59.241).

17. *St. Jerome in the Cave* by Albrecht Altdorfer (CMA 49.528); *St. Jerome in the Cave* by Albrecht Dürer (CMA 49.529); *The Martyrdom of St. Sebastian* and *The Small Playing Cards: Playing Card with King and Helmet* by Master E. S. (CMA 49.7 and 49.564); *Battle in a Wood* by the Master of the Year 1515 (CMA 49.34); *Christ with Crown and Glory in Benediction* and *The Life of the Virgin: The Massacre of the Innocents* by Israhel van Meckenem (CMA 49.530 and 49.563, resp.); and *The Agony in the Garden* attributed to Francesco Rosselli (CMA 49.540).

18. *Battle of the Nudes* by Antonio Pollaiuolo (CMA 67.127).

# REPORT OF
# HUBERT LANDAIS

C O N S E R V A T E U R

D E P A R T M E N T  D E S  O B J E T S  D ' A R T

M U S É E  D U  L O U V R E

P A R I S ,  F R A N C E ,  1 9 5 3

Year in and year out numbers of scholars visit the Museum to study the collection and meet with Curators; they enrich the life of the Museum immeasurably. While a young Curator at the Louvre, Hubert Landais spent two months in 1953 as the Museum's guest, studying the collection. William Milliken asked him to speak about his experience to the Advisory Council, meeting in joint session with the Trustees in December of that year. Presented here with his permission, that report shows his delight in the collection and is seen as representative of the countless appreciative words and letters that the Museum has received from colleagues throughout the world over the years.

Hubert Landais later became the Director of the French Réunion des Musées Nationaux and in that position repeatedly furthered this Musem's efforts to create vital programs for the Cleveland community.
E. H. T.

r. Clark, President of The Cleveland Museum of Art, Ladies and Gentlemen:

It is with pleasure that I respond today to the invitation of Mr. Milliken, very sensible of the honor which you do me in permitting me to say a few words. I hope you will excuse me for my faults of pronunciation.

Several people have asked me recently if I had experienced great difficult in adjusting myself to the life of Cleveland. Aside from the question of politeness, this has surprise me and I must say that in your busy Museum I have not had a moment to think of it, except to feel from the first moment that I was completely at home (chez moi). This very agreeable impression is due to the very cordial welcome I have received here and I would like to thank everyone and this impression is due also to your Museum.

How indeed could the medievalist, which I hope to be, not feel himself at home in your wonderful Treasure Room where objects of the very first quality are shown which would honor the greatest museums of the world? Many times with a magnifying glass have I looked at photographs of many of these objects. Many times have I turned the pages of the fine book of Von Falke and Swarzenski on the Guelph Treasure. What an entirely different sensation it was to have been able to see the objects themselves and to be able to study them out of a case and discover many details which the photographs did not show. In those pieces we are at the very source of western art in the Middle Ages, at the source from which our culture comes.

For a French man as I am, as well as an art historian, what could be more moving I ask you, than to be able to examine at my ease, one of the most ancient enamels which was made on the soil of France, the Christ Medallion, which was so wisely chosen from the objects included in the Guelph Treasure and now a part of the J. H. Wade Collection.

Permit me equally to call attention to the great Limoges cross which came from the Spitzer Collection, a great French collection, and, which is surely one of

*Quadrilobed Plaque,*
about 1300, by Circle
of Guillaume Julien,
French. The Mary
Spedding Milliken
Memorial Collection,
Gift of William
Mathewson Milliken.
CMA 32.537

Milliken gave a total
of 205 works of art to
the Museum—107 of
them were *May Show*
purchases—as well as
an acquisition fund in
honor of his mother.

the finest of all, in any case the only one which is complete. It would take a place of importance in a case full of the finest objects in the Colonnade of The Louvre. This piece, bought during Mr. Wade's lifetime, is a marvelous tribute to his taste and [with] the other objects purchased from his fund makes the Cleveland medieval collection one of the greatest in the world.

In a neighboring case you will remember your small translucid quatrefoil enamel plaque, dear above all to your Director, Mr. Milliken. Do you know that it is without a doubt one of the few pieces one can attribute to Guillaume Julien, the favorite goldsmith of Philip le Bel?

Your enamel triptych in the Wade Collection is not as yet on exhibition in your galleries. Who can tell us the history of this unique object? What beautiful hands have opened it to pray to the Virgin? What Maecenas ordered it and by what good fortune has it come to Cleveland after having testified finally in the Kremlin to the taste and ability of our goldsmiths?

I cannot enumerate all the objects which have held my attention. Will you mount with me to the main floor? There we are received by two little heads in white marble, given by the late William G. Mather. I love to think the artist wished to represent Heloise and Abélard as tradition says and I beg you to dream

with me of one of the most beautiful love stories of the Middle Ages which has been so well told by Etienne Gilson.

The adjoining Gallery II evokes perfectly our eighteenth-century interiors forever lost. The furniture there creates the atmosphere—the Savonnerie tapestry, the tapestries of Beauvais and Gobelin cover the walls. It is truly the Paris of the eighteenth century which relives and one almost awaits the entrance of one of the great ladies such as the Marquise de Pompadour who might have ordered then the bronzes and porcelains which have been assembled here. We do not hear the sound of her feet because they are muffled by the high nap of a Savonnerie carpet which came without a doubt from the Château de la Muette.

En route to the second floor where in two galleries Louis XVI reigns always, we salute Georges de la Tour, Degas, Renoir, Picasso. But, it is difficult for us to mount to the second floor because so many beautiful objects hold our attention. The walls of the galleries on the main floor attract us like [a] magnet and it seems as if one hears always the sound of organ music. It is Bach, César Franck and, by a happy chance for me, it is André Marchal who interprets them so profoundly.

I will not forget the loving effort which is made here not only to acquire beautiful objects, not only to present them well, but also, through your Educational Department, to explain them.

As the father of five children, I will treasure always your unforgettable Saturday mornings in the Cleveland Museum, the memory of innumerable children, happy in living in the midst of the masterpieces under the watchful eyes of devoted teachers.

In all this, the ancient Museum which I have the honor of representing, expresses to you its admiration. We have certainly much to learn from each other but, is it not encouraging from time to time to feel the communion of interest, the communion of spirit which unite us? All of that I am sure you have felt, but for me it is a great joy and pleasure to emphasize it.

Respectfully submitted
Hubert Landais

*Heads of a Man and Woman,* second decade 16th century, by an artist in the Circle of Michel Colombe, French. Gift of William G. Mather. CMA 21.1003-.1004

*La Montagne Sainte-Victoire,* 1894-1900, by Paul Cézanne, French (1839-1906). Bequest of Leonard C. Hanna, Jr. CMA 58.21

hen Leonard Colton Hanna, Jr., died in 1957, he left a bequest of over $33 million dollars to the Museum. Becoming a member of the Museum's Advisory Council in 1914, Hanna was among the founding members of The Print Club in 1919. He was named to the Museum's Board in 1920, serving on the Accessions Committee. Among the beneficiaries of his Hanna Fund, incorporated in 1941, were Karamu House, the Cleveland Play House, University Hospitals, and Western Reserve University as well as the Art Museum. Besides collecting art, he loved the theater, boxing, and baseball.

When the 1958 wing opened, William Milliken wrote: "There is, however, one great regret and that is that Leonard C. Hanna, Jr., could not have lived to see the actual completion of the new structure. He would not have asked for special mention, in fact, he would have shrunk from it. He wished no wing named after him, no special honor of any kind; he merely wished to be recorded with the thousands of friends who, according to their means, have united to create a great civic institution dedicated to the service of all—The Cleveland Museum of Art."

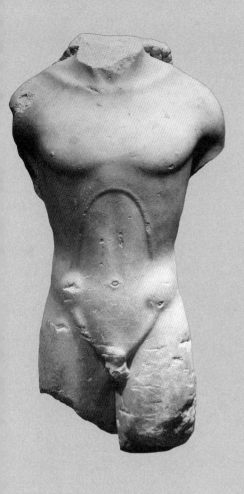

*Kouros Torso*, Greek,
second quarter of the
sixth century BC. Gift
of the Hanna Fund.
CMA 53.125

*Head of a Boy* by
Pablo Picasso, Spanish
(1881-1973). Bequest
of Leonard C. Hanna,
Jr. CMA 58.43

*In Memoriam, Le-
onard C. Hanna, Jr.,*
marked the first ex-
hibition of the works
of art bequeathed
to the Museum by
Hanna. It was dis-
played in the special
exhibition gallery of
the 1958 wing.

**R**alph Coe's enthusiasm for collecting modern French painting as well as contemporary American art began while he was a student at Yale and was confirmed during a trip to Europe just after graduation. His collection of Impressionist and Post-Impressionist paintings became one of the best known and most selective in the country. Although these works are highly sought after now, in the 1920s they were considered too avant-garde to be desirable.

He was a member of the Accessions Committee for 30 years and a Trustee of the Museum 1928-1959. Coe was also active in The Print Club. The author of his memorial wrote: "His wit and friendly advice, his knowledge and enthusiasm were an inspiration to a staff with whom he maintained sympathetic relations." Ralph Coe, his wife Dorothy, and their children were particular friends of William Milliken.

Ralph M. Coe (1883-1959) was a graduate of University School and Yale University. President of the family-founded Cleveland City Forge and Iron Company, he was also president and director of the Western Reserve Investing Company and the Medical Center Company.

*Three Bathers,* 1897, by Pierre Auguste Renoir, French (1841-1919). Gift from J. H. Wade. CMA 39.269 This canvas once belonged to the Ralph M. Coe collection.

*The Pigeon Tower* at *Bellevue,* about 1894-1896, by Cézanne. The James W. Corrigan Memorial. CMA 36.19

In one of his memoirs, Milliken recalled how furious Laura (Mrs. James W.) Corrigan was about the Museum's choice for her gift: she "stormed into the Museum, asked the head guard where the Cézanne was, snatched the label off it, and tossed the pieces in the face of the guard, who had meanwhile managed to get between her and the picture. Then she flounced away, saying it was a disgrace to have bought such a picture and it certainly should not be a memorial to her husband."

Milliken consoled himself that the painting, from the Coe collection, was "one of Cleveland's finest."

*Lion,* Donvide School, Republic of Benin, Fon, Gvaname, about 1940s. Gift of Mrs. Ralph M. Coe in memory of Ralph M. Coe. CMA 65.323

Coe's interests embraced Asian porcelains and Cambodian sculpture, as well as pre-Columbian and African works.

One of the largest and most successful of all regional shows, the *Annual Exhibition of Work by Cleveland Artists and Craftsmen*—better known today as the *May Show*—began in 1919. That first show included over 500 objects submitted by local residents and businesses. Exhibitors were allowed to install their own objects, an experiment that has not been repeated. All entries were juried, and citations were presented to the most accomplished artists from a wide range of categories.

In charge of the exhibition from the start, Milliken stressed sales rather than monetary awards and de-

serves credit for building a local market for Cleveland art. During the 1930s and 1940s *May Show* sales were a significant part of the income of some artists, especially since there was no limit on the size of editions for sale. In 1984 the then-Curator of Contemporary Art, Edward B. Henning, recalled: "row after row of little ceramic squirrels (or were they chipmunks?) in storage waiting for their purchasers...."

Some people may have feared that when Sherman Lee became Director, he would end the show. But he was too conscious of the important role it played in the life of the community and, as he noted in 1977, of the importance for artists of exhibiting their work

The Ninth Annual *Exhibition of Work by Cleveland Artists and Craftsmen*, May 1927. Frank N. Wilcox's prize-winning oil painting *The Reunion* can be seen toward the center of the wall to the left, while

Alexander Blazys's sculpture *City Fettering Nature*, which won first prize in the Models or Finished Work for Sculpture in Marble or Bronze category, dominates the gallery.

The Eighteenth Annual *Exhibition of Work by Cleveland Artists and Craftsmen*, May 1936. Leon Kroll chaired the jury composed of Gifford S. Beal and Sidney Waugh also of

New York City. They stated in the *Bulletin* that "Cleveland artists working with and for the Museum have made the city one of the few major art centers of the United States."

Further, that "The Cleveland group of water-color painters, in the opinion of the Jury, is as fine as any in the country."

"where it can be seen, criticized, and supported by the community." Changes were in order, however, and the changes occurring "over the years in the mechanics of the exhibition have been largely dictated by changed economic conditions and efforts to respond to the needs of the growing professional art community in Northeastern Ohio." Such modifications encompassed merging many of the early categories into four general classifications, successive broadenings of the definition of local artists from the city boundaries to embrace the thirteen counties of the Western Reserve, refinements in the selection of the jury (from all outsiders, to all staff, to some of each), shifting to new quarters as the Museum itself expanded (even to outside the Museum in 1958 and a suspension of the show in 1970 while the Breuer wing was finished), and finally the decision to use slides for the preliminary selection of objects since the number of entries had increased until simply handling all of the works submitted was nearly impossible.

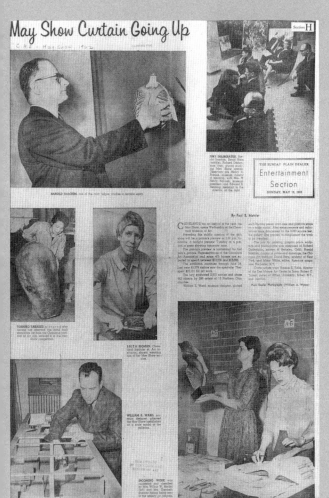

The Fifty-Fourth *Annual Exhibition by Artists and Craftsmen of the Western Reserve,* May 1973.

For the third year the jury was composed entirely of Museum staff: James A. Birch, Edward B. Henning, Sherman E. Lee, Janet L. Mack, Janet G. Moore, Alexander Saulsberry, and Dorothy G. Shepherd.

In his introduction to the catalogue, Henning remarked on the artists' tendency to work on increasingly larger scale, the burgeoning art of photography, the strength of the textile category, and the continuing vitality of crafts entries such as metalwork, enamels, and pottery—not to mention the jury's difficulty in deciding which of several excellent paintings would receive the $1,000 Award.

*The May Show* always receives excellent coverage in the local and regional press. This photo-story from *The Plain Dealer* for Sunday, May 13, 1962, conveys some of the behind-the-scenes activities involved in mounting this exhibition each year. The jurors were Harold Joachim, David Hare, and Richard Diebenkorn, as well as Minor White.

Functionally designed to handle large crowds, the 1958 wing permitted the creation of a central outdoor garden court. Designed and landscaped by Gilmore D. Clark-Michael Rapuano of New York, the court-yard itself was largely the gift of Elizabeth Ring (Mrs. William G.) Mather, in memory of her husband, who had served as President of the Museum from 1936 to 1949.

A focal point that can be seen from many parts of the Museum, the outdoor garden court provides light in the galleries, a terrace dining area, and space for modern sculpture.

# OVERVIEW: 1958-83

EVAN H. TURNER

The year 1958 marked a major turning point in the Museum's history. With Leonard C. Hanna's spectacular bequest—the income of which was to be divided equally between operations and acquisitions—the Museum would for the next two decades or so be in the enviable position of becoming all that its founders could possibly have desired! And in appointing the Museum's Curator of Oriental Art, Sherman E. Lee, as the new Director, the Board of Trustees chose a person fully capable of rising to the challenge.

The impact of that bequest quickly became evident in an awesome succession of acquisitions. Director Lee's effective blend of brilliant connoisseurship, scholarly method and—yes, the best word is *daring* —ensured that the Museum acted effectively, again and again, on the international art market. It was soon apparent that his approach reflected a quite different point of view from that of William Milliken. The earlier Director had had no formal training beyond his bachelor's degree from Princeton, but had developed his eye through the first-hand experience of working at the Metropolitan Museum with the medieval treasures gathered by that most voracious of collectors, J. P. Morgan. The Milliken acquisitions were characterized by a refinement of detail and often by an opulent elegance; they tended by-and-large to be small in scale. As one recognizes in considering his acquisitions in the aggregate, his taste was thoroughly appropriate to opportunities then appearing on the market. In contrast, Director Lee had a formal art historical training—his selection of American watercolors as the topic for his doctoral dissertation was dictated by wartime travel restrictions—but, not unimportant, he had also worked as an artist. The method of his training was reflected in his policy of acquiring in all fields; his knowledge was evident in the stature of those acquisitions. Repeatedly his colleagues at the Museum, his students, even the most casual of acquaintances, discovered new rewards in the visual arts as he fondly handled an object and verbalized his delight in its qualities. Cleveland's collec-

On March 4, 1958, a ribbon cutting ceremony was held for the opening of the new wing. Left to right: Sherman E. Lee, Museum President Harold T. Clark, and Director Emeritus William M. Milliken.

Clark (1882-1965) was Museum President from 1950 until 1962. He had joined the law firm of Squire, Sanders, and Dempsey, while it was working out the legal complexities of consolidating the three bequests founding the Art Museum, and became the son-in-law of William Sanders, the Museum's first President. Clark served—first as a member of that law firm and later in his own practice—as the Museum's legal counsel with great skill and devotion until his death.

However, as the Board's memorial put it: "He was a many-sided man and, in the interstices of a busy professional life, found time to interest himself actively in an amazing number of educational, cultural, civic, and welfare causes." It concluded: "Without belittling in the least the many magnificent contributions of wealth and high service which the Museum has received through other sources, it may well be said, paraphrasing Ralph Waldo Emerson's famous aphorism, that The Cleveland Museum of Art ... is in many respects the lengthened shadow of Harold Clark."

tion grew in an orderly manner seldom seen elsewhere in America, and the individual acquisitions perceptibly changed in character from those of the earlier years. Frequently the acquisitions were more monumental in scale, the eccentric crept in from time to time, while wit and humor as well as charm frequently appeared. The collection assumed new character even as standards of quality were maintained. The Museum's long-standing interest in Asian art became an aggressive commitment, pursued with a method evident in no other American collection of such material. Major strides were also made in the representation of nineteenth-century American art, in seventeenth-century Dutch landscape, and in Italian baroque painting. In fact, outstanding treasures were acquired in every field.

Naturally, the acquisitions had a high visibility, but the scholarly standards now associated with the Museum were steadily developed during these years as well. Thanks also to Hanna's funds, a distinguished art history library was achieved, and the Museum's monthly *Bulletin*, which regularly publishes its acquisitions, established new standards of scholarship for American museums.

Perhaps as a just compensation for the courage with which the painfully straitened years of the 1930s were handled, the Cleveland Museum enjoyed a charmed, truly carefree existence, during the 1960s and the 1970s. And during these years the Board of Trustees was led successively by three Presidents who maintained the earlier generation's commitment with an energy that would have done honor to their forebears: the Liberty Holdens' granddaughter, Emery May Norweb, the wife of a diplomat whose fascination with South America greatly influenced the development of the Museum's pre-Columbian collection; Lewis C. Williams, who led the Board with a quiet resolve and carried on his father's generosity in presenting family treasures to the Museum; and James H. Dempsey, the son of one of William B. Sanders's original partners. While quite different in character, the last two epitomize the virtues of the Museum's

Board members over the years, men and women who by-and-large did not expect to have great knowledge about the visual arts but who, through their own experience, had an unequivocal sense of the importance of the arts as a factor in the civilized life. Yet another leader among these second generation descendants of the founders was Severance A. Millikin, who as Chairman of the Accessions Committee gave the Director and staff impeccable support.

With the retirement of Sherman Lee in 1983, The Cleveland Museum of Art was thoroughly established. Having had a singular evolution, it was justly recognized as one of the nation's major public collections. But the halcyon years were over. Looming was the reality that the Museum must consider new options if it was to maintain the institution—so much more impressive today than the one envisioned at its founding—that the community had come to expect.

The North Entrance of the 1958 wing, by J. Byers Hays of Hays and Ruth, architects. Barber, Magee, and Hoffman were the consulting structural engineers; John Paul Jones, Cary, and Miller, consulting mechanical engineers; and The Sam W. Emerson Company, general contractors.

Gray Minnesota granite was chosen not only to blend with the weathered gray-white patina of the original Georgia marble but also for its durability and easy maintenance. Extending from the middle of the west and north facades, the new wing was built on three sides of a hol-low square, the original building forming the fourth side.

Accessibility was emphasized in designing the floor plans; the desirability of using natural light wherever proper was accomplished by using clerestory lighting.

The third Director of
the Museum, Sher-
man E. Lee, earned
his undergraduate
degree at the Ameri-
can University in
Washington and his
M.A. at the Phillips
Memorial Gallery. He
obtained his Ph.D. at
Western Reserve
University in 1941.
Experience as Curator
of Far Eastern Art at
Detroit led to his
becoming an advisor
to the Allied arts and

monuments commis-
sion in Tokyo. After
the war, he was Assis-
tant, then Associate
Director of the Seattle
Art Museum.
    Lee came to Cleve-
land in 1952 as Cura-
tor of Oriental Art
but was also in charge
of classical and Egyp-
tian art.
    He has written such
widely respected
books on Far Eastern
Art as: *Chinese Land-
scape Painting, Japa-*

*nese Decorative Style,*
*Chinese Art Under*
*the Mongols: The*
*Yüan Dynasty (1279-*
*1368), Colors of Ink*
and *A History of Far*
*Eastern Art.*
    Here, Sherman Lee
is contemplating
the arrangment of
Dutch paintings for
a major gallery rein-
stallation following
the construction of
the 1971 wing.

# THE CLEVELAND MUSEUM OF ART: 1958-1983

SHERMAN E. LEE

Sherman Lee retired on June 30, 1983, after a quarter of a century as the Museum's Director.

t was the best of times ..."[1] and the most fortunate of situations. In 1958 the bequest of Leonard C. Hanna, Jr., made the Museum even more than well endowed, providing the fiscal means for achievement, not only in the acquisition of works of art, but in such activities and responsibilities as conservation, education, library, extension exhibitions, musical arts, the physical plant, and last, but not least staff. The bequest was especially significant because it revealed not only generosity but wisdom. The advice of Harold T. Clark, who was then President of the Board of Trustees as well as Hanna's legal advisor, was warmly received by that avid and discerning collector and, when put into practice, became the Museum's salvation for the next quarter century. The advice was simple yet profound—pay equal attention to acquisitions and to activities. Consequently, half of the income from the final bequest of some $34 million (not counting the remarkable group of Impressionist and Post-Impressionist paintings) was designated for building the collection, and the other half for protecting, conserving, and elucidating those works of art—in short all those tasks gathered under the dismal budgetary term *operations.*

The overwhelming importance of this inheritance cannot be exaggerated. Even before Leonard's untimely death, the Museum had tasted some of the benefits of his personal generosity by means of his private foundation, Hanna Fund. That considered generosity had largely made possible the construction of the new wing that opened in early 1958: it doubled the size of the Museum and made possible the then-inevitable expansion of both operations and collection. But consequently a plan was needed so that all development could be purposefully and economically achieved. The opportunities were too great to be exploited through whim or accident.

The Museum had achieved great distinction since its opening in 1916. A positive tradition of excellence provided a substantial foundation for the possibilities afforded by its new financial independence. What had been achieved? What was to be done? And what

Thomas Munro's influence in innovative programs integrating various art forms continued under his successor James Johnson.

Here, Barbara Beach is showing young people how the Museum collection relates to her particular art: dance.

Held on March 7, 1970, this was one of four sessions in the Saturday morning class "Viewpoints in the Galleries." Others featured a musician and a writer, while the fourth involved all three artists working together with the young people.

would be the relationship between these two questions? An evaluation of the Museum's achievement could be reasonably and rationally done, not only from internal discussions but from outside comments and publications. For a hard look at one's position, one logically looks to one's rivals. Cleveland's collection was admired in any of the areas represented by more than just a few objects. The superb holdings in medieval art, European decorative arts, pre-Columbian art, textiles, and prints and drawings were praised by all. The small holdings in ancient and Asian material, although considered excellent indeed, lacked in depth and breadth. Most significantly though, the main Western tradition of post-Renaissance art was unevenly represented in both quality and quantity. Late nineteenth-century painting was stronger, but the twentieth century was only feebly represented. One measure of this was the absence of any abstract paintings, aside from a few works by local artists acquired from the annual *May Show*. Only one abstract sculpture, Brancusi's *Male Torso* (CMA 3205.37), had been acquired—oddly enough from a dealer specializing in ancient and medieval art.

The special exhibition program was dominated by a few, though fine, monographic shows, partially funded by Hanna Fund and organized by New York's Museum of Modern Art. The Curator of Oriental Art, Howard Hollis, had mounted one of the first major loan exhibitions of Chinese ceramics in 1940 (with which I was privileged to assist) and an Islamic show in 1944. But by-and-large the Museum had not given any new or revisionary ideas to the visual arts through loan exhibitions or, for that matter, catalogues of the collection itself.

This was not true of the Museum's educational programs. Dedicated from the beginning to outreach and to educating children, the department under Thomas Munro during the years 1931-1967 became the leading, most innovative instrument for children's art education in the museum world. The only area needing further development was that of adult and university-level education in art, and that was begun by 1933. The policy of placing displays of art in public and private schools and libraries, initiated even before the Museum's doors opened, had been effectively broadened by the Extensions Division of the Education Department.

Conservation, a primary responsibility, was the least developed area, having neither facilities nor staff. The little that was done had been farmed out to conservators based in New York City or Boston. The Museum Library, although understaffed, was on the other hand excellent in classical art, European decorative arts, prints and drawings, and Old Master paintings. The Musical Arts Department, which enjoys its own endowment, had a superb reputation for the quality of its visiting artists program and the McMyler Memorial Organ recitals, but was feeling the pinch of increased concert fees and the limits of an inadequate auditorium.

Fortunately, the Trustees, Director, and staff were united in their dedication to an art museum philosophy embodying free access, quality and breadth of collection and programs, and in their conservatism, in the best sense of that word, toward collecting, preserving, displaying, and elucidating the art of the world from earliest times to the present day. The Museum's now considerable income was to be carefully—some even said parsimoniously—spent for these four major purposes, and not on such ancillary activities as entertainment, social affairs, or public relations frills. Art was the Museum's specialty and all who were or could be interested in the visual arts were welcome indeed, to a free and open institution.[2]

First, however, a master plan had to be developed for the future, both near and far, but not one so detailed and rigid as to prohibit change; the Museum tried to maintain or improve the admirable parts of a rich tradition while adding innovative elements or changing some less rewarding aspects of the past. An analysis of the monies spent on acquisitions from 1916 to 1958 revealed, not surprisingly, that the decorative arts had received the major proportion. The low percentage spent on Western paintings, however, was a revelation. Without Hanna Fund appropriations—particularly for Impressionist and Post-Impressionist works—the figure would have been far lower. Ancient and Asian art purchases amounted to even less, while modern art barely figured at all. The new master plan called for at least 50 percent of the total available purchase funds to be spent on Western paintings. Four other areas would share the balance—prints and drawings (10 percent), the decorative arts including textiles and Pre-Columbian art (15 percent), ancient art (10 percent), and Asian art (15 percent). It was understood that special exceptions might be made due to the vagaries of the art market. Since the income from the new Leonard

C. Hanna, Jr., Fund had more than doubled the annual acquisitions budget, we found that we were for the first time in the Museum's history able to compete on equal terms with larger and older art museums. Thus, we could expect to implement the plans for developing the Museum collection, achieving balance without sacrificing quality.

To conserve and present both the collection and special exhibitions, two new departments were established. The Conservation Department (then titled Restoration) began with two Preparators (now called Conservators): Joseph G. Alvarez for paintings and Frederick L. Hollendonner for objects. The position of Museum Designer was established and filled by William E. Ward; later he was joined by an Assistant Designer, Joseph Finizia. From the beginning the Conservators were overloaded, and subsequent years were to see major increases in personnel, equipment, and housing, but for the first time Curators could exercise ongoing observation and consultation with Conservators as they worked on the "patients" in the studio and laboratory. Further, they could jointly examine works being considered for acquisition, which saved the Museum some potentially costly errors. The Designer was a particularly important addition to the Museum's capabilities, since setting up each special exhibition requires a sensitive and professional approach, one as distinctive as either curatorial or educational expertise. The 1958 wing had included an exhibition area specifically designed to be flexible in partition placement, artificial and natural lighting, and case positions. The combination provided a major financial bonus by effectively reducing the cost of installing special exhibitions.

The Department of Education responded in 1967 to its new challenges in adult and higher education by beginning a formal joint program in art history with Case Western Reserve University and by expanding its courses, lectures, and programs for adults. To reflect the changes under which several members of the Museum staff were appointed adjunct professors at the University, the Department's name was changed to Art History and Education. A balance among art historians, educators, and studio personnel was made the norm, assuring that no single approach would dominate, while maintaining the close relationship between teaching and the Museum collection and exhibitions. The Extensions Division (formerly called Circulating Exhibits) added exhibition galleries at Karamu House (1959) and Lakewood High School (1961) to its already large and complex program.

Broadening and balancing were also the goals of the Trustees in their consideration of the Museum's new situation. The Operations Administrator, Albert Grossman, reorganized budgeting procedures to reveal monthly the state of the budget and programs in greater detail. The Trustees enlarged the number of Board members and broadened representation of key elements in the cultural community. Trustee members of the Board's Finance Committee reviewed not only their own investment program but also those of the various trust funds, and achieved a greatly improved yield without sacrificing quality or reliability. Equal opportunity within the Museum staff was examined, tested, and strengthened. Under President Clark's able leadership, staff fringe benefits were substantially improved in 1960 to reach at least an acceptable minimum in the pension and hospitalization plans. He was also instrumental in establishing a firm and mutually respectful relationship with the union (AFL-CIO) representing the operations staff, which has persisted through the years to the benefit of all.

The election of Emery May Norweb as President of the Board in 1962 signaled a shift of emphasis on this high level. The Museum had benefitted on many occasions from Harold Clark's unmatched legal and administrative knowledge; but Mrs. Norweb, with her love of collecting and her long diplomatic experience, gave the Museum full speed ahead on its acquisitions program and the inestimable aid of her knowledge of international matters.

Although the Museum had a regional, national, and international status in other areas by 1958, activity in contemporary art was largely centered on the excel-

lent annual exhibition, the *May Show*. Confined to local residents or natives, the exhibition had become rather stereotyped; its content and standards—particularly in "multiples"—had declined as cash receipts had increased. Further, important and active studio departments in the area's many colleges and universities outside of Cleveland were barred from competition. Some of these problems had solutions; others appeared to be intractable. The show's parochial character was easily changed by enlarging the eligibility area to include the area of the old Western Reserve, roughly Northeastern Ohio. This action not only avoided treading on other regional toes in Toledo, Columbus, and Cincinnati, but also provided welcome competition and professionalism from some fine practicing artists previously frozen out of the Museum's annual service to local artists. Selecting the show proved to be daunting. The traditional jury system had been varied by expanding or decreasing the number of jurors, who were selected from different regions or, contrariwise, locally. The one constant factor was the vocal dissatisfaction of artists, critics, and public—despite the show's increasing popularity, proven by attendance and sales figures alike. Staff morale when considering the next annual show was not good. Finally, a mix of germane staff and outside jurors was instituted for each of the recognizable disciplines in the exhibition: painting, sculpture, crafts, graphic arts, and photography. This arrangement put the burden of responsibility on the Museum. If it was reproached—and it was—then at least the criticism would not be provoked by visiting jurors who would be far away when the show opened.

Modern art represented the major anomaly in the acquisitions program. The Trustees were unenthusiastic, even suspicious of spending money on the international art of the present century; the *May Show* was headache enough for them. But the Director along with the Curator of Contemporary Art, Edward B. Henning, by dint of heavy "politicking," rhetoric, and sheer tenacity, finally persuaded them to provide a contingency fund for modern purchases. This "mad money" was to be spent at the discretion of the said Director and Curator subject to annual review; the initial sum of $15,000 marked at least a beginning and was regularly increased. One of the first purchases was Robert Motherwell's collage, *Mallarmé's Swan* (CMA 61.229) for $4,500, at the end of 1961. Since that time, until the useful but unnecessary subterfuge ended in 1971 with the acceptance of responsibility for such purchases by the Board's Accessions Committee, about thirty works were acquired under the rubric *Contemporary Collection of The Cleveland Museum of Art.* These included major works by Arp, Caro, Cornell, Stuart Davis, de Kooning, Gorky, Guston, Hofmann, Kelly, Klee, Louis, Miró, Mondrian, Motherwell, Noguchi, Porter, Rothko, David Smith, and Tobey.[3] Despite our justifiable pride in this accomplishment, when we made our last "mad money" report before ending the charade—and emphasizing current market value compared to the puny initial purchase price—a sepulchral voice (Charles Bolton's) from the back of the Board Room pronounced an unreconstructed "sell!" But the contest was over, as evidenced by the almost simultaneous acquisition of major Cubist canvases by Picasso and Braque from regular purchase funds at not inconsiderable prices.[4]

The traditional acquisition program proceeded at

full throttle. Anyone perusing the annual *Year in Review* exhibition catalogues cannot but be impressed with the unprecedented growth of the Museum collection in both breadth and depth. It was a halcyon time on the art market for a museum with a high regular purchase income. The Old Masters came on in numbers. Hitherto little-represented genres such as still life and landscape were cultivated and much enlarged. Spanish painting suddenly appeared as a major part of the collection; the Dutch "little masters" took their rightful place. American painting became more than Winslow Homer, Thomas Eakins, Albert P. Ryder, and William Merritt Chase. While the ancient and Asian art holdings were particularly enriched, at relatively little cost, traditional strengths such as textiles and medieval art were not forgotten; key acquisitions, particularly of complete manuscripts and sculpture, bolstered previously weak areas. Auction opportunities in medieval art, notably the von Hirsch and Stoclet sales,[5] were not ignored. The decorative arts, too, had their days in the sun—the most celebrated one occurring in 1977, when the Museum collaborated with Baron Heinrich Thyssen-Bornemisza to acquire against all bidders the Kingston Tureens made by Meissonier in 1735-1737.[6] But this much-publicized event and an earlier failed effort to acquire Rembrandt's *Aristotle Contemplating the*

Commissioned from the French artist Juste-Aurèle Meissonier by Evelyn Pierrepont, second Duke of Kingston (1711-1773), the so-called Kingston Tureens are perhaps the most important works in silver made in Europe since the Renaissance.

When the Museum acquired one of the pair (CMA 77.182), Sherman Lee remarked: "With their asymmetrical design, graceful curves, and imaginative treatment of natural motifs, these tureens represent the purest expression of the 18th-century rococo style of which Meissonier was one of the principal originators."

*Bust of Homer* from the Erickson collection in 1963, signaled a future, unwelcome certainty in the art auction market—the vast inflation of prices and publicity in the sale of famous and popular works of art. The Rembrandt "contest" between Cleveland and the Metropolitan Museum of Art was horrendous at the time, although it now seems as nothing when compared with more recent theatrical performances in New York, London, and Hong Kong. Fortunately, the negative effect on this Museum's program was long delayed, in large part due to its restraint and its traditional interest in a wide range of art.

The special exhibition program escalated in number and quality, matching the rate of increase at major art museums. In retrospect, all directors and staff should probably have been restrained, but public demand was heavy and Trustee and staff satisfaction with the results was gratifying. The quality and innovative nature of the larger loan exhibitions were remarkable, not because they were "blockbusters"— a few were, but most were not—but because, in keeping with both staff and Trustee policy, they contributed to knowledge about art. The shows did not simply assemble a heterogeneous collection of masterpieces. Some of them—for example, the Miró sculpture exhibition of 1972, the *Sculpture of Thailand* in 1973, and the Giacometti show of 1975—were

organized by other museums but were recognized as being particularly useful for the education and delectation of our varied publics. Clevelanders had not had the exposure to modernism taken for granted in New York, London, or Chicago. Most of the shows, however, were organized by this Museum, either by one of its Curators or by a Guest Curator selected by the Museum. The list that follows reveals the varied nature of the subjects, the individual and creative thought behind the exhibitions, and the need for each particular display. It also demonstrates the fulfillment of a staff-set quota of one Cleveland Museum organized exhibition about every two years, except 1968-71 due to the construction of the Breuer Wing.

| | |
|---|---|
| 1961 | *Japanese Decorative Style* |
| 1963 | *Style, Truth, and the Portrait* |
| 1964 | *Neo-classicism: Style and Motif* |
| 1966 | *Fifty Years of Modern Art* |
| 1966-67 | *Treasures from Medieval France* |
| 1968 | *Chinese Art Under the Mongols: The Yüan Dynasty (1279-1368)* |
| 1968 | *African Tribal Images: The Katherine White Reswick Collection* |
| 1971 | *Caravaggio and His Followers* |
| 1973 | *Dutch Art and Life in the Seventeenth Century* |

The journal *Arts of Asia* found *Eight Dynasties:* "the largest exhibition of Chinese painting ever assembled in the western world..., made up entirely from the collections of ... the Nelson Gallery, and the Cleveland Museum of Art...." It provided an unrivaled "opportunity for the western viewer to become acquainted with the Orient through the eyes of the greatest masters in Chinese painting...."

Important to the exhibition were the intended gifts of Mr. and Mrs. A. Dean Perry, purchased to complement the Museum holdings.

On the far wall in this gallery view can be seen *A Pair of Peacocks* (CMA 64.242) by Lin Liang; it was part of the collection that Severance Millikin (John L. Severance's cousin) and his wife Greta so generously bequeathed to the Cleveland Museum.

An urgent need for increased, more appropriate space resounded from various sources, all related to the Museum collection. As we gained experience with special exhibitions we learned about other possibilities for displaying the collection itself. The logic of the current arrangement left much to be desired, a shortcoming mirrored in the curatorial organization inherited from the pre-World War I system prevailing at Boston and New York. The separate departments—for example, Painting, Decorative Arts, and Oriental Art—were based on long-obsolete categories divided according to medium and to an assumed hierarchy defined by the supposed distinction between the "fine arts" and the "minor arts," and also between a Western tradition and the arts of exotic outlands. Thus, in order to see the artistic productions of our own culture, one had to visit four different and often widely separated departmental galleries. In contrast, the arts of the ancient world, Asia, pre-Columbian America, and tribal cultures could be seen in cross-media galleries where the painting, sculpture, ceramics, metalwork, and textiles of the same periods could be studied in a single space. Why one way for Europe but another for the other cultures? Why should the metalwork and textiles produced in fourteenth-century Florence by the workshops of artists such as Antonio Pollaiuolo and Andrea del Verrocchio not be seen with the painting and sculpture also produced under their direction?

A question of power and money was also involved. Five departments served the European tradition, which already had a purposefully enlarged budget, while only two served the rest of the world. When pies were divided, five to two seemed a bit distorted. There were repercussions for personnel as well. How could a curator know only European, or Northern, or Italian paintings and not understand the other arts of the same region and time? Gallery space was involved too. Paintings occupied walls, while objects populated pedestals and cases. What of the wasted floor space in

John Russell in *The New York Times* noted that the purpose of the exhibition *Reflections of Reality in Japanese Art* was "not to recycle any of the traditional panoramas of Japanese art, but to watch for the points at which the bruise of reality shows through the pale smooth skin of period style."

The exhibition was organized jointly by the Museum, The Agency for Cultural Affairs of the Japanese Government, and The Japan Foundation. Additional support, for the exhibition or programs, came from the Federal Council on the Arts and the Humanities under the Arts and Artifacts Indemnity Act, the National Endowment for the Arts, the Ohio Arts Council, the Japan-United States Friendship Commission, and the Asian Cultural Council.

On February 2, 1971, Director Lee cut the ribbon at the grand opening of the second new wing. Assisting him were Cleveland's Mayor Carl B. Stokes and Museum President Emery May (Mrs. R. Henry) Norweb. Mrs. Norweb had been named a Trustee in 1941. Elected President in 1962, she served until 1981, when she was made an Honorary Trustee.

In a 1970 interview with Wilma Salisbury, Mrs. Norweb had explained the genesis of the addition: "'Sherman and I felt that a museum which just housed material could become a mausoleum.'" She also noted: "We were both anxious to bring Western Reserve [University] to the realization that education in the history of art is right here in the museum. Also, the Musical Arts program had developed in a way we had not expected.'"

Probably no one was more enthusiastic about the new wing than James Johnson, Head of the Education Department, who was quoted in *The Plain Dealer* as saying: "'We're the lucky ones. In most museums the education department is the stepchild. Here the museum gives us very generous support. We're one of the oldest and as of now we probably are the most magnificently housed museum education department in existence.'"

the painting galleries and the often empty walls in the decorative arts galleries? Then, there was the overall historical and philosophical question: Isn't any major tradition the product of combined factors—the ideas, activities, technology, literature, material culture, works of art, and more? How can these be sensed, understood, and savored if they are artificially fragmented?

The report to the Trustees from the senior staff studying these questions articulated the obvious need for still more room. Thus came the call for another new wing—the same size as each of the two previous buildings but designed to allow a total rearrangement of the collection along historical-cultural lines merging the separated artistic media. All galleries in the 1916 and 1958 buildings would be devoted to displaying the collection, while particular quarters for the Education and Musical Arts departments and for special exhibitions would be built in a new wing. Staff members developed plans for an ideal program providing for some future expansion of gallery, library, and conservation areas. Plans for the special exhibition galleries in particular were grounded in our experience with the innovative 1958 facilities.

Staff and Trustee discussions took place with remarkable amity and agreement, as was the selection of an architect, which was to be made not by competition or endless "shopping around," but by considering various post-World War II museum designs by distinguished architects. The President and the Director fully agreed that the Museum would be acquiring a work of architectural art for its distinguished collection and programs, and that an international approach was appropriate. They found themselves agreeing on the firm of Marcel Breuer and Hamilton Smith, whose Whitney Museum of American Art in New York City had mightily impressed them. Trustees and staff were equally enthusiastic. The easy part was finished. Three years of anticipation, hard work, misery, vigilance, argument, negotiation, nagging, exhortation—all the experiences of humankind save pestilence, death, and destruction—followed hard on

In designing the 1971 wing Marcel Breuer and Hamilton Smith placed this heroic canopy of architectural concrete at the Museum's North Entrance. In effect it gave the Museum a new front door, although the new 11,400-sq.-ft. gray-striped granite wing respectfully confined itself to the back, leaving the building's historic south facade untouched.

The Breuer wing provided a grand lobby, two special exhibition galleries, a 740-seat auditorium, two 154-seat lecture or recital halls, classrooms, specially equipped audio-visual rooms, and offices. Interior courtyards belie its windowless exterior.

Paul Weidlinger and H. W. H. Associates, Inc., served as engineers; Dan Kiley and Partners as landscape architects; Turner Construction Company as general contractor.

A portion of Isamu Noguchi's sculpture *Rock Carvings: Passage of the Seasons* (CMA 81.46) is seen in this view.

one another. But the results were worth it, not only in terms of a building as a work of art but in the realization of a complete—for the moment—long-range plan for the Museum as a whole.

The Education Wing was inaugurated in 1971 with the exhibition *Caravaggio and His Followers* in the new, vastly improved special exhibition galleries. The new home for the educational program and a new auditorium proved eminently suited to the Museum's varied musical programs, lectures, and films, as well as the many meetings, symposia, and other programs. It is now, of course, largely taken for granted, but to have had it in all its freshness, scale, and efficiency was a heady experience. All concerned know it was a real achievement, even, and especially, as it was disliked by many for being too strong, too uncompromising, and too different. Naturally, these remarks were taken as compliments, especially since the new "Breuer wing," finished thirteen years *after* the same-sized 1958 wing, had actually cost less to construct. By 1977, for the first time in the Museum's history, it was possible to

view a continuous sequence of art from Neolithic to modern times, organized according to the present curatorial departments: Ancient Art, Early Western Art, Later Western Art, Modern Art, Asian Art, and the two traditional departments specializing in particularly light- and atmospheric-sensitive media, Prints and Drawings, and Textiles.

The North Entrance on Wade Oval was landscaped anew and a cubic-formed stand of sycamore trees became a foil for the mound with the three-part monumental stone sculpture *Rock Carvings: Passage of the Seasons* by Isamu Noguchi (CMA 81.46), given by the Mildred Andrews Fund. Now, the north side could begin to match the wonderful South Entrance of 1916 by the firm of Hubbell and Benes, with its neoclassic facade and the marble *Fountain of the Waters* by Chester Beach.

While planning and achieving the new dispensation was time-consuming, we would be the first to admit that the program of collection and publications development was not allowed to decelerate after the

President Lewis C. Williams (1912-1990), previewing the 1979 *May Show*. He is looking at Janice Diller's low-fired clay creation *Progress of Aviation Through the Eyes of a Hamburger Fanatic* and a marble and slate sculpture

by Charles Laylin Herndon, *Lamabed*.

Elected to the Museum's Board in 1967, Williams took the place of his father, the noted banker and print collector Lewis B. Williams. In announcing Williams's election as President

in 1971, Sherman Lee wrote: "His financial experience and demonstrated interest in the arts guarantees that continuity of leadership, constant in quality for fifty-six years, is maintained."

Museum celebrated its golden anniversary with *Fifty Years of Modern Art*, organized by Edward B. Henning, and *Treasures from Medieval France*, curated by William D. Wixom.[7] The dinner orchestrated by Mrs. Norweb was a tented wonder housed in the Armor Court, a fitting celebration of an exhibition observing the Museum's fifty-year commitment to the glories of medieval art. *The Year in Review for 1966* was strengthened by some particularly significant gifts and purchases held back from the previous year. If, as Evan Turner noted in the introduction to *The Year in Review: Selections 1989*, a close perusal of the *Bulletin*-catalogue for the 1959 *Year in Review* reveals much about what has happened to dampen the acquisition prospects of all American art museums during the last ten to fifteen years, then the rich catalogue of the Golden Anniversary acquisitions makes the point even more dramatically.[8]

Following the establishment of a Department of Publications in 1959 with the appointment of Merald E. Wrolstad as Editor, an effort was made at last to move ahead on producing in 1966 a copiously illustrated *Handbook* (revised and enlarged in 1970 and 1978), improving the *Bulletin*, and publishing real catalogues of the Museum collections. American museums have lagged behind their European peers in offering visitors adequate handbooks, to say nothing of serious catalogues of homogeneous collections. Rather than a glamorous but brief color extravaganza, the Cleveland *Handbook* was precisely that: a *hand*book, capable of being easily handled and stowed, despite its over one thousand illustrations arranged in the same historical-cultural sequence as the collection it served to recall. The *Bulletin* was enlarged somewhat, allowing for a scholarly exploration of Museum holdings.

Collection catalogues were a tougher nut to crack, given the busier schedules of all personnel concerned, the increased responsibility for loan and educational exhibition catalogues, and the specific expertise required to attempt exhaustive entries in all categories. The catalogues of European paintings were begun, and two were accomplished by 1982, with Wolfgang Stechow as Consulting Curator and the Curator of Paintings, Ann Tzeutschler Lurie, bearing the brunt of the task. A catalogue of The India Early Minshall Collection, *Fabergé and His Contemporaries* by Henry Hawley was published in 1967. In an unprecedented collaboration, *Eight Dynasties of Chinese Painting[9]* served as a complete catalogue, as of 1980, for the Chinese painting collections of both the Cleveland and Kansas City art museums as well as a catalogue for a show of their combined collections. *Indian Miniature Paintings and Drawings* by Linda Leach appeared in 1986.

Under four successive presidencies—those of Harold T. Clark, Emery May Norweb, Lewis C. Williams, and James H. Dempsey, from April 1958 to June 1983—the *Bulletin* containing the Museum's annual report included an introduction written by the Director (during Mrs. Norweb's tenure, 1962-1971, it was jointly signed by the President and the Director). Carefully prepared as brief essays on specific Museum problems and policies of particular and current interest, the subjects of these reports ranged from special loan exhibitions through the philosophy of educational outreach, the choices available in acquisitions policy, the relationship of art museum architecture to the contents of a building, and many more. In a sense the report offered a fortuitous "bully pulpit," an occasion for Museum strategies to be proposed, explicated, or confirmed. In the development of this continuing text, I hope that the Museum's advocacy of a middle-way between the extremes of reaction and "avant-gardisme" was understood by its readers. Conservation is manifestly a conservative requirement, charged with the need to preserve the objects collected. Education is a liberal requirement if one is to understand the art of the past and the changes of the present. The acquisitive responsibilities of the art museum are neither conservative nor liberal, but rest in that continuum of value judgments exacting a balance among the requirements of quality, necessity, and fiscal and knowledge capabilities. I

Sherman E. Lee, Edith (Mrs. Paul) Vignos, and James Dempsey, at the July 19, 1982, groundbreaking ceremony for the third new addition. Dempsey was the Museum's eighth President, having been elected at the end of 1980, and serving for five years. A partner in the law firm Squire, Sanders and Dempsey, he had been a Museum Trustee since 1964, a member of the Executive Committee for more than a decade, and First Vice-President of the Museum since 1972.

have written elsewhere of the hazards and responsibilities of acquisition, under the title "Collecting and the Seven Deadly Sins"[10]—and only partly in jest. Nevertheless, the union of these museum obligations —collecting, preservation, display, and elucidation— is the beginning, middle, and end of an art museum's justification for accomplishing its particular and peculiar task.

The final phase in this twenty-five year period was dominated by further refinements in overall planning. It resulted in the decision to construct yet another addition—the Library Wing, completed in the fall of 1983. Far less spectacular in appearance and size than the buildings of 1916, 1958, and 1971, the fourth wing nevertheless made possible major improvements in all areas of Museum responsibility. The architect, Peter van Dijk, succeeded admirably in stressing the interiors while modestly blending the new wing with the two major architectural exterior statements of the Museum. The provision of an adequate future for the art library—now named the Ingalls Library, one of the best such libraries in the world—on ground and basement levels made it possible to build new galleries above it at precisely that point in the historical circuit where they were most needed: for nineteenth- and twentieth-century Western art. The growing modern collection was backing up on the Impressionists and Post-Impressionists, while the equally increasing number of early nineteenth-century works—from both purchases and the important 1980 bequest of paintings by Noah L. Butkin[11]—was moving forward into the hard-pressed galleries of the later nineteenth century. With the Library Wing, some nine new galleries made the Museum's strengths more evident than ever before.

This difficult "jigsaw" puzzle of providing for new gallery and library facilities had still a third part, conservation. The capabilities of this department had been enormously enlarged with new personnel for object, metal, and painting conservation. An intern program, begun and continued with substantial grants from the Andrew W. Mellon Foundation of

New York, added to the intensifying problem of space and equipment in this area. The enormous growth of the collection in all areas compounded the department's task—more works meant more patients needing treatment. Fortunately, the expanse on the third floor of the 1958 wing vacated by the old Library was structurally strong and suitable for conservation use. Venting equipment for the fumes and by-products of conservation treatments could be installed without endangering the public areas below. *Serendipity* is the only word that describes this "fit" made possible by the decision to build a Library Wing. As of 1983 and for an as-yet-undetermined number of succeeding years, the long task begun in the 1950s to present the art of the world in quality and depth thorough unified and purposeful contexts, to be able to use this collection educationally at many levels, and to preserve the objects themselves for future generations, had been achieved.

The victories and defeats of connoisseurship supported by science are staples of the gossip in the art world and among journalists. One example of each will suffice to demonstrate the perils of the trade. The authenticity and priority of the Museum's masterpiece by Nicolas Poussin, *The Holy Family on the Steps* (CMA 81.18) of 1648, was firmly established after its acquisition in 1981. Its authenticity was confirmed in fact by the x-rays revealing the arched arcade of the preliminary drawing in the Louvre beneath the final paint surface.[12] Equally certain, but damning, was the final proof by the Museum laboratory that the much-heralded Matthias Grünewald *St. Catherine* bought in 1974 was a recent forgery. The initial suspicions of a distinguished visitor, Konrad Oberhuber, set the Director and the staff to soul-searching and reexamination leading to strong doubts about the picture on the grounds of connoisseurship alone. We had the doubtful privilege of first announcing the grievous error. Here wishful thinking was the seductive motive—the splendid group of German works of art and paintings, begun by William Milliken, would have been fittingly crowned by a Grünewald; we had "discovered" Hans

The *Holy Family on the Steps* (CMA 81.18), with Elizabeth and the young St. John, is one of the most accomplished and purest expressions of the French artist Nicolas Poussin's mature style.

Holbein the Younger's *Terminus, The Device of Erasmus of Rotterdam* (CMA 71.166), why not an even rarer find? As aptly noted by Guglielmo Ferrero in the nineteenth century, "What makes good judgment? Experience! What makes experience? Bad judgment."

Other purposeful, rewarding activities in these years include the projection of prime museum responsibilities into local, national, and international spheres. In collecting it was possible to encourage and advise on the development of private collections that would someday augment Museum holdings. The patience, enthusiasm, and generosity of these collectors was wonderful to experience, and since most of them were interested in Asian art, those experiences were very personal ones for the staff of the Oriental Art Department. Without the gifts, bequests, and promised gifts of these individuals, the remarkable development of the Asian collection into one of the best known and most complete such assemblages in the United States would never have been possible. (Moreover, we cannot forget that the policy commitments to adding Old Master and modern works in major ways were real and were achieved within the possible confines of the art market.) George Bickford has given some of the Museum's key monuments in Indian painting and sculpture. The late Kelvin Smith added immeasurable strength to the holdings of Japanese and Chinese painting, as the catalogue of his

bequest demonstrates.[13] The bequests of the late Severance and Greta Millikin have just recently been memorialized by a splendid exhibition showing the range of their interests,[14] but particularly meaningful for the Museum were their holdings in Chinese and Japanese porcelains. The carefully chosen group of significant Chinese paintings collected by Mrs. A. Dean Perry and intended as a gift to the Museum was gathered at the same time and from the same sources as that formed by the Museum; together with the Museum's Yuan paintings, they make up a whole for the fourteenth century that cannot now be duplicated or even approached.

The twenty-five-year task of representing the Museum on the Fine Arts Advisory Committee of the City Planning Commission was rewarding in its opportunities for influencing the city's development and appearance in general and its new construction in particular. Working with the Director of the Cleveland Institute of Art, the Museum Designer, and local artists and architects, the often painful but sometimes stimulating weekly sessions had positive results. Perhaps the most notable were the improved redesign of the Justice Center and placement of important sculptures by Isamu Noguchi, Richard Hunt, and George Segal near the building. The Museum was also influential in locating major works by George Rickey, Tony Smith, and Athena Tacha in the city.

*The European Vision of America* was a joint effort with the National Gallery in Washington and the State Museums of France. It traveled to Washington and Paris as well as Cleveland.

Mounted to honor the nation's bicentennial, the exhibition focused on works of art by European artists, created in the years 1493-1876, showing how they depicted the New World. Most of the objects were lent by 140 museums and private collectors, largely European.

A grant from Central National Bank marked the first corporate sponsorship of an exhibition at the Museum.

Extracurricular activities reflect real responsibilities for the Museum and its representatives. On national and international levels the pressures and tensions in the wide expanse of the art world can directly affect local institutions and determine climates of opinion that can both help and hinder the community of art museums and of individual institutions. The old and still-honorable concept of free work for the public good is part of the Museum's responsibility. Some of the national and international contributions of the Museum are inevitably a part of this record of a quarter century.

The annual meeting of the Association of Art Museum Directors in 1962 was significant for both the Association and the Museum. The necessary step was then taken by the assembled members to incorporate the organization since, while operating as an informal club of directors, it could neither act officially nor receive grants to investigate or improve the art museum profession. The new path marked the beginning of a steady increase in responsibility and action, and the Cleveland Museum was one of the leaders in persuading the membership to take this necessary step. We were not so successful in trying to influence the American Association of Museums (AAM) at its annual meeting in Cleveland on June 3-7, 1979. It seemed evident to many of us here that the AAM had shifted its emphasis almost exclusively toward political, social, and technological problems, becoming over-involved in details. We invited the leading philosopher-aesthetician in the world, Nelson Goodman of Harvard University, to deliver the convocation address. His excellent, thoughtful, and succinct speech, however, fell on obviously deaf ears.

In art and museum educational studies this Museum administered in 1978 a study by the Council on Museums for Education in the Visual Arts. It was supported by grants from the National Endowment for the Arts, National Endowment for the Humanities, Rockefeller Brothers Fund, Edward John Noble Foundation, and Ford Foundation, and resulted in the publication of *The Art Museum as Educator: A Collection of Studies as Guides to Practice and Policy.*[15] This major study, with a range of educational beliefs from right to left, from pragmatic to theoretical, was complex in its practical applications but single-minded in its concern that art museums be major educational institutions using art as a path to general education. It still presents an agenda that cannot be ignored despite present ephemeral concerns about "relevant" attitudes toward art. The place of the visual image alongside the word as a tool for humanistic education remains a major proposition not yet accounted for.

The Museum's national and international position as a leader in examining art museum theory and practice was recognized by the prominent role it was given in the American Assembly of Columbia University's conference and study of art museums in the fall of 1974, which was followed in the spring by a European conference in England. The resulting publication *On Understanding Art Museums*[16] is a forceful, influential presentation of the necessarily conservative functions of the art museum in society. The current "high" intellectual fashion for emphasizing the social, political, and practical relevance of art and museums remains unconvincing before the visual facts provided by the works of art fortunately conserved in the world's museums.

This Museum was much concerned in reviewing the tax laws with regard to donations of works of art to non-profit charitable foundations such as art museums. Abuses of tax deduction privileges for such gifts had reached unacceptable levels by the late 1960s. The Cleveland Museum, represented by its Director, was one of the founding participants on the Art Advisory Panel of the Internal Revenue Service. Providing expert assistance and evaluation to the undermanned art section of the Internal Revenue Service, it and subsequent panels were instrumental in substantially reducing fraud and over-evaluation at the taxpayer's expense.

The support of the federal government for the arts and humanities has enormously benefitted American culture for the last thirty years. Again, this Museum assisted in the early development of these programs, particularly those under the Humanities Endowment where the Director served as councilor for six years and was active in at least partially convincing the Endowment that the arts firmly belong with the humanities. Further, when the arts found the pressing need for a "lobbying" voice in Washington, this Museum and its professional organization—the Association of Art Museum Directors—worked with other art, theater, music, and dance organizations through the American Arts Alliance to present their needs and goals to legislators and government agencies. Cleveland's Director served as Chairman of the Alliance for three years in its formative period.

Equally active in the international art world, both West and East, the Museum's involvement in the celebration of the nation's Bicentennial in 1976 was particularly notable. Cleveland's best-known contribution was the exhibition *The European Vision of America*, shown in Cleveland, in Washington at the National Gallery, and then in Paris at the Grand Palais.[17] Also, the United States-Japan Conference on Cultural and Educational Exchange (CULCON) asked the Museum to act as chief organizer of a bicentennial exhibition held in Tokyo and Kyoto in 1976. The theme, *Masterpieces of World Art from American Museums*, admittedly a popular one, presented the international character of American museum collections, in contrast to the more customary national displays of Asian museums. In Tokyo the show opened at the National Museum of Modern Western Art in a building designed by Le Corbusier (1959); the display in Kyoto, however, was held in the first Western-style art museum built in Japan (1897), the Kyoto National Museum, now registered as a National Treasure.

Earlier, in 1959, Cleveland had been invited by Munich's Haus der Kunst to organize the large American section of *1000 Jahre Chinesische Malerei*, which also traveled to Amsterdam. The exhibition emphasized later Chinese painting, especially works by the *literati* painters of the Ming and Qing dynasties. It was one of the first two such efforts in Europe, the other being the painting section of *Arte Cinese* (1959), a Venetian exhibition celebrating the travels of Marco Polo. The joint effort of Cleveland and Kansas City, *Eight Dynasties of Chinese Painting*, was circulated in 1982, under the name *Chinese Painting from Two American Museums*.

Close ties to the Far East extended to working committees and missions. The Director served on CULCON, which was charged with drafting a minimum code for the conservation of works of art in exhibitions exchanged between the United States and Japan; this encounter led to a beginner's education in the diplomatic arts of patience and good humor,

In late 1973 Sherman
Lee headed a group
of American special-
ists in art and archae-
ology on a 30-day
tour of China at the
invitation of the
Communist govern-
ment. The trip was
arranged by the
Committee on Schol-
arly Communication
with the People's
Republic of China.

qualities difficult to master for the unaccustomed neophyte. Similarly, I represented the Museum on the first official art and archaeology delegation to the Peoples' Republic of China in 1973, soon after the opening of relations with China. The improvements during the next fifteen years of cultural relations between the two countries have been remarkable both for educating the West and for substantially increasing public interest in the cultural relics of the oldest continuous culture known to the world.

Much more could be written of the years 1958-1983—particularly about the Museum's collecting activities. To select any number of acquisitions would be arbitrary, however, and would give a false impression: whether masterpieces of painting by Zurbarán, Poussin, Church, and Dong Qichang,[18] great sculptures like the Cambodian *Krishna Govardhana* (CMA 73.106) from the Stoclet collection or the Mayan limestone *Relief Part of a Stela* (CMA 67.29), rare and beautiful decorative arts embodied in the previously mentioned Kingston Tureen or the three Chaumont tapestries (CMA 60.176-.178), a unique first state of the greatest of all early Renaissance prints, *Battle of the Nudes* by Pollaiuolo (CMA 67.127), or in such modern paintings as Picasso's *Si Tu Veux* of 1918 (CMA 75.2) and Kline's *Accent Grave* of 1955 (CMA 67.3). If

*Krishna Govardhana*, carved in Cambodia, Phnom Da, during the first half of the 6th century (CMA 73.106). Besides its great historical significance, it ranks in purely aesthetic terms as one of the sculptural masterpieces of the world.

When acquired by the Museum in 1974, the lower part of the body was missing. Since then curatorial research led to the excavation of missing fragments in a garden in Brussels.

*The Holy House of Nazareth* (CMA 60.117). Much like the early Flemish panel painters who influenced him, the Spanish artist Francisco de Zurbarán cast a mystical spell on this simple interior through the isolation of the two figures and the pronounced corporeality of his objects, charged with symbolism.

looking at these and the unnamed others can be pure delight, listing them is sheer hell.

In this survey of a quarter century, stress has been laid on a conservative art museum philosophy and practice—not a reactionary stance but a *conservative* one that highlights the peculiar nature of an art museum, as contrasted with an art center or the art market. Changing times may encourage shifts in emphasis but cannot wholly remove the responsibility for the conservation, study, and enjoyment of the past. Abraham Lincoln expressed his understanding of this idea

at the Cooper Union in 1860: "What is conservatism? Is it not adherence to the old and tried, against the new and untried?" This is not the philosophy of a research center, a "think tank," or an inventor. But conservatism is a healthy part of human understanding in the right place and the right time.

Ruth Ward Lee and Sherman E. Lee enjoying the program in their honor during the June 1983 staff farewell party at the Museum.

In *The New York Times* on March 27, 1983, John Russell reported: "On July 1 of this year Sherman E. Lee retires after 25 years as the director of the Cleveland Museum of Art. I know of no one in the field who does not agree that the American museum world without Mr. Lee will be a thinner and less interesting place."

1. Charles Dickens, *A Tale of Two Cities*, bk. 1, ch. 1.

2. This philosophy is perhaps best summarized in my article published in 1972 ("The Art Museum as a Wilderness Area," *Museum News* 51 [October 1972]: 11-12), comparing the art museum to a designated "wilderness," an area preserved to allow people a direct empathetic experience of nature uncontaminated by any often-invasive constructs. The experience of unpolluted nature does have a relation to the direct experience of original works of art without the gimmickry and hype that can overwhelm the defenseless works of art—to say nothing of the visions of dollars dancing above them. The knee-jerk and cant reply that such a vision is somehow "undemocratic" is both thoughtless and misguided. To the contrary, the homogenization of approaches and responses induced by unbridled popularization is truly undemocratic. It can only be countered by open access to museum collections and educational programs and by the creation of an environment where the free individual can learn from and about works of art, and experience their most particular and special character as visual objects capable of bestowing delectation upon the beholder. If they cannot do this or are not permitted to do so, then the justification for art museums becomes a purely utilitarian and brutish exploitation of things. These beliefs obviously have both specific and general implications for museum philosophy and program.

3. *Forest* by Jean (Hans) Arp (CMA 70.52), *Wending Back* by Anthony Caro (CMA 70.29), *Video* by Joseph Cornell (CMA 64.143), *Composition Concrete (Study for Mural)* by Stuart Davis (CMA 64.2), *Figure* by Willem de Kooning (CMA 64.1), *Landscape* by Arshile Gorky (CMA 63.152), *Sleeper I* by Philip Guston (CMA 61.21), *Smaragd, Red, and Germinating Yellow* by Hans Hofmann (CMA 60.57), *Red Blue* by Ellsworth Kelly (CMA 64.142), *Karneval im Schnee (Carnival in the Snow)* by Paul Klee (CMA 69.46), *Number 99* by Morris Louis (CMA 68.110), *Constellation: Woman with Blond Armpit Combing Her Hair by the Light of the Stars* by Joan Miró (CMA 65.2), *Composition with Red, Yellow, and Blue* by Piet Mondrian (CMA 67.215), *Elegy to the Spanish Republic* by Robert Motherwell (CMA 63.583), *Woman with Child* by Isamu Noguchi (CMA 66.48), *Nyack* by Fairfield Porter (CMA 68.3), *Red Maroons* by Mark Rothko (CMA 62.239), *Pilgrim* by David Smith (CMA 66.385), and *Composition Circulaire* by Mark Tobey (CMA 63.150).

4. Picasso's *Harlequin with Violin (Si Tu Veux)* of 1918 (CMA 75.2), *Bottle, Glass, and Fork* of 1912 (CMA 72.8), and *Fan, Salt Box, Melon* of 1909 (CMA 69.22), and Braque's *Guitar and Bottle of Marc on a Table* of 1930 (CMA 75.59), *Still Life with Violin* of ca. 1913 (CMA 68.196), and *The Crystal Vase* of 1929 (CMA 75.82).

5. Sotheby's, London, June 20 and 22, 1978, for von Hirsch (Raphael and Rembrandt drawings, CMA 78.37,78.38, and medieval objects, resp.) and Sotheby's, London, December 12-13, 1979, for Adolf Stoclet's 12th-century French *Corpus of Christ* (CMA 80.1).

6. Christie's, Geneva, November 8, 1977, lot 339. *Tureen* by Juste-Aurèle Meissonnier (CMA 77.182). See Henry Hawley, "Meissonnier's Silver for the Duke of Kingston," CMA *Bulletin* 65, 10 (December 1978): 311-352.

7. William D. Wixom was later lured from us by the Metropolitan Museum of Art and the Cloisters, New York.

8. *CMA Bulletin* 77, 2 (February 1990): 37-80, see p. 39; *CMA Bulletin* 46, 10 (December 1959): 211-231; for further comparison of the shift in the art market, see *CMA Bulletin* 53, 7 (September 1966): 179-286, which presents the 50th anniversary acquisitions.

9. *Eight Dynasties of Chinese Painting: The Collections of the Nelson Gallery-Atkins Museum, Kansas City, and The Cleveland Museum of Art*, Wai-kam Ho, Sherman E. Lee, Laurence Sickman, and Marc Wilson (Cleveland, 1980).

10. "The Sins and Virtues of Collecting" in *Quest of Excellence: Civic Pride, Patronage, Connoisseurship*, ed. Jan van der Marck (Miami: Center for the Fine Arts Association,

11. See "The Year in Review for 1980," *CMA Bulletin* 68, 6 (June 1981): 161-220, esp. 165-182.

12. See Ann Tzeutschler Lurie, "Poussin's 'Holy Family on the Steps' in The Cleveland Museum of Art: New Evidence from Radiography," *The Burlington Magazine* 124 (November 1982): 663-671.

13. *CMA Bulletin* 75, 7 (September 1988): 237-296.

14. *Catalogue of the Severance and Greta Millikin Collection* (Cleveland, 1990).

15. Edited by Barbara Newsom in New York and Adele Z. Silver of The Cleveland Museum of Art (Berkeley, Los Angeles, London: University of California Press, 1978).

16. Englewood Cliffs, NJ: Prentice-Hall, 1975.

17. The exhibition was held at the Grand Palais, September 17, 1976-January 3, 1977: *L'Amérique vue par l'Europe* (Paris: Éditions des musées nationaux, 1976).

18. *The Holy House of Nazareth* by Francisco de Zurbarán (CMA 60.117), *Holy Family on the Steps* by Nicolas Poussin (CMA 81.18), *Twilight in the Wilderness* by Frederic Edwin Church (CMA 65.233), and *The Qingbian Mountains* (CMA 80.10) and *River and Mountains on a Clear Autumn Day* by Dong Qichang (CMA 59.46).

*The Thinker*, bronze, 1880-1881, signed by the artist, Auguste Rodin, French (1840-1917). Gift of Ralph King, 1917. CMA 17.42

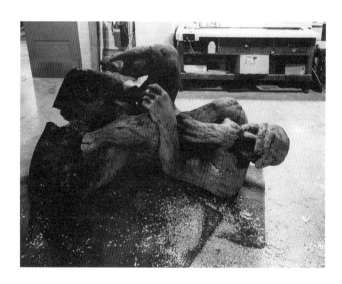

The sculpture was removed temporarily to the Museum's packing room so that the damage could be fully assessed.

A traumatic experience, unique to this art museum among its peers, occurred on March 24, 1970. The great cast of Rodin's *Thinker* in front of the Museum's south facade, a cast made in Rodin's lifetime and supervised by him, was dynamited and damaged. A scrawled *graffiti* made it clear that this was a symbolic attack on what the perpetrators described as "the ruling class." Most of us remember the extraordinary intellectual and social climate of the time, polarized by the unnecessary tragedy of the Vietnam War. From a radical point of view, the Museum was probably seen as the cultural face of the "establishment," an error born of frustration and misidentification. The reasons for Cleveland's selection as the only such institution to be physically savaged remain unclear and debatable. What is reasonably certain is that the bombing signaled an attack on art and educational institutions in their traditional position "above the fray" of social and political contention. *Relevance* was the cant word of the day and for some time to come, but its application to museums threatened greater harm than good. Relevant to what? And how can the visual content of a Titian painting be made a text for revolution without distorting its nature as historical document beyond any recognition?

The Museum's answer, misunderstood and criticized at the time, was to reinstall the damaged sculpture on a black granite pedestal bearing a new legend on the back: *Damaged 24th of March 1970.* Virtually unanimous in insisting on the historical nature of the event, Trustees and staff were also influenced by Rodin's own attitude toward chance and accident when these affected his own clay and wax models—let the event remain as a part of the making of the work.

With *The Thinker*, the consequences remain part of its history. And, in an ironic way, the violated work has the last word, for it was not conceived in isolation but as the main figure in the lintel above Rodin's *Gates of Hell*, seated in tortured contemplation of Dante's *Inferno* represented below.

S. E. L.

*Gloria,* 1956, by
Robert Rauschenberg,
American (born
1925). Gift of The
Cleveland Society for
Contemporary Art.
CMA 66.333

*Knight Series OC #1,*
1971, by Jack
Tworkov, American
(born 1900). Pur-
chased with a grant
from the National
Endowment for the
Arts and matched by
gifts from members
of The Cleveland
Society for Contem-
porary Art. CMA 76.102

Formed in 1961, The Contemporary Arts Society has the principal objectives of encouraging, supporting, and stimulating the collection and study of the contemporary visual arts for its members and the Museum. Among its regular activities are lectures by artists, critics, curators, dealers, and others important in the visual arts. Members also take trips to visit exhibits, galleries, and private collections in the area, the United States, and foreign countries, and enjoy annual house tours. The Society has established an endowment fund, the income from which is used to supplement their annual dues and goes toward the purchase of contemporary art for the Museum.

Membership in the Society is open to people with a substantial interest in contemporary art who are also members of The Cleveland Museum of Art and who are not professional dealers, or otherwise active in the sale of art. Jeannette (Mrs. John B.) Dempsey, Katherine White, Frank Porter, Lockwood Thompson, and the then-Curator of Contemporary Art, Edward B. Henning, among others, were instrumental in the Society's formation.

Preserving the works of art it collects has the highest priority among a museum's responsibilities. Cleveland's Conservation Department (then titled Restoration) was first set up in March 1958, when Joseph G. Alvarez started working in a specially designed room in the new wing. Earlier, various conservators had either come to the Museum on a temporary basis or objects had been sent out for treatment. Since Alvarez specialized in paintings, prints, and drawings, another Conservator, Frederick Hollendonner, was soon hired to care for sculpture, furniture, and decorative arts objects.

Over the years, with the growth of both the Museum's building and its collection, the Department's facilities and personnel have expanded. Today, it enjoys spacious quarters in the vacated space formerly occupied by the Library in the 1958 wing. Previously separated paintings and objects conservation studios are now located next to an analytical laboratory, documentation area and darkroom, preparation and mat cutting areas, an environmental chamber, workshop, solvent storage, and spray booth, and office.

The importance of conservation in achieving the Museum's mission can scarcely be overstated, and the routine care of objects in the collection remains a central task. In performing technical examinations of works of art before acquisition and after—using scientific equipment and techniques—Conservators make major contributions not just about dating and authentication but about an object's condition. Such examinations can also expand knowledge about art, as attested by articles appearing regularly in the Museum's *Bulletin*.

In 1984 Sherman Lee summed up another aspect of the Conservators' art: "although accepted tradition has it that a work of art does not change only the views of its beholders—some objects do change and sometimes for the better. Damages, deterioration, or ill-conceived and poorly executed cleaning and restoration can alter a work for the worse, while some more fortunate conservation activities can transform a well-known and problematic work into what amounts to a newly discovered object with strong claims to both beauty and importance. Such is the case with a sculptured Buddhist image acquired by this Museum [CMA 83.86] ... [when it was] carefully cleaned and minimally restored by Frederick Hollendonner ..." (*Bulletin*, March 1984).

This documentary photograph of the Museum's Tang dynasty, hollow dry lacquer *Bodhisattva* (CMA 83.86) shows how it looked in June 1983 while undergoing treatment.

The Museum's late Chief Conservator Frederick Hollendonner and Conservator Bruce Christman working in the newly opened Objects Conservation Studio.

Hollendonner meticulously used surgical knives and etching tools to uncover the sculpture's original polychromy and gilding, hidden beneath layers of protective varnish and paint. The Song Dynasty *Seated Kuanyin* (CMA 84.70) had mostly recently been used as a garden sculpture.

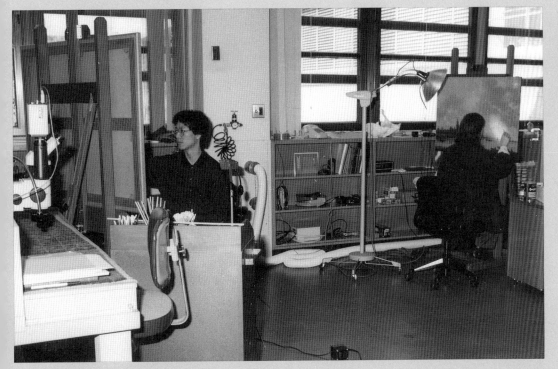

Assistant Conservator of Paintings Kenneth Bé (left) and Conservator of Paintings Marcia C. Steele at work in the Paintings Conservation Studio.

Minor treatments on paintings, such as removing surface grime and repairing flaking paint, are sometimes done in the galleries.

Since its founding, the Museum has seen the Library as a central component in meeting its responsibility to acquire, exhibit, publish, preserve, and study works of art. The first issue of the Museum *Bulletin* (April 1914) contained the following plea: "Friends can assist by donating suitable art volumes, or by contributing funds for the purchase of needed books." Early gifts were from such sources as: J. P. Morgan (New York), John G. Johnson (Philadelphia), Josiah Wedgwood & Sons, the Metropolitan Museum of Art, and the Smithsonian Institution, as well as significant Cleveland donors such as Mr. and Mrs. John L. Severance, Hermon A. Kelly, Mrs. Amasa Stone Mather, and Samuel Mather. Purchases from the John Huntington Art and Polytechnic Library Purchase Fund began in 1915. Marian Comings was appointed acting Librarian in Charge in October 1916. Since she left in 1919, eight people have held the position of Head Librarian: William McC. McKee (1920-1921), Neil G. Sill (1921-1947), Ella Tallman (1947-1966), Elizabeth Halbe (1966-1968), Jack C. Schuman (1969-1970), Daphne C. Roloff (1971-1977), Jack Perry Brown (1977-1984), and Ann B. Abid (1985-present).

Today, the Library comprises approximately 650,000 volumes, including bound periodicals, as well as thousands of art sales catalogues, and 237 drawers of clippings. The photographs number well over 300,000, and the slide count is close to 400,000. The Library grows by some 5,000 books, 7,000 photographs, and 10,000 slides annually since it must increase its holdings in response to each new addition to the Museum collection, archaeological discovery, or significant publication in the history of art. Two-thirds of the Library's holdings have been acquired over the past 30 years. Primarily dedicated to serving staff members by supporting research on works of art in the collection, Ingalls Library also welcomes Museum members, researchers, and graduate students. It is open to the public on Wednesdays.

Over the past 33 years, the Library's development as a preeminent research facility has been aided by three events: First, the Leonard C. Hanna, Jr., Bequest in 1958, then the construction of the Ingalls Library in 1983, and finally the receipt of a grant in 1987 from The Reinberger Foundation (a private Cleveland foundation). The first provided regular funding for Library acquisitions, the second guaranteed new, spacious facilities, and the third enabled automated access to the Library's vast resources.

When the Museum opened in 1916, provisions were made for a Library and photograph room on the first floor. The projected size of the Library was 10,000 volumes and even more photographs and lantern slides, but its growth was envisioned as being related to the size of the Museum collection itself.

In 1934 Library's slide department was moved to new quarters in the mezzanine. That year's amazing circulation total of 204,879, from a collection of 32,174 lantern slides, makes clear the reason for the move. A grant from the Carnegie Corporation assisted in the acquisition of both lantern slides and photographs.

The 3-1/4-by-4-inch lantern slides were phased out in favor of 2-by-2-inch slides beginning in 1958. The acquisition in the 1980s of microfiche editions of major photograph archives has increased the available resources of the photograph library to 2,700,000 images of works of art and architecture.

Reading Room, Ingalls Library. The Library in the 1983 wing is named for two Museum Trustees: Jane Taft Ingalls and Louise Harkness Ingalls.

The shelves at the end of the room are used for volumes held on reserve for the Case Western Reserve students enrolled in the joint program in art history.

# OBSERVATIONS: 1983-91

EVAN H. TURNER

With admirable generosity Clevelanders have sought to achieve a community with wide-ranging social and cultural benefits for all. Possibly nurtured at the outset by the staunch Puritan background of the city's first settlers from New England, this impulse found a receptive response among the successive waves of immigrants coming from all parts of Europe. They too trusted that the lands along the banks of the Cuyahoga River and the shores of Lake Erie would provide for their children's prosperity if not for their own. As the city flourished, the comforts of life were the presumed goal, but ostentation never took root here to the degree it did so often elsewhere. Immense sums were spent first on churches and on education, then upon a broader range of institutions, all established for the common good. It comes as no surprise that the idea for the Community Chest was established first in Cleveland (in 1919) and that, for its size, the city has such a remarkable variety of cultural resources. Few have enjoyed the benefits of Cleveland's generosity as much as its Art Museum.

The Museum has been well served by that sense of conviction and personal assurance which so often occurs in a fast-growing, thriving community. The Museum's leaders have had the courage and the wisdom to entrust its operation and the creation of its collection to a succession of professionals who have become very much a part of the city's life. The Board's shrewd support of two men in particular, William M. Milliken and Sherman E. Lee, has meant that for well over two-thirds of its history, the Museum has been led by two comparably inspired and dedicated men whose differences of personality have only enriched the collection's character. (Milliken became Director in 1930 but had played a dominant role in developing the collection since he first arrived in 1919.) Without question, the "distinct individuality" of the Museum that we know today is the result of the longevity of its staff and the absolute support of its Board. Is there another museum in America with such a record?

At the beginning, perhaps more than it realized, the

Museum's collecting goals had been deeply influenced by a nineteenth-century tradition, particularly characteristic of New England, which found an object quite as rewarding for the lesson it taught about a past civilization or a distant faith, as for its intrinsic aesthetic quality—perhaps more so. Whether it be the educated tourist (which surely Horace Kelley and John Huntington represented) or a voracious connoisseur such as Boston's flamboyant Mrs. Jack Gardner (from whom Whiting had once hoped to receive a gift for the new Museum), such collectors were always aware of the instructive value of their treasures.

Nonetheless, the height of Cleveland's initial goals for its Art Museum was evident in its construction of such a splendid building, even though there was little to put inside it. The dreams, however, were not so clearly defined when it came to what the Museum should collect and display. Indeed, Whiting's early plan firmly stated that "the Museum of today is primarily an educational institution" as he realistically recognized that "the widest possible opportunities ... [were] in this direction." Accordingly, the Museum's educational mission influenced the initial tentative acquisitions for the permanent collection. Associations with past cultures evinced by quite ordinary objects apparently satisfied early, hesitant aspirations. It is not without significance, however, that at the same time a distinct and separate collection was established for the use of an Extensions Division. Even today that department puts together displays of objects chosen for their educational value for the area's schools, libraries, and cultural centers.

Whiting's 1914 report, nonetheless, urged "a definite policy to buy only the best examples available," not knowing of course what might actually be for sale. World War I could hardly have been envisioned when he expressed that belief, but after the war major opportunities did occur. Thus, as William Milliken's well-grounded connoisseurship was given a freer range, the principle of quality as the basis for choice became absolute—and, indeed, remained the guiding force during the Lee years, as it has ever since.

Evan H. Turner became the Museum's fourth Director, on July 1, 1983. With a B.A., M.S., and Ph.D. in art history from Harvard, he had been Curator and Assistant Director at the Wadsworth Atheneum, Hartford, 1955-59; Director of the Montreal Museum of Fine Arts, 1959-1964, Director of the Philadelphia Museum of Art, 1964-1977; and Director of the Ackland Art Museum at the University of North Carolina at Chapel Hill since 1978.

Vice-President of the American Federation of the Arts at the time of his appointment in Cleveland, Turner is a former President of the Association of Art Museum Directors, Chairman of the museum panel of the Japan-United States Cultural and Educational Cooperation Joint Committee, and a member of the Joint Museum Committee of the Indo-U.S. Subcommission on Education and Culture among other positions in the art world. His principal area of curatorial interest is American and European painting of the 18th and 19th centuries.

Visiting Egypt in 1988 on Museum business, Evan Turner took time out to see the Great Pyramid at Giza. He and Curator Arielle Kozloff were arranging loans for *Egypt's Dazzling Sun: Amenhotep III and His World,* scheduled for July 1-September 20, 1991. A fitting affirmation of the founding Trustees' interest in Egyptian art, this show will be the final special exhibition celebrating the Museum's 75th anniversary.

Artist John Moore, then-Assistant Curator in the Education Department, teaching a drawing class for adults in the Museum galleries in July 1981.
    Although the Museum seeks new ways of involving people in the arts, it continues traditions like this in the 1980s and 1990s.

By 1930 the two parts of the collection contained some 18,253 objects of which 4,000 were in the Extensions Division. Not too surprisingly, given more critical standards and the lean years of the 1930s, between 1930 and 1957 the permanent collection did not grow at a comparable rate—10,000 objects—but the Extensions collection nearly doubled: in all 18,339 objects entered the Museum. The increase in the collections during Sherman Lee's directorship was much more modest, some 4,000 for the permanent collection and 6,500 for Extensions.

Consistently throughout the Museum's history, perhaps reflecting Cleveland's conservative management patterns, however, the Museum has avoided succumbing to fashion or to those passing enthusiasms that have played such an important role elsewhere. The money it has received from benefactors has, therefore, been shrewdly spent. Splendid opportunities emerged—especially during the early years of the collection's formation. Scholarly frenzy, at times impelled by market pressures, has resulted in the discovery of whole bodies of material scarcely known before. The Museum has repeatedly been at the forefront in considering such material and then, as appropriate, in pursuing its acquisition. As is evident in the galleries, the Museum has always reacted to the contemporary with caution—outstanding works have been acquired but never in numbers. Maintaining a relative balance among the parts of the collection has been such a concern that the temptations of large special collections offered as gifts have even been shunned. In sum, due to this thoughtful planning, the Museum has achieved a collection that to a rare degree is as interesting as it is distinguished.

Since 1983, under the fourth Director, myself, the commitment to earlier goals has remained constant, but the potential for acquisitions has changed significantly. Prices have soared astronomically in certain areas, opportunities are perceptibly declining, and the Museum faces competition such as it has not experienced for thirty years. The acquisitions made since 1983 are proportionately somewhat fewer in number,

The artist Sol LeWitt, who is internationally known for his site-specific, temporary installations, furnished a dynamic, engaging geometric design that incorporated every wall in the Museum's Gallery 40.

Following the artist's instructions and diagrams, locally recruited assistants superimposed ink washes of rich, warm colors directly onto the walls. As previously agreed, at the close of the show on June 21, 1987, the installation was painted over.

about 1,300 for the permanent collection. Because of the eccentricities of the market, major Old Master paintings, the Impressionists and their followers, and American art are disproportionately expensive so the Museum has tended to turn more toward other areas, concentrating somewhat more upon objects than on paintings, very much as was done in the 1920s and the 1930s. Deliberately, there has been significant growth in the classical collection, while the commitment to Asia has also increased, appropriately, given the importance of the material that has emerged.

Attitudes toward the history of art change from one generation to the next, so responding to such changes has been a considered strategy during these years. The complexities of Korea's contribution to the field of Asian Art have much greater appeal today; consequently, the Museum has been collecting more actively in this area. Possibly influenced by a contemporary fascination with the eccentric, scholarly opinion now recognizes South Italian vase painting as being more notable in the history of classical art, so the Museum has sought important examples to broaden its vase collection. And the emergence of startling new material clarifying the complexities of the East-West exchange in central Asia between 1000 and 1300 has opened up a most exciting new chapter in the Museum's acquisitions. Such occurrences once again underline the point that however much one may plan and plot, the most exciting acquisitions are repeatedly—and happily—the result of chance.

One major new element in the growth of the collection during the 1980s has been the systematic introduction of the history of photography into the collection as a whole.

Today, the collection remains small in total numbers—about 30,000 objects plus another 19,500 works of art in the Extensions Division—but the balanced breadth with which it presents an overview of the history of art is matched by few other museums. Without question, Frederic Whiting's initial concern that Cleveland's new Museum should have a "distinct personality" may safely be put to rest.

Education has been of paramount importance throughout the Museum's history. A nearly missionary zeal at the outset is evident in Whiting's early report on his meetings with the Committee on Industrial Education, which was deeply committed to Huntington's declared polytechnic goals; the Director noted "how eagerly certain elements in the community are reaching out for any form of sympathetic cooperation in their efforts to develop higher capacities in the rising generations." Exhibiting the collection was not enough; the works of art had to be explained—face to face—to nurture a full and genuine understanding.

Throughout the years, there have been many audiences: school children (kindergarten to sixth grade, middle school, and high school), art students, college students, various adult groups, and since the early 1970s even preschool children. Lectures remain a constant feature, but gradually other routes have been explored. Students could copy works in the collection, for example, or use those works as a point of departure for other pursuits. Under Thomas Munro, interdisciplinary programs were much favored, not too surprisingly given the Museum's long-standing commitment to music. In the aggregate the classes are not unlike a braid, each audience being one of its strands; at one point greater effort might be invested in one audience, then in another. Elementary and middle school students received more attention in the early years, for instance; whereas secondary school students were of greater interest in the 1930s, particularly with the Munro testing programs. The sudden decline in school field trips to the Museum in the early 1970s, caused by diminished school funding, coincided with an increasing commitment to the adult audience and especially to the college student, specifically with the launching of a more active joint program in art history with Case Western Reserve University. The Andrew W. Mellon Foundation's decision to fund a joint appointment at the Museum and the University only strengthened that bond.

Although the degree of emphasis may have varied

This view of Gallery 208 as it was rein-stalled in 1988 results from a thoughtful reevaluation of the space and its ancient Greek and Roman occupants by Curator Kozloff with Director Turner and Chief Designer Ward. The acquisition of a life-size Roman bronze in 1986, *The Philosopher as Emperor* (CMA 86.5), mandated major installation changes.

In the process, earlier acquisitions, some of which had been purchased by the Huntington Trustees, were installed elsewhere in the building so that attention could be focused on works of art more in harmony with the Museum's present standards.

The Teacher Resource Center (TRC) was established in 1982, with Penelope D. Buchanan as Coordinator, to aid individual Ohio teachers in using the Museum's resources to enrich their students' understanding of the arts.

The TRC offers structured workshops (often with guest instructors who can share a special expertise), a lending library of books and slide packets, and an opportunity to browse and talk with members of the Museum's Education Department staff. The *TRC Newsletter* is sent to over 3,000 teachers in northeastern Ohio to keep them apprised of TRC offerings.

Many of the TRC programs and workshops center on special exhibitions at the Museum. In this instance it was *Comfortably Seated*, a survey of seating furniture from ancient Egypt to modern times, organized by Henry Hawley, Chief Curator of Later Western Art, and shown in 1986-87. Sharon Cica (standing to the right) taught the workshop; among the participants were Kathy Buckner (left), Beatrice Alexander (front), and Joan Van Osdal (in the back).

from period to period as staff turnovers brought new skills and interests, all audiences were served. Nonetheless, schools remain of paramount concern; for at least twenty years, 70 percent of the Museum staff lectures have been addressed to school students.

The goals of the education program have shifted in two significant ways during the 1980s. As early as 1918 the local school board funded teachers on the Museum staff, sometimes as many as six. However, with the end of that commitment in 1978, the Museum had to find another way of interacting with teachers. A Teacher Resource Center (TRC) was inaugurated in 1981; and in the years since, the Museum staff, working with a Teacher Advisory Council, has designed monthly programs suggesting a wide variety of possible activities involving the Museum collection. The State of Ohio has recognized the validity of this venture by accepting participation in TRC workshops for credit in its continuing education program for teacher recertification.

Potentially much more far-reaching is a new effort created in response to the increasing numbers of visitors, because even though the area's population is declining, audiences are clearly expanding. Over the years Museum attendance has remained remarkably steady, averaging about 460,000 between 1947 and the early 1980s. During the last half of the 1980s, however, because of the special exhibitions and delib-erate staff efforts, those figures have increased—in one year by as much as 50 percent. Significantly, many more people come on the weekends. The Museum can no longer hope to deal with such numbers using traditional face-to-face methods like gallery tours, and these visitors frequently do not wish such interaction. The traditional programs are, of course, maintained, but the Museum eagerly seeks new routes of communication.

Alternative modes of instruction are being considered, whether by explanatory labels in the galleries, video tapes, films, printed brochures, or other media. Simultaneously, much research is underway, through questionnaires and interviews, to gain insight about the public's perceived needs.

The aim, of course, is to demystify the works of art, to end aimless rambles through the galleries, and instead to nurture an active curiosity—but to do so in ways that will avoid compromising the Museum's standards. This effort is made even more challenging by the reevaluations offered by art historians of long-standing interpretations of works of art and the cultures that produced them, the fruits of continuing research. Also, given the changing national population patterns and other cultural developments as the century ends, the Judeo-Christian tradition no longer dominates. Various new audiences exist with just expectations and different viewpoints. The ways of making the Museum experience more involving thus proliferate. During its initial years the Museum did express a concern for its ethnically varied local audiences, but with the aim of melding all into a common point of view. Today, that concern has yielded to an awareness of the particular rights of each audience in its search for its own unique heritage. A sensitive resolution to these challenges is further complicated because on the one hand today's audiences are in many ways less informed than earlier ones, even as, thanks to television, they are visually far more sophisticated and capable of a swift (if at times subliminal) intake of summary information.

Inevitably, making the collection available to Museum visitors affects every decision. As the Museum has always aspired to have a small but distinguished collection, so a goal has been to have a building which can be visited easily with minimum fatigue. Such an effort is achievable when there is no wish to amass extensive study collections. The declared restriction in space has an undeniable merit; for example, the experience of the ever-absorbing achievement of ancient Egypt, so eagerly desired by the Board at the outset, may be for many far better grasped in Cleveland's few galleries than, say, in the awesome miles devoted to such material at the Metropolitan Museum of Art, New York. Although each approach has its validity and its rewards, Cleveland has at least remained consistent in pursuing its goals.

In 1983 the latest addition to the Museum building created new galleries for the area of the collection experiencing the greatest recent growth. In contrast to the collectors of the Museum's first years, who acquired diverse works of art to create a civilized ambience in their households, today's collectors tend to develop a specialty, and then to accumulate objects methodically. Thus, Noah Butkin's eager pursuit of the conservative nineteenth-century French academic painters, who had for so long been condescendingly dismissed, epitomizes such imaginative collecting. His bequest beautifully complemented the Museum's holdings and, much more to the point, fulfilled a genuine need. Given that bequest, as well as Leonard Hanna's gifts and the number of nineteenth- and twentieth-century acquisitions made under Sherman Lee, this portion of the collection most needed expanded exhibition space.

Although further construction is not desired for its own sake, one yearning need, nonetheless, exists: space for the adequate presentation of the Museum's extraordinary collection of Asian art. With the possible exception of contemporary art, this remains the area of greatest growth, whether by purchase or by gifts, such as the examples of Indian art from George P. Bickford and the promised collection of Chinese paintings formed by J. H. Wade's granddaughter, Mrs. A. Dean Perry. Initial studies are, therefore, in hand for an increase in the exhibition space devoted to this material with a minimal impact upon the exterior appearance of the building. It is hard to believe that with time such an addition will not be made—but, as happened with the 1958 and 1971 expansions, a lengthy planning period seems inevitable. However, the West desperately needs an enhanced understanding of Asia—a region no longer so remote as when Americans first began collecting there—and the Museum's holdings present a considered overview of the Asian achievement not found elsewhere in this country. Its proper presentation is a genuine responsibility.

From the beginning the Museum has been a leader in encouraging cooperation among the city's cultural institutions. In the 1920s, for example, Whiting led the effort to establish the Cleveland Conference for Educational Cooperation, to foster efficiency and effectiveness among the city's various educational programs. In the 1950s the Museum actively supported the creation of University Circle, Incorporated—an effort energized by Mrs. William Mather, the widow of the Museum's third President—and it has remained as committed as it is admiring of that organization's energetic concern for the area.

In the past three years the Museum has become active in the development of the new Cleveland Arts Consortium. This organization, vigorously considering the joint programming and marketing concerns of twenty-one of the city's theaters, musical groups, dance companies, and museums, resulted from a study funded by The Cleveland Foundation. All concerned rightly believe that much is to be gained by having these organizations address common goals together. Clearly, the Consortium members have, in the aggregate, an inestimable potential that can assist the City of Cleveland, absorbed in a total reorganization of its economic base, in developing a more positive national image. Such involvement in the greater well-being of the city seems only appropriate on the part of the Museum that owes so much to earlier generous attempts to enrich the local quality of life.

The Museum's finances, however, have increasingly become a major concern during the 1980s. For many years, Hanna's bequest essentially carried the institution, the income often even being sufficient to form a reserve fund against the unexpected. But the expenses of operating a museum have so spiraled up that the day of reckoning has come. The difficulties faced, however, are not so different from those of its peers.

Five years ago the Cleveland Museum started a fund-raising department—with immense success—and now follows its peers in seeking income producing programs. It finally pursues the route that has been the American museum norm for at least much of the 1980s. Providentially, one might say that, in comparison with many institutions, such actions are dictated by need rather than desperation. Nonetheless, aggressive planning is essential to avoid such a fate. For the first time in its history, therefore, the Museum's Board is involved in analyzing the possible routes before it and the means necessary for funding them. Through such planning, the Museum's course for the next quarter century will become evident.

Nine new galleries connect the 1958 and 1983 wings, permitting an expanded, continuous display of the 18th-, 19th-, and 20th-century art in the collection.

Four mini-galleries provide intimate spaces that are appropriate for the works in the Noah L. Butkin bequest: French 19th-century paintings, sculptures, and drawings. Personally preferring works of a small size with a largely figural content, Butkin, a Museum Trustee, focused on works by Realist and Academic masters long before the work of these artists was seriously reevaluated. This in-depth view, thanks to the generosity of Muriel Butkin, adds greatly to the Museum's capacity to present a broad range of 19th-century art.

In this gallery view the Sèvres *Vase with Portrait of President MacMahon* (CMA 79.40) dominates the space. A tour-de-force of ceramic and metalwork, it was acquired thanks to the bequest of Thomas L. Fawick, the Cleveland inventor and industrialist.

Canvases by Jean-Léon Gérôme and Léon Cogniet (CMA 80.254 and 80.249) from the Butkin bequest can be seen on the wall behind the vase.

Tucked between two stairwell towers on the Museum's west side the latest addition is not monumental or luxurious. Clad in a red-and-gray granite that matches the adjoining building, the 33,650-sq.-ft.-wing is made of quality materials, serves its purpose, and is designed to fit its location without being obtrusive. Peter van Dijk of Dalton, van Dijk, Johnson & Partners was the partner in charge of the project; Byers Engineering Company were the mechanical and electrical engineers; the structural engineers were Gensert Bretnall Bobel, Inc.; while R. P. Carbone Construction Company served as general contractors.

A $500,000 National Endowment for the Arts challenge grant assisted in the successful $6.5 million campaign for the new Library, nine new galleries, renovations of existing space for the Conservation Department, and an operating endowment for the addition. The Kresge Foundation of Troy, Michigan, also set up a challenge grant of $400,000 to supplement the $6.3 million raised with major gifts from the Andrew W. Mellon Foundation (another challenge grant), the Andrews Foundation, the Cleveland Foundation, the GAR Foundation, the Ingalls Foundation, the Ireland Foundation, and the Elizabeth Ring Mather and William Gwinn Mather Fund. Corporate gifts were received from more than 70 Cleveland businesses plus many private donations.

orporate sponsorship of exhibitions and corporate membership in the Museum have become vital elements in the Museum's maintaining a dynamic series of exhibitions and programs for the city. Although production costs for many special exhibitions fall in the $1 million range, the Museum presents many significant, exciting exhibitions for less than $100,000.

Corporate sponsors of exhibitions have included: American Greetings Corporation, AmeriTrust Company, Ameritech, BP America, Inc., Central National Bank, Columbiana Boiler Company, Forest City Enterprises, International Business Machines Cor-

poration, National City Bank, Ohio Bell Telephone Company, Squire, Sanders & Dempsey, and United Technologies Corporation. The support of such corporations and foundations—not to mention the National Endowment for the Arts, the Federal Council on the Arts and the Humanities, and the Ohio Arts Council—has enabled the Museum to make available to the citizens of Cleveland many of the major international exhibitions seen here during the last six years.

The gallery labels for the *Paul Klee* exhibition were carefully conceived—building on visitor surveys made during the extremely popular exhibition *Impressionist and Post-Impressionist Master-* *pieces: The Courtauld Collection.* The aim was to assist the viewer in more fully experiencing each work of art.

The extra effort paid off. The exhibition's 98,764 visitors lingered longer in the galleries and were clearly moved by the work of this foremost master of modernism. This 1987 show was sponsored by National City Bank.

Alton W. Whitehouse was elected President of the Museum in 1985; he had been a member of the Board since 1975. Whitehouse has served as Treasurer and Chairman of the Trustees' Finance Committee, and his appointment to the Board signalled the Museum's greater involvement with Cleveland's corporate community.

Not only did National City Bank significantly underwrite the costs of the Cleveland showing of the *Paul Klee* exhibition, but it funded a handsome city-wide publicity campaign.

The exhibition, the first major Klee retrospective in 20 years, featured 249 of his paintings, drawings, and prints. It was organized by Carolyn Lanchner of the Museum of Modern Art, New York. Support was provided in part by the National Endowment for the Arts, Nestlé Holdings, Inc., The International Council of The Museum of Modern Art, and other benefactors. An indemnity for the exhibition was provided by the Federal Council on the Arts and the Humanities. The Ohio Arts Council also provided assistance.

Given the number of hours of staff effort and the funds necessary to bring an exhibition to Cleveland, it is only proper that the city should be made aware of the opportunity. Well-designed banners are one method of doing so. The cheerful yellow banners with Klee's dancing stick figure, displayed downtown and in the University Circle area, contributed to the exhibition's success.

# EPILOGUE

n so many ways the Museum's story is the story of Cleveland. It is an account of pride, of deep commitment to the quality of life in the city and in the area. A story of caring, it is a statement of absolute conviction that the city's cultural energy is essential to achieving a vital Cleveland.

This volume has recounted the many factors leading to the achievement of a great Museum—the construction of the large handsome building that opened in 1916, its gradual growth, and the all-important gathering of a collection that, as it turned out, would be the envy of any great cosmopolitan center.

As appropriate, it is an account of the many who brought it all about and of the audience whose interest and enthusiasm became so significant to the realization of its programs.

It is the story of the past—but at the same time we all recognize that those very qualities that over the years brought about the creation of Cleveland's remarkable Art Museum are the same ones that will assure its vitality in the years to come.

E. H. T.

The Department of Education and Public Programs in cooperation with the Department of Musical Arts sponsors a series of public events at the Museum during July. These Wednesday Evening Festivals include musical programs, slide lectures, feature-length and art films, and family workshops.

The Festivals typify the sort of events that the Museum sponsors for its members and for the public to foster a broader involvement with the community.

Box suppers in the Museum's outdoor Garden Court are perennially popular with the large and responsive audiences drawn to the Festivals. These annual events began in 1974.

# MUSEUM TRUSTEES, 1913-1991

1913   Frederic Allen Whiting
       named Director.

Original Trustees and signers of incorporation:

1913   Dudley P. Allen (-1915)
       Charles W. Bingham (-1920)
       Mariett L. Huntington (-1921)
       Hermon A. Kelley (-1925)
       John H. Lowman (-1919)
       Samuel Mather (-1931)
       Charles L. Murfey (-1936)
       David Z. Norton (-1928)
       Edwin R. Perkins (-1915)
       William B. Sanders (-1929)
       Jeptha H. Wade (-1926)
       George Worthington (-1924)

1915   John L. Severance and Ralph King elected
1919   William G. Mather elected
1920   Leonard C. Hanna elected
1921   John Huntington Hord elected
1924   Francis F. Prentiss elected
1925   Edward B. Greene elected
1926   Henry G. Dalton elected
1928   Chester C. Bolton and Ralph Coe elected
1929   Harold T. Clark elected

1930   William Mathewson Milliken
       named Director.

       Chester C. Bolton (1928-1939)
       Harold T. Clark (1929-1965)
       Ralph M. Coe (1928-1959)
       Henry G. Dalton (1926-1939)
       Edward B. Greene (1925-1957)
       Leonard C. Hanna, Jr. (1920-1957)
       John H. Hord (1921-1949)
       Samuel Mather (1913-1931)
       William G. Mather (1919-1951)
       Charles L. Murfey (1913-1936)
       Francis F. Prentiss (1924-1937)
       John L. Severance (1915-1936)

1932   Lewis B. Williams elected
1936   Mrs. B. P. Bole elected
1937   Mrs. Francis F. Prentiss elected
1939   Laurence H. Norton elected
1940   George Garretson Wade elected
1944   Mrs. Albert S. Ingalls elected
1947   Severance A. Millikin elected
1949   Mrs. R. Henry Norweb elected
1952   Ralph S. Schmitt elected
1956   George P. Bickford, Charles B. Bolton, Fay-
       ette Brown, Jr., James N. Sherwin, and John
       S. Wilbur elected

1958    Sherman Emery Lee
named Director.

George P. Bickford (1956-)
Charles B. Bolton (1956-1963, *honorary*)
Harold T. Clark (1929-1965)
Ralph M. Coe (1928-1959)
Edgar H. Hahn (1958-1970)
Mrs. Albert S. Ingalls (1944-1962)
Severance A. Millikin (1947-1985)
Laurence H. Norton (1939-1960)
Mrs. R. Henry Norweb (1941-1981, *honorary*)
Ralph S. Schmitt (1952-1974)
James N. Sherwin (1956-1971)
John S. Wilbur (1956-1981, *honorary*)
Lewis B. Williams (1932-1966)

1960    Robert I. Gale, Mrs. David S. Ingalls, and
A. Dean Perry elected
1964    James H. Dempsey, Jr., and James D. Ireland
elected
1967    Willis B. Boyer, Mrs. Alfred M. Rankin, Paul
Vignos, Jr., and Lewis C. Williams elected
1970    Daniel J. Silver elected
1973    Frances P. Taft and George Oliva, Jr., elected
1975    Noah L. Butkin and Alton W. Whitehouse,
Jr., elected
1978    George M. Humphrey, Mrs. Edward A. Kilroy, Jr., and Norman W. Zaworski elected
1981    Ruben F. Mettler elected
1982    E. Bradley Jones and S. Sterling McMillan III
elected

1983    Evan Hopkins Turner
named Director.

George P. Bickford (1956-)
James H. Dempsey, Jr. (1964-1988, *honorary*)
George M. Humphrey II (1978-)
James D. Ireland (1964-1987, *honorary*)
E. Bradley Jones (1982-1988)
Mrs. Edward A. Kilroy, Jr. (1978-)
S. Sterling McMillan III (1982-)
Ruben F. Mettler (1981-1988)
George Oliva, Jr. (1973-)
A. Dean Perry (1960-1983, *honorary*)
Mrs. Alfred M. Rankin (1967-1989, *honorary*)
Daniel J. Silver (1970-1989)
Frances P. Taft (1973-)
Paul Vignos, Jr. (1967-)
Alton W. Whitehouse, Jr. (1975-)
John S. Wilbur (1956-1981, *honorary*)
Lewis C. Williams (1967-1985, *honorary*)
Norman W. Zaworski (1978-)

1984    Jack W. Lampl, Jr., and Donna S. Reid elected
1985    Quentin Alexander elected
1987    Michael Sherwin elected
1989    Morton L. Mandel and Richard T. Watson
elected
1991    Mary Manning Wasmer and Ruth Swetland
Eppig elected

# PHOTO CREDITS

Courtesy of the Western Reserve Historical Society, pp. 2, 16 (left), 19 (top), 78; Courtesy of Archives, University Hospitals of Cleveland, p. 6; Courtesy of Photograph Collection, Cleveland Public Library, pp. 17 (top), 26, 64 (top right), 108, 124 (left), 161, 170, 178; Courtesy of Frances K. (Mrs. Gilbert P.) Schafer, p. 28; Courtesy of The Cleveland Press Collection/Cleveland State University Archives, pp. 39, 40, 56, 102, 160; Courtesy of Elizabeth Travis Dreyfuss, p. 51; Courtesy of Mrs. A. Dean Perry, pp. 60 (top), 61 (bottom); Courtesy of Anne Halle (Mrs. Robert A.) Little, p. 83; Courtesy of Musart Society, pp. 98, 137; Courtesy of the Department of Later Western Art, p. 105; Courtesy of Ingalls Library, pp. 114, 157 (left), 187 (top, middle); Courtesy of Mrs. Anthony Sroka, p. 123; Courtesy of Extensions Division, Department of Education and Public Programs, pp. 138-139 (all); Courtesy of *The Plain Dealer*, Cleveland, Ohio, pp. 157, 170, 172; Courtesy of Conservation Department, pp. 184, 185 (bottom); Archives of The Cleveland Museum of Art, frontispiece, pp. x, 3 (top, bottom), 5, 8-9, 19 (bottom), 33, 43 (top, bottom), 64 (top left, bottom), 65, 80, 82, 84, 86, 93, 95 (top), 113 (bottom), 116 (top), 118, 119, 127, 128, 130, 131, 136, 154, 161, 162, 164, 171, 190, 194, 199 (top).

Generally, illustrations of objects in the collection and gallery views were taken by the Museum Photography Studio and are available from the Museum Registrar. Photographers where known (including those on the Museum staff) include: H. V. Perkhammer, p. 3 (top); Edd A. Ruggles, p. 33; James J. Meli, pp. 86, 93; William Wynne, pp. 116, 172; Parade Studios, Cleveland, p. 118; Richard Godfrey, pp. 133, 131; Martin Linsey, pp. 138, 139 (left), 161, 164; Andrew T. Chakalis, p. 139 (right); John Cook, p. 162; James A. Hatch, p. 170; Robert Falk, pp. 173, 180; Joan T. Neubecker, p. 185 (bottom); Copyright 1991 by David M. Thum, pp. 185 (top), 187 (bottom), 196, 197; Arielle P. Kozloff, p. 189; David Heald, p. 190; Stephen Kovacik, pp. 191, 193, 194, 198, 201; Copyright 1991 by Emily S. Rosen, Cover, p. 199 (bottom).